101
QUESTIONS & ANSWERS
S E R I E S

LAW OF TORT

SECOND EDITION

DR VICKNESWAREN KRISHNAN
LLB (Hons),LLM, MA, Barrister at Law,
ACI, Arb, AIPFM, AFSALS, ACII, PhD

OLD BAILEY PRESS

OLD BAILEY PRESS
at Holborn College, Woolwich Road,
Charlton, London SE7 8LN

First published 2000
Second edition 2004

ISBN 1 85836 516 3

British Library Cataloguing-in-Publication Data

A catalogue record for this book is available from the British Library.

Printed and bound in Great Britain.

Contents

Contents

Foreword

This book is part of a series designed specifically for those students studying at undergraduate level. Coverage is not restricted to any one syllabus but embraces the main examination topics found in a typical examination paper.

This book is concerned with the law of tort in the context of examinations. Each chapter contains an Introduction setting out the scope of the topic, together with important recent cases and reports.

Additionally, in each chapter there are Interrograms and Examination Questions. The Interrograms are designed as short questions testing knowledge of the fundamentals of the topic being covered. The Examination Questions are a selection of actual questions taken from papers set by a university, and have been selected because they represent the most typical examples of how knowledge of the syllabus is tested. It is intended that students should work through the Interrograms and Examination Questions before checking their knowledge (and presentation style) against the suggested answers contained in each chapter (skeleton answers for Interrograms, full-length essay answers for the Examination Questions). The law is stated as at 1 October 2003.

Acknowledgement

Examination questions are the copyright of the University of London.

The questions are taken or adapted from past University of London LLB Degree for external students examination papers. Our thanks are extended to the University of London for their kind permission to use and publish the questions.

Caveat

Table of Cases

Part I: Negligence

1

Duty of Care: Protected Interests and Parties

Introduction

The duty of care in tort has three vital elements:

1. the defendant must owe the plaintiff a duty of care;
2. the defendant must be in breach of that duty;
3. the plaintiff must suffer a loss or damage (which must not be too remote) consequently.

Donoghue v *Stevenson* (1932) laid the foundation for a general test to determine liability in negligence. It broke away from the shackles of contract (*Winterbotton* v *Wright* (1842)) and Lord Wilberforce in *Anns* v *Merton London Borough Council* (1978) extended the utility of the general principle in the two-tier test of proximity and policy, which was subsequently criticised as being too wide: *Leigh & Sillivan Ltd* v *Aliakmon Shipping* (1986), *Yuen Kun Yeu* v *Attorney-General of Hong Kong* (1988) and *Murphy* v *Brentwood District Council* (1991). The three-stage test or incremental approach was formulated in *Caparo Industries* v *Dickman* (1990) requiring three elements for the justification of a duty of care, ie reasonable foreseeability (*Bourhill* v *Young* (1943)); proximate relationship (*Alcock* v *Chief Constable of South Yorkshire* (1991)); and, is it just fair and reasonable to impose a duty of care (*Governors of the Peabody Donation Fund* v *Sir Lindsay Parkinson & Co Ltd* (1985)). Considerations of policy (*McLoughlin* v *O'Brian* (1983)) and the availability of alternative remedies (*Junior Books* v *Veitchi* (1983)) also justify the non-imposition of a duty of care. In this respect, see the recent House of Lords decision in *McFarlane* v *Tayside Health Board* (1999) where duty of care was denied. See also *Law Society* v *KPMG Peat Marwick* (2000) and, more recently, *Vowles* v *Evans and Another* (2003).

PROTECTED INTERESTS

Economic loss – negligent misstatement

In order to succeed, the plaintiff must show that the defendant had particular knowledge or skill or expertise; that the defendant knew or ought to have known that the plaintiff would rely on it and it was reasonable to do so; and, finally, that there was a 'special relationship' without any disclaimer of responsibility: *Hedley Byrne* v *Heller* (1963). The position before *Hedley Byrne*'s case is illustrated in *Candler* v *Crane Christmas* (1951). After *Hedley Byrne*, the view of the courts can be seen in *Caparo Industries* v *Dickman* (1990) and *Mutual Life* v *Evatt* (1971). See also *White* v *Jones* (1995), *Welton* v *North Cornwall District Council* (1997), *Harris* v *Evans and Another* (1998) and *Williams and Another* v *Natural Life Health Foods* (1998). See also the recent cases of *Gorham* v *British Telecommunications plc* (2000) and *Grim* v *Newman and Another* (2003).

Pure economic loss

There is no recovery for economic loss, simpliciter. To succeed, the plaintiff must show that he has a proprietary interest and that the act is sufficiently proximate. On proprietary interest: see *Cattle* v *Stockton Waterworks* (1875) and *Electrochrome* v *Welsh Plastics* (1968). On sufficient proximity: see *Ross* v *Caunters* (1980), *Junior Books* v *Veitchi* (1983), *Muirhead* v *Industrial Tank Specialitites* (1985), *British Celanese* v *Hunt* (1969) and *SCM* v *Whittall* (1970). And see *Spartan Steel & Alloys* v *Martin* (1973) on consequential loss. See also, recently, *Carr-Glynn* v *Frearsons* (1998). The more recent case of *Walker* v *Geo H Medlicott & Son* (1999) also bears significance, as does *Hooper* v *Fynmores (A Firm)* (2001).

Nervous shock or psychiatric damage

It means the plaintiff must suffer a mental injury of psychiatric illness which is directly attributable to the defendant's negligence. Initially the courts were quite reluctant to impose a duty of care: *Victorian Railway Commissioners* v *Coultas* (1888). The modern formulation was laid down in *McLoughlin* v *O'Brian* (1983) as requiring three elements: the class of persons recognised by the law; the issue of proximity of the plaintiff; and the means by which the injury was caused (sight, sound or immediate aftermath). Note the controversial decisions flowing out of the Hillsborough disaster: *Alcock* v *Chief Constable of South Yorkshire* (1991), *Page* v *Smith* (1995), *Vernon* v *Bosley* (1997), *Frost* v *Chief Constable of South Yorkshire* (1997), *McFarlane* v *Wilkinson* (1997) and *White* v *Chief Constable of South Yorkshire* (1999). See also the Law Commission Report No 249 (March 1998) entitled *Liability for Psychiatric Illness* and, more recently, see *W* v *Essex County Council* (2000) and *Greatorex* v *Greatorex* (2000).

PROTECTED PARTIES

Police

They do not have any general immunity from the law (*Rigby* v *Chief Constable of Northamptonshire* (1985)) but, in many situations where negligence is alleged, the courts may find insufficient proximity to impose a duty of care: *Hill* v *Chief Constable of West Yorkshire* (1989), *Alexandrou* v *Oxford* (1993), *Hughes* v *National Union of Mineworkers* (1991), *Clough* v *Bussan* (1990) and *Ancell* v *McDermott* (1993). See also, recently, *Bennett* v *Commissioner of Police of the Metropolis* (1998), *Reeves* v *Commissioner of Police of the Metropolis* (1999) and *Costello* v *Chief Constable of the Northumbria Police* (1999). More recently, see *Waters* v *Commissioner of Police of the Metropolis* (2000), *Vellino* v *Chief Constable of Greater Manchester Police* (2001), *Orange* v *Chief Constable of West Yorkshire* (2001) and *Cullen* v *Chief Constable of the Royal Ulster Constabulary* (2003).

Judges and legal representatives

They cannot be sued for the way in which they conduct their case: *Rondel* v *Worsley* (1969), *Saif Ali* v *Sydney Mitchell* (1978) and, recently, *Atwell* v *Michael Perry & Co and Another* (1998). There will however be liability for the giving of negligent advice. However, this position is now subject to the principle established in *Arthur J S Hall & Co* v *Simons* (2000).

Third parties

As regards a person's duty to prevent third parties from inflicting damage on the plaintiff: see the House of Lords' decision in *Smith* v *Littlewoods Organisation* (1987).

Fire brigade

Generally they do not owe a duty of care to property owners when fighting a fire: see *Nelson Holdings Ltd* v *British Gas* (1997) and *Capital and Counties plc* v *Hampshire County Council* (1997). On the liability of coastguards: see *OLL Ltd* v *Secretary of State for Transport* (1997).

The exercise of a statutory power

In this context, a distinction is drawn between policy and operational decisions, the latter being capable of being exercised negligently: *Sheppard* v *Glossop Corporation* (1921) and *Home Office* v *Dorset Yacht Co* (1970). See the recent case of *Barrett* v *Enfield London Borough Council* (1999) for an illustration. Judicial review, an administrative law remedy, is more applicable.

Questions

INTERROGRAMS

1. What did *Donoghue* v *Stevenson* do to the notion of the 'contract fallacy'?
2. Who is a neighbour under the *Donoghue* principle?
3. What was the state of law prior to *Hedley Byrne*?
4. What is meant by pure economic loss and consequential economic loss?
5. What is the current status in determining liability for nervous shock cases?
6. Is there a general duty to rescue?

QUESTION ONE

Lewis and his twin sister Megan went for a week's holiday to the seaside resort of Fishmouth where they hoped to participate in water-skiing. The weather was unsuitable, and none of the water-ski operators was prepared to venture out in the conditions. On the last day of their holiday the weather improved and Megan was determined to water-ski. Owen, one of the operators, agreed to take her out. Lewis refused to go and went for a drink in a pub near the harbour. While he was drinking, he heard a commotion from the harbour and someone rushed in to the pub, saying that there had been an accident and that the young woman who had gone water-skiing had been swept out to sea. Megan's body was not found until it was washed ashore three days later. Lewis has had a serious mental breakdown as a result of the tragedy and has not been able to complete his university course. Some water-ski operators say that they would not have gone out in the conditions, but others disagree.

Advise Lewis on his behalf and Megan's.

University of London LLB Examination
(for external students) Law of Tort June 2001 Q2

QUESTION TWO

Aileen and Betty have entered their cars in a rally of vintage and veteran cars from London to Dover. As Aileen reaches the foot of a hill, a car ahead of her stalls. She knows that, if she stops or slows down, she will have great difficulty in restarting on the hill and so she pulls out sharply in order to get past. Betty, who is driving immediately behind with Carla as her passenger, is unable despite careful driving to avoid colliding with Aileen's car. The cars are only slightly damaged, but Carla is thrown forward and hits the dashboard. Carla complains that she is in severe pain, but Betty tells her not to make a fuss and that they must push on in order to reach the finishing line. When they reach the terminus of the rally, Carla is taken to hospital where it is discovered that she has suffered serious internal injuries. She requires major surgery and a long period of convalescence. It is probable that, if she had sought medical assistance when the accident happened, she would have made a quick recovery.

Advise Carla.

University of London LLB Examination
(for external students) Law of Tort June 2001 Q8

QUESTION THREE

In 1997 Gigantic Industries plc contracted with Superdig Ltd to reconstruct their factory premises. The plans included the building of a light railway to carry finished goods from the factory to the distribution warehouse on another part of the site from which they were despatched throughout the country. Under sub-contracts Superdig engaged Hugetrains Ltd to build the light railway and also engaged Maxigardens Ltd to landscape the site. Maxigardens planted a large selection of trees and shrubs. The weather has been much warmer since 1997 than was forecast then, and during exceptionally hot weather in 1999 the railway line buckled, damaging a train travelling on it. The line was out of action for some weeks. The trees and shrubs have grown so as to overhang the railway line, and the Health and Safety Executive reported in 1999 that they obscured the line of vision of drivers to such an extent that they threatened the safety of those operating the railway. Accordingly Gigantic Industries had to have many trees felled, shrubs removed and a large area replanted at considerable expense.

Superdig Ltd have gone out of business. Advise Gigantic Industries as to the possibility of an action against Hugetrains and Maxigardens.

University of London LLB Examination
(for external students) Law of Tort June 2000 Q6

QUESTION FOUR

Joseph collected his car from the Knock-u-Down garage after its annual service. He drove out of the garage and into a busy road. Before he had got up any speed, a pedestrian, Leila, crossed a pedestrian crossing ahead of him. Joseph applied the brakes but the car did not stop. He was able to swerve and bring the car to a halt without any damage, but Leila was struck a glancing blow and fell over. Leila was taken to the casualty department of the local hospital, where the nurse at reception accorded her a low priority and she had to wait several hours for attention. When she was eventually called, she found that she could not stand up. It was found that she had sustained a more serious back injury than at first thought, and she is likely to suffer permanent paralysis. If she had been given a suitable support and seen promptly, these consequences would probably have been avoided. Joseph, who was of a very nervous disposition, was shocked by the accident and has suffered a permanent breakdown in his mental health. It has been established that the garage had failed to reconnect the brakes before the car was returned to Joseph.
    Advise Joseph and Leila.

University of London LLB Examination
(for external students) Law of Tort June 2000 Q8

QUESTION FIVE

A party of schoolchildren from London went on a week's adventure holiday in Devon. One afternoon they went on a river expedition organised by Titanic Cruises. Twelve of the children were on a boat piloted by Amos, an employee of Titanic Cruises. As the boat approached a dangerous section of river, the steering mechanism failed and Amos was unable to stop the boat being carried towards a weir. The boat crashed over and everyone was thrown overboard and carried down by a raging current. Bianca was standing on the bank. She tried to climb down the bank but saw at once that she would herself be carried away. She watched helplessly as the children were carried past. Most children were drowned, but two together with Amos were rescued. News of the tragedy was given on the evening news bulletin together with an emergency contact number in Exeter. Cleo telephoned the number from London to ask about her daughter Daphne, who had been on the expedition, and was told that Daphne had drowned. This was a mistake; Daphne had not been on the trip that afternoon.
    Amos, Bianca and Cleo have all suffered psychiatric injury. Advise them.

University of London LLB Examination
(for external students) Law of Tort June 1999 Q4

QUESTION SIX

'… in *Henderson* v *Merrett Syndicates Ltd*, it was settled that the assumption of responsibility principle enunciated in the *Hedley Byrne* case is not confined to statements but may apply to any assumption of responsibility for the provision of services.' (*Williams* v *Natural Life Health Foods Ltd* (1998) per Lord Steyn.)

Discuss this statement and comment on the use of the concept of 'assumption of responsibility' as the basis of liability.

University of London LLB Examination
(for external students) Law of Tort June 1999 Q3

QUESTION SEVEN

Juliet is a doctor who works for the Laburnam Street Surgery, a National Health Service practice in an inner-city area. Because there have been several attacks on doctors on night call, the practice has an arrangement with Owlish Security Services to provide a guard to drive the doctor's car. Juliet is called out one night to a patient living in a large block of flats. She went into the flats leaving Dale, a guard from the security firm, sitting in the driver's seat. Two men attacked the car. One of them distracted Dale's attention by trying to open the back door. While Dale dealt with him, the other opened the passenger door, removed a pad of prescription forms which Juliet had left in the glove compartment and ran off. Juliet did not discover the loss until the next day. Meanwhile the thieves had given some prescription forms to their friends, one of whom, Liam, used a form to obtain a supply of drugs from a pharmacy. Liam suffered permanent brain damage as a result of taking the drugs.

Advise Liam's father.

University of London LLB Examination
(for external students) Law of Tort June 1998 Q2

QUESTION EIGHT

Every month a national newspaper The Clarion publishes the serial numbers of premium bonds which have won large prizes in that month's draw. Louisa read the list one month, checked her numbers and saw that one of her bonds had won a prize of £100,000. A week earlier in her public library she had been reading a copy of The Dabbler, a weekly periodical which gives investment advice. She remembered readers being advised to consider purchasing shares as soon as possible in Dentache plc, whose research scientists were said to be on the brink of a revolutionary new technique for arresting tooth decay. This information was seriously misleading and The Dabbler published a correction in the next issue, but Louisa had not read this. Louisa immediately decided to invest a large part of her prize money in Dentache plc and purchased shares to the value of £80,000.

In the list of prizewinners in The Clarion two digits had been transposed incorrectly and Louisa had not won a prize. The shares in Dentache plc have not risen in value. They fell slightly after she purchased them, but have now risen to the price at which she purchased them.

Advise Louisa.

University of London LLB Examination
(for external students) Law of Tort June 1998 Q3

QUESTION NINE

'Can a mere failure to speak ever give rise to liability in negligence under the *Hedley Byrne* principles? In our view it can, but subject to the all important proviso that there has been on the facts a voluntary assumption of responsibility in the relevant sense, and a reliance on that assumption' (*Banque Financière de la Cité CA* v *Westgate Insurance Co Ltd* (1989)).

Discuss.

Written by the Author

Answers

ANSWERS TO INTERROGRAMS

1. Under the tort of negligence, one can now sue another without having to establish a contractual or fiduciary relationship for personal injury or property damage. This was made possible after the *Donoghue* v *Stevenson*'s 'neighbour' principle.
2. The law defines 'a neighbour' as persons who are or could be so closely and directly affected by a person's actions that that person ought reasonably to have them in contemplation when he is directing his mind to the acts or omissions which are called in question.
3. Prior to *Hedley Byrne*, economic loss was only recoverable where there was a pre-existing contractual relationship between the parties, or where there is a fiduciary relationship in existence: *Nocton* v *Lord Ashburton* (1914).
4. Pure economic loss is purely financial loss without any personal injury or property damage, whereas consequential economic loss refers to losses which arise as a result of physical injury, eg loss of earnings, or property damage like cost of repair.
5. Claimants who bring an action in respect of nervous shock must satisfy the requirements of proximity of relationship, proximity in time and space, and proximity of perception. Medical evidence is needed to support the claims for mental injury or psychiatric illness.
6. Unless a person is under a legal duty, there is no general duty to rescue. Where responsibility is however assumed, then negligent execution of that responsibility will attract liability (where none was existing previously!)

SUGGESTED ANSWER TO QUESTION ONE

General Comment

At a glance this question appears to focus on general negligence, but on a closer examination it also gives rise to a discussion of psychiatric injury and issues of causation and breach.

Key Points

- Did Owen owe a duty of care to Megan?
- Was Lewis owed any duty or was he a secondary victim?
- Issue of breach by Owen
- Any defences?
- Lewis's claim for psychiatric injury
- The *McLoughlin* v *O'Brian* criteria
- Chances of recovery

Suggested Answer

The first point is to determine whether Owen owed a duty of care to Megan. Subsequent to the *Donoghue* v *Stevenson* (1932) neighbour principle, the case of *Caparo Industries plc* v *Dickman* (1990) established a three-stage test to determine whether a duty of care is owed. The first stage is to establish reasonable foreseeability. The second stage is to determine the proximity of relationship between the parties. The final stage is to consider the reasonableness or otherwise of imposing a duty of care under the circumstances. Applying this criteria, there is no doubt that Owen, the water-ski operator, owed his client Megan a duty of care in tort.

The more crucial issue in relation to liability is whether Owen was in breach of his duty to Megan. In considering the issue of breach several factors must be addressed. First, the test of establishing a breach of duty. In *Blyth* v *Birmingham Waterworks Co* (1856) the standard of care was stated to be that of the reasonable person, and a breach of duty was defined as the omission to do something that a reasonable man would do, or doing something that a prudent or reasonable man would not do. This requires an objective assessment of the situation. The question is not whether the defendant acted reasonably, but whether a reasonable person placed in the position of the defendant would have acted as the defendant did: *Glasgow Corporation* v *Muir* (1943). In considering how a reasonable person would acted, the following guidelines are material:

1. the magnitude of the risk: *Paris* v *Stepney Borough Council*;
2. the likelihood of the risk or injury materialising: *Bolton* v *Stone*;
3. the relationship of the risk to the object to be attained: *Watt* v *Hertfordshire County Council*;
4. the practicality of precautions taken, if any: *Knight* v *Home Office*;
5. the knowledge and skill of the defendant (is he/she a professional?): *Bolam* v *Friern Hospital Management Committee*;
6. the common practice surrounding the defendant's activity, ie was the defendant conforming to or departing from established practices: *Johnson* v *Bingley*.

Considering the above, the facts disclose first that the weather was unsuitable for water-skiing. Second, none of the water-ski operators were prepared to venture out under those conditions. These factors obviously support the contention that Owen was in fact in breach of his duty of care. Other considerations, such as could he have negligently controlled the boat or was he incompetent in some way so as to cause the accident, are also relevant. Even if there is no negligence in Owen's management of the boat, could he have been negligent in simply venturing out in those conditions? Alternatively, was the boat sufficiently or adequately equipped to negotiate adverse weather conditions, even though the question merely states that the weather was unsuitable? What about Megan's role in the whole scenario? She had been there for a week: the bad weather had persisted and deterred water-skiing throughout her stay. But she was determined to go water-skiing even though she knew the weather was unsuitable. Could Megan's determination to go water-skiing in any way be said to attract any liability on her part? It is likely that Owen could invoke contributory negligence under the Law Reform (Contributory Negligence) Act 1945, but no more than that. In any case, above all, there is nothing on the facts to indicate that the accident was caused by the bad weather or the unseaworthiness of the boat. It could have been any extraneous factor that could have caused the accident. If this is the case, then Megan's death would be deemed as a misadventure. If, on the other hand, it isn't, then the causation argument is what will pin liability on Owen, ie 'but for' Owen taking the boat out, would Megan have suffered a fatal injury? The answer would be an obvious 'no' and that is enough, it is submitted, to establish liability on Owen's part: *Cork v Kirby MacLean Ltd* (1952). Owen's standard must be compared with other water-ski operators, and on balance it is arguable that most of them would not have ventured out under those conditions, even though we are told that some would have gone nonetheless.

As such, Megan's estate or dependants may sue Owen if he is the owner, or his employers under the principles of vicarious liability if he is working for another. Section 1(1) Law Reform (Miscellaneous Provisions) Act 1934 provides for the estate of the deceased to sue the defendant. Alternatively, the dependants of the deceased may sue under the Fatal Accidents Act 1976.

Lewis has suffered a serious mental breakdown or psychiatric injury. Can he hold Owen liable for this condition? In *McLoughlin v O'Brian* (1983), the court established the principles of recovery in psychiatric injury cases. Three conditions must be fulfilled. First, the claimant's relationship to the primary victim must be sufficiently close that it was reasonably foreseeable that he might suffer psychiatric injury. Second, the claimant's proximity to the accident or its immediate aftermath must be sufficiently close both in time and space. Third, the claimant must have suffered the nervous shock through seeing or hearing the accident or its immediate aftermath. In *Alcock v Chief Constable of South Yorkshire Police* (1992) the House of Lords held that a claimant would only recover if he satisfied both the test of reasonable foreseeabilty (that he would be so affected because of the close relationship of love and affection with the primary victim), and the test of proximity to the tortfeasor in terms of the physical and temporal connection between the claimant and the accident. Being twins, Lewis would stand a better chance of establishing a special closeness with Megan. As far as proximity is concerned, Lewis was there, and although he did not see or hear the accident directly, he came within its immediate aftermath. No one else had gone water-skiing that day. It was only Owen, who had taken his sister Megan, who had done so. On the basis of *McLoughlin* v *O'Brian* it is submitted that Lewis would be able to recover for psychiatric injury as against Owen.

SUGGESTED ANSWER TO QUESTION TWO

General Comment

A question of this nature would evidently be a hit with candidates as it requires a discussion of general issues of negligence, such as a duty of care, breach and consequential loss. Care has to be taken, however, in analysing each party's role and contribution in determining liability. As there are several parties involved, a structured appraisal is necessary.

Key Points

- Aileen: is she negligent?
- Standard of care of competitors in a rally such as this
- Betty: did she fail in her duty? – could she have obtained medical assistance sooner for Carla?
- The effect of Betty's act or omission on the scope of Aileen's liability
- Is Carla contributorily negligent?

Suggested Answer

Each party's liability will now be assessed in turn.

Aileen

There is no problem in establishing that Aileen owed a duty of care to all other competitors in the rally of vintage and veteran cars which were travelling from London to Dover. Applying the principle in *Donoghue* v *Stevenson* (1932), it is evident that all the other competitors would be defined as a proper 'neighbour' to Aileen. Further, the *Caparo Industries plc* v *Dickman* (1990) elements seem to have been discharged as well. There is foreseeability, proximity and it is just, fair and reasonable under the circumstances of the case for there to be the imposition of a duty of care.

The enquiry should be, however, one of a breach of duty. Did Aileen fall below the standard of care expected of her? And, if so, what is the standard of care expected of a competitor in such a rally? Answering these questions will determine if Aileen was negligent. The standard of care is that of a reasonable person. In *Blyth* v *Birmingham Waterworks Co* (1856), a breach of duty was defined as an omission to do something that a reasonable and prudent man would do, or doing something that a reasonable and prudent man would not do. This is an objective test. Thus, as regards drivers of motor vehicles, it was held in *Nettleship* v *Weston* (1971) that a learner driver or impaired driver is judged by the standard of the reasonably competent driver. Aileen's manner of driving and her reasons for such driving (that she would have difficulty in restarting on the hill) clearly indicate negligence on her part. Aileen, therefore, is a potential defendant for Carla.

Betty

Betty is driving immediately behind Aileen. Betty has Carla as a passenger. When Aileen pulled out sharply, Betty, despite careful driving, collided into Aileen's car. Although the cars were only slightly damaged, Carla was thrown forward onto the dashboard and was complaining of severe pain. Despite Carla's complaint, Betty carried on driving, telling Carla not to make a fuss. Clearly her main aim was to finish the rally and reach the end. This blatantly careless attitude is clearly negligent. Betty owed her passenger, Carla, a duty of care and she breached that duty of care by not stopping the car to see if Carla was okay, or, alternatively, to seek medical assistance. Clearly, another reasonable person in Betty's shoes would have done just that. Applying *Glasgow Corporation* v *Muir* (1943), the breach is evident on Betty's part. Under the principle of passenger liability, Betty owed Carla a non-delegable duty to ensure her safety at all times during conveyance. Betty has evidently failed to discharge this duty. Carla would be able to recover against her successfully, in the first instance, for all her injuries. On the issue of causation, it must be remembered that despite the defendant owing the plaintiff a duty of care and being in breach of that duty, the defendant will not be liable unless his/her conduct has caused the plaintiff's damage, and that damage is not too remote in law. The test that is generally used in determining causation is the 'but for' test, as illustrated in *Cork* v *Kirby MacLean Ltd* (1952). Therefore, but for Betty's failure in seeking immediate medical assistance for Carla, would Carla still have suffered the injuries she sustained? The question states that had medical assistance been sought at the time of the accident, Carla would have probably made a quick recovery. Clearly Betty's omission in not seeking immediate medical help causes a problem in applying the but for test: *McWilliams* v *Sir William Arrol & Co Ltd* (1962), but on the balance of probabilities, negligence can be made out against Betty: *Fairchild* v *Glenhaven Funeral Services Ltd* (2002). The fact that Betty's breach did in fact materially contribute to Carla's injury would be significantly relevant following *McGhee* v *National Coal Board* (1973).

Potentially, therefore, as far as Carla is concerned, there are two defendants, Aileen and Betty, who have successively and in their own independent way caused Carla's injury. The court may apportion liability on the basis of the Civil Liability (Contribution) Act 1978. Additionally, the court may adopt the approach taken in *Baker* v *Willoughby* (1970) in finding each of the defendants liable to the extent of their involvement. Therefore, Aileen may only be liable to Betty for the damage to Betty's car, and Betty may be wholly responsible to Carla for Carla's injuries.

All that remains is to see whether Betty would have any defence available. If Carla was not wearing her seat belt, then Betty could invoke contributory negligence on the basis of *Froom* v *Butcher* (1976), and under the Law Reform (Contributory Negligence) Act 1945. Apart from this defence, there is no indication on the facts of any other defence being available.

SUGGESTED ANSWER TO QUESTION THREE

General Comment

This is a question on pure economic loss and the principles governing the recovery of such loss. Matters are made difficult by the fact that the main contractors, Superdig, have gone out of business, leaving Gigantic Industries to question whether they can proceed against the sub-contractors in tort.

Key Points

- The general principles of the tort of economic loss
- Recovering economic loss in tort
- The relevance of *Junior Books Ltd* v *The Veitchi Co Ltd*
- Negligence in relation to railway line
- Physical damage to train and economic loss
- Liability of Maxigardens for economic loss caused by tree plantings

Suggested Answer

In the late 1970s and early 1980s, a number of successful attempts were made to circumvent limitations in the law of contract by framing the cause of action in the tort of negligence. Two such cases were *Ross* v *Caunters* (1980) and *Junior Books Ltd* v *The Veitchi Co Ltd* (1983). Academics seem divided over the justification of such circumvention. Jaffey (1985) states that it goes against the established rules of privity of contract, whilst Markesinis (1987) on the other hand argues for a possible expansion of tort law.

However, in the late 1980s, and certainly in the 1990s, a string of cases emerged to bring this expansion of the tort of negligence to a grinding halt. In its place has been inserted a new restrictive approach. Such a restrictive approach can clearly be seen in cases such as *Yuen Kun Yeu* v *Attorney-General of Hong Kong* (1988) and *Curran* v *Northern Ireland Co-ownership Housing Association Ltd* (1987). The culmination of this restrictive approach can be seen in the decision of the House of Lords in *D & F Estates Ltd* v *Church Commissioners for England* (1989), where it was held that damages in tort did not generally extend to the cost of repairing the defect in the product itself; such a claim lay, if at all, in contract. Cases such as *Junior Books* and *Anns* v *Merton London Borough Council* (1978), which had allowed the recovery of damages in tort in respect of repairing the defect in the product itself, were held to be anomalous cases, which their Lordships felt were not to be extended. Hence, there is no recovery for pure economic loss.

In the instant case, if Superdig had not gone out of business and were still solvent traders, Gigantic Industries would have no problem at all in framing an action for breach of contract, but Superdig are insolvent and have gone out of business. The question, therefore, is whether Gigantic Industries can file a claim against Hugetrains for the buckled railway line and the damaged train. There is also the issue of the line being out of action for some weeks, generating a loss of revenue. It this recoverable as well?

The second question relevant to Gigantic Industries is whether there is any liability on the part of Maxigardens, who have planted trees and shrubs along the railway line which have overgrown to the extent that they are posing a threat, resulting in additional expense as a result of felling, removing and replanting. Each issue will now be dealt with in turn.

Liability of Hugetrains

Hugetrains were contracted by Superdig to build a railway line for Gigantic Industries. Hugetrains did build a railway line, but it buckled under exceptionally hot weather. Did Hugetrains owe Gigantic Industries any duty of care in constructing the railway line free from any defect or free from negligence? Hugetrains were in the business of building trains. They should have foreseen and guarded against extreme weather conditions. It is no defence, nor it would not be logical or sensible, to say that the railway line could only be used in mild weather conditions. The weather in the United Kingdom is unpredictable, and the added benefit of hindsight would compound the issue of foreseeability. On this basis, it could be said that Hugetrains owed Gigantic Industries a duty of care, that they breached that duty, and as a result Gigantic Industries suffered loss and damage. Any physical injury or damage is recoverable, but not pure economic loss flowing from the negligence. Whilst Gigantic Industries would be able to recover for the damage to the train and all other consequential losses flowing from it on the basis of *Spartan Steel and Alloys Ltd* v *Martin & Co (Contractors) Ltd* (1973), the defective railway line and loss of revenue resulting from the railway line being out of action for some weeks would amount to economic loss. Unless Gigantic Industries is able to show reliance on their part and an assumption of responsibility and the existence of a fiduciary relationship on the part of Hugetrains, it is highly suspect that Gigantic Industries would be able to recover for pure economic loss.

Liability of Maxigardens

The trees and shrubs planted by Maxigardens along the railway line have overgrown and have begun to overhang the railway line. The trees and shrubs, although described by the Health and Safety Executive as posing a threat to drivers of trains and other potential users as well as to those operating the railway line, have not caused any physical injury to any person or property damage. There seems to be no possibility of any negligent act on the part of Maxigardens in planting these trees and shrubs. They seem to have discharged their contractual obligations properly. The duty to maintain the trees and shrubs falls to Gigantic Industries themselves as owners, and there is nothing on the facts to suggest otherwise. Hence the cost of felling the trees, removing the shrubs and replanting a large area amounts to pure economic loss and is thus irrecoverable on the basis of *Lancashire & Cheshire Association of Baptist Churches* v *Howard & Seddon Partnership* (1993).

SUGGESTED ANSWER TO QUESTION FOUR

General Comment

The question raises general issues in relation to an action in negligence. Students should be vigilant and rope in the garage as a party to the action, and not merely focus on Joseph. The other pertinent issue is whether Joseph can recover for psychiatric injury against the garage.

Key Points

- Negligence: duty of care, breach, loss or damage – foreseeability – causation – remoteness
- Garage's liability to Leila: hospital's liability, if any – if so, the effect of that on garage's liability
- Psychiatric injury: principles establishing recovery in *McLoughlin* v *O'Brian* – is Joseph a primary or secondary victim?
- Garage's liability to Joseph

Suggested Answer

Winfield and Jolowicz define the tort of negligence as 'the breach of a legal duty to take care which results in damage, undesired by the defendant, to the plaintiff'. In order to succeed in an action for negligence, the plaintiff has to satisfy three primary elements:

1. that the defendant owed the plaintiff a duty of care;
2. that the defendant breached that duty; and
3. that as a result of the defendant's breach, the plaintiff suffered loss or damage which is not too remote.

The crucial issue here for Leila is whether she can bring an action against Joseph. Looking at the facts of the case, there is no suggestion that Joseph was negligent or fell below the standard of care expected of a reasonably competent driver. On yet closer examination, the facts seem to rule out negligence on the part of Joseph and point inescapably to liability on the part of the garage. The question clearly states that Knock-u-Down garage was negligent in leaving the car with the brakes unconnected. Was Leila their neighbour, based on the 'neighbour' principle enunciated in *Donoghue* v *Stevenson* (1932) so that the garage owed her a duty of care? Yes, surely the garage must know or foresee that if the car was not roadworthy, then there would be other victims apart from the owner alone. Therefore, Leila was a foreseeable victim and on that basis was owed a duty of care. Applying *Caparo Industries plc* v *Dickman* (1990), there is no problem establishing proximity and foreseeability. Knock-u-Down garage failed to discharge their duty properly in leaving the brakes unconnected. Therefore, they are in breach of their duty, and it is that breach that causes loss and damage to Leila consequently. It is therefore just, fair and reasonable to impose a duty on Knock-u-Down garage: *Peabody Donation Fund (Governors of)* v *Sir Lindsay Parkinson & Co Ltd* (1985). Leila would be able to bring an action directly against Knock-u-Down garage for negligence.

However, the garage may only be liable for the initial injury sustained by Leila, and not the ultimate injury. This is dependent on whether there could be any liability attributed to the hospital in failing to prioritise Leila's case as urgent. The facts disclose that the nurse at casualty diagnosed Leila's case as one of low priority, which meant that Leila had to wait for several hours to be seen. For there to be any liability on the hospital's part, it must be proven that they fell short of their duty of care to Leila. Was the hospital in breach of their duty to Leila? It is submitted not, on the basis that there were not any physical injuries suffered by Leila apart from the glancing blow. Presumably Leila was still standing and was not showing any other signs or symptoms apart from mere discomfort. This may have led the nurse to conclude that there was no urgent treatment required. The issue is one of breach and causation. Would any other nurse have acted in the same way on the basis of *Bolam v Friern Hospital Management Committee* (1957)? The standard of care owed by this nurse must be judged according to the standard of care expected of nurses of equal standing. The *Bolam* test was given approval in *Shakoor v Situ* (2000). In deciding breach, the House of Lords in *Paris v Stepney Borough Council* (1951) remarked that the seriousness of the injury must be taken into account. On that basis, since the nurse could not see any patent serious injury, she did the right thing by according Leila a low priority. This would probably be the same course of action taken by another nurse under the same circumstances. This, however, does not break the chain of causation and Knock-u-Down garage will still be liable to Leila.

If, on the other hand, it can be established that the hospital was indeed in breach of its duty of care to Leila in failing to sufficiently diagnose the extent of her injury, by successfully using the 'but for' test as established in *Barnett v Chelsea and Kensington Hospital Management Committee* (1969), then Knock-u-Down garage's liability could be limited to the initial injuries only and the hospital would be liable for the subsequent and ultimate injury suffered by Leila on the basis of *Baker v Willoughby* (1970). The court is empowered under the Civil Liability (Contribution) Act 1978 to apportion liability as between as many defendants as may be relevant and appropriate or blameworthy.

As far as Joseph's claim for psychiatric injury against Knock-u-Down garage is concerned, Joseph would have to satisfy the principles of recovery for psychiatric injury as laid down in the celebrated case of *McLoughlin v O'Brian* (1983). Joseph will only be able to recover if:

1. his relationship to the primary victim was sufficiently close that it was reasonably foreseeable that he might suffer nervous shock; and
2. his proximity to the accident or its immediate aftermath was sufficiently close both in time and space; and
3. he suffered nervous shock through seeing or hearing the accident or its immediate aftermath.

On a strict application of these principles, it is evident that Joseph would not be able to satisfy the first condition and would not be able to recover for nervous shock. However, the decision of *Page v Smith* (1995) would prove otherwise. In this case, it was held that where the defendant was under a duty to avoid causing personal injury to the plaintiff, it did not matter whether the injury caused was physical, psychiatric or both; and that the control mechanisms for nervous shock only applied to secondary victims and not primary victims. This therefore implicates Knock-u-Down garage. Another possibility is to proceed on the basis of the decision in *Frost v Chief Constable of South Yorkshire Police* (1999), in which it was held that where the defendant causes the plaintiff to suffer psychiatric injury either through fear for himself (which is not the case as far as Joseph is concerned), or through witnessing what happened directly (which is the case here), there there could be liability. Joseph is filled with fear that he was the sole cause of all that has happened to Leila, when in fact it is Knock-u-Down garage's negligence that has produced these consequences. Hence, his fear has been induced by the garage's negligence, and this gives rise to liability. Therefore Joseph would be able to successfully bring an action against Knock-u-Down garage for negligence.

SUGGESTED ANSWER TO QUESTION FIVE

General Comment

This should have been a relatively straightforward question for those candidates who revised the law concerning the recovery of compensation for psychiatric injury, provided they were up to date with the most recent case developments. It must of course be remembered that 'nervous shock' is a type of damage rather than a tort, and therefore candidates would first have needed to identify the basis upon which the defendant might be held liable to those involved in the accident.

Key Points

- Identify and discuss the basis for liability
- Elements of negligence: duty – breach (res ipsa loquitur) – causation – remoteness of damages
- Discuss each potential claim for recovery in respect of psychiatric illness: Amos as a primary victim – Bianca and Cleo as secondary victims
- Does Cleo have an alternative claim for a negligent statement made by the Exeter authorities?

Suggested Answer

Basis for liability

It appears that Titanic Cruises may well be liable in negligence to the primary victims of the accident, ie Amos and the children, on the basis of their apparent failure to properly maintain the boat, if indeed this was the case. The elements of the tort of negligence are briefly as follows.

1. The defendant must have owed the claimant a duty of care. The modern approach for determining whether a duty of care should be imposed in a novel case was recommended by the House of Lords in *Caparo Industries Ltd plc* v *Dickman* (1990). The question is approached in the three stages shown below.

   a) Assuming Titanic had failed to properly maintain the boat, were the consequences of that failure reasonably foreseeable? It would have to be proved that the failure of the steering mechanism was a reasonably foreseeable consequence of a failure to properly maintain the boat. If this were the case, it is submitted that the resulting inability to properly navigate the boat in fast moving rapids would almost inevitably result in a crash, causing injury to the occupants of the boat.

b) Was the relationship between the defendant and the claimant(s) sufficiently proximate? This requirement is easily satisfied on the facts, because it is the negligent infliction of physical injury which itself appears to create the required degree of proximity.

c) Would it be 'fair, just and reasonable' in all the circumstances for the courts to impose a duty of care? This requirement is heavily influenced by policy considerations, and it is submitted that it would certainly be fair, just and reasonable to impose a duty of care upon Titanic in these circumstances. Titanic are likely to be insured against claims arising from its business activities, and to allow this type of claim would certainly not result in an opening of the 'floodgates of litigation'. It might be argued that imposing a duty in these circumstances will encourage other similar operators to take care.

2. The defendant must be in breach of that duty. This involves deciding whether Titanic's conduct fell short of the standard of care which would have been adopted by reasonable persons in the circumstances. The amount of care required in each particular case will depend upon different factors, such as the likelihood of people suffering injury from the hazard, balanced against the practicality of taking precautions in terms of cost and otherwise: *Bolton* v *Stone* (1951). The extent of the potential damage may also be relevant.

   In this case, the maxim 'res ipsa loquitur' (the thing speaks for itself) may apply, as the facts appear to be sufficient to give rise to an inference of negligence on Titanic's part. If such were the case, the court would not require the claimant to give detailed evidence regarding Titanic's failure to maintain the boat. Instead, it would fall to Titanic to rebut the inference of negligence.

   For the maxim to apply, the claimant must show that Titanic was in control of the thing (ie the boat) which caused the loss or damage, and that the accident was of such a nature that it would not have occurred in the ordinary course of events with proper care. It might be suggested that a steering defect would have been unlikely to occur had the boat been properly maintained. Finally, the cause of the accident must be unknown in that it cannot be easily explained. This criterion may apply assuming that no cause can readily be advanced for the failure of the steering mechanism.

3. The breach of duty must have caused the claimant to suffer reasonably foreseeable damage/loss. Assuming that the failure of the steering mechanism resulted from a breach of a duty owed by Titanic, there can be no doubt that the deaths of the children and the psychiatric injuries suffered by the various claimants were direct factual causes. The question as to whether the psychiatric injuries were reasonably foreseeable is dealt with below. The following analysis assumes that Titanic were negligent in respect of physical harm suffered by Amos and the other primary victims of the accident.

Can Amos recover as a primary victim of the accident?

The law relating to the recovery of compensation for psychiatric illness in tort makes a distinction between primary and secondary victims. Primary victims are those who are physically threatened by the negligence, and either suffer personal injury or are put in fear of suffering injury. A secondary victim is someone who is a witness to the consequences of a negligent act or omission in respect of a primary victim.

Amos is a primary victim as he was directly involved in the accident and must have feared for his own life and/or was an active participant in an accident caused by Titanic's negligence: *Dooley* v *Cammell Laird & Co Ltd* (1951). This level of direct involvement in the accident automatically establishes a relationship of proximity between Amos and Titanic. The fact that Amos is Titanic's employee does not automatically give him the status of a primary victim. In *White* v *Chief Constable of South Yorkshire Police* (1999) the House of Lords decided that an employer is not under a duty to protect employees from psychiatric injury unless the employer is in breach of a duty to protect employees from physical harm. Assuming that Titanic were negligent in respect of the latter, there is no requirement that Amos' psychiatric injury should have been reasonably foreseeable and Amos will be able to recover compensation accordingly. It does not matter whether or not Amos actually suffered physical injury: it is sufficient that physical harm was reasonably foreseeable in the circumstances, even if psychiatric harm was not: *Page* v *Smith* (1995).

Can Bianca recover as a primary victim of the accident?

Bianca is a secondary victim of Titanic's negligence in that she was a mere bystander or witness to the accident rather than an active participant: *Robertson* v *Forth Bridge Joint Board* (1995). She was not put in fear for her own safety, as it is for this reason that she desisted in her initial attempts to climb down the bank of the river. Bianca is therefore in the position of having to show, in addition, that her psychiatric injury was a reasonably foreseeable consequence of Titanic's negligence. This will require Bianca to satisfy a number of extra criteria which were first established in the case of *McLoughlin* v *O'Brian* (1983) and subsequently refined in *Alcock* v *Chief Constable of South Yorkshire Police* (1992). These criteria have been imposed in order to limit the class of potential claimants in such cases. The criteria are as follows.

1. It must have been reasonably foreseeable that Bianca would suffer psychiatric illness as her relationship with at least one of the primary victims was sufficiently close. This would normally require a relationship based upon close ties of love and affection between the claimant and the primary victim, comparable to those of a normal parent, spouse or child. Whilst three of the Lords in *Alcock* suggested obiter that claims by unrelated bystanders might not be excluded where a particularly horrific catastrophe occurs within very close range, this suggestion was not subsequently followed by the Court of Appeal in *McFarlane* v *EE Caledonia Ltd* (1994). The Court reasoned that to exclude the requirement of close ties of love and affection between the claimant and primary victim would be to base the test for recovery upon foreseeability alone.

   It is the requirement for a relationship of proximity which almost certainly excludes Bianca's claim in the instant case, given that she appears to be unrelated to any of the primary victims. The other criteria for recovery in *Alcock* would, however, have been satisfied in Bianca's case.

2. The claimant must have been proximate in both time and space to the accident or its immediate aftermath.

3. The psychiatric injury must have been sustained through direct perception of the accident (or its immediate aftermath) with the claimant's own unaided senses.

Can Cleo recover as a secondary victim of the accident?

Any claim by Cleo for psychiatric injury as a secondary victim of Titanic's negligence would certainly be excluded under the aforementioned criteria in *Alcock*. Whilst the relationship between parent and child is one of sufficient proximity (see *McLoughlin* v *O'Brian* (1983)), Cleo was neither close in time and space to the accident or its immediate aftermath, nor did she perceive the events with her own unaided senses. A news report cannot equate with the direct sight or hearing of an event, and being told about an accident does not, by itself, suffice.

However, whilst Cleo might not have a claim against Titanic under the present state of the law, she might have a claim against the Exeter authorities on the basis of their incorrect statement, provided it could be established that they owed a duty of care to callers on the emergency number to take reasonable care to give accurate information.

SUGGESTED ANSWER TO QUESTION SIX

General Comment

This question would have suited those candidates who were keeping themselves fully up-to-date with current developments in tortious liability in the House of Lords. Such contemporary developments are always possible areas for examination, although a more in-depth analysis and comment upon the law will usually be required to compensate for predictability. Candidates should have concentrated their efforts on describing recent case law concerning liability for the provision of services, rather than the historical development of the *Hedley Byrne* v *Heller* principles relating to negligent misstatements. The two cases mentioned in the question were obvious starting points.

Key Points

- Describe the notion of 'assumption of responsibility' as a criterion for liability in respect of negligent statements under *Hedley Byrne*
- Explain how the concept has been used to extend liability to the provision of services
- Discuss specific examples, in particular *Henderson, White* v *Jones* and *Williams*
- Criticise the concept of 'assumption of responsibility' as a basis for liability, describing the different attitudes of the judges to it

Suggested Answer

In *Hedley Byrne & Co Ltd* v *Heller & Partners Ltd* (1964) the House of Lords established that pure economic loss, suffered as a consequence of reasonable reliance by the claimant upon the defendant's negligent statement, is recoverable.

All of their Lordships justified their decisions upon the basis of one party having assumed a responsibility towards the other. Lord Devlin in particular held that the 'special relationship' necessary for a duty of care to arise occurred in relationships which '… are equivalent to contract'; that is, there is an assumption of responsibility in circumstances in which, but for the absence of consideration, there would be a contract.' Lord Devlin also stated: 'Cases may arise in the future in which a new and wider proposition, quite independent of any notion of contract, will be needed.'

This essay will concentrate on how notions of 'assumption of responsibility' have been used by the courts since *Hedley Byrne* to extend the principles established in that case to the negligent performance of services in addition to negligent statements and advice. Such extensions were made in order to do individual justice in cases where the claimants concerned had suffered pure economic loss, and would therefore have been unable to recover under normal negligence principles.

The extension of the Hedley Byrne *principle to the provision of services*

A suggestion that *Hedley Byrne* was not simply to be confined to 'statement' cases came in the judgements of Lord Oliver in *D & F Estates Ltd* v *Church Commissioners for England* (1989) and Lord Keith in *Murphy* v *Brentwood District Council* (1990). Their Lordships classified the decision of the House of Lords in *Junior Books Ltd* v *The Veitchi Co Ltd* (1983) as an example of Hedley Byrne-type liability. However, *Junior Books* was a case concerning the recovery for economic loss arising from a defective product rather than a negligent statement.

The extension of *Hedley Byrne* principles to cover negligently provided services is, perhaps, unsurprising. Many professional services are based wholly or partly upon the giving of advice. A significant extension of liability eventually occurred in *Henderson* v *Merrett Syndicates Ltd* (1994), a case arising out of the losses suffered by Lloyd's 'names' following advice given by their underwriting agents as to the risks involved. The House of Lords decided that a duty of care would exist where a person assumed responsibility to perform professional or quasi-professional services for another who relied on those services. Lord Goff stated:

> '… though *Hedley Byrne* was concerned with the provision of information and advice, the example given by Lord Devlin … and his and Lord Morris's statement of principle show that the principle extends beyond the provision of information and advice to include the performance of other services.'

The scope of this extended duty will necessarily be limited, because service providers are only likely to assume responsibility to specific individuals, or to a limited class of specific recipients, in respect of their services. Thus, liability can be maintained within acceptable bounds.

Similarly, in *White* v *Jones* (1995) Lords Goff and Browne-Wilkinson applied Hedley Byrne in order to impose liability upon a solicitor who had negligently failed to carry out instructions in preparing a new will, resulting in financial loss to the intended beneficiaries. The lack of privity of contract between the solicitors and beneficiaries did not prevent a claim in negligence, because a 'special relationship' arose between the parties, the defendant having assumed a responsibility for the economic welfare of the beneficiaries. A point of particular difficulty in this case was that the beneficiaries could not necessarily be said to have relied upon the defendant's expertise as a matter of fact, given that beneficiaries are usually unaware of the provisions which have been made for them in a will. However, in order to allow the beneficiaries a claim, their Lordships held that reliance is not a necessary condition for the creation of a 'special relationship' in every case under the extended *Hedley Byrne* principle.

White v *Jones* therefore, clearly indicates that *Hedley Byrne* principles may be extended to the provision of services, even if those services were provided at the request of a third party.

The case of *Williams* v *Natural Life Health Foods Ltd* (1998) involved a claim for substantial economic losses following the failure of a franchisee's natural health business. It was claimed that the loss arose from negligent advice provided by the franchisor, a company run by the defendant (who was the principal shareholder and managing director). However, the franchisor had been wound-up and dissolved, and so the claimants sued the defendant, attempting to prove that he had personally assumed responsibility for the negligent advice. On the facts, the House of Lords held that the defendant had not assumed personal responsibility for the advice and the claim failed.

Lord Steyn confirmed that 'assumption of responsibility' is the basis for liability under the extended *Hedley Byrne* doctrine. The test is an objective one, not depending upon the state of mind of the defendant but upon evidence of statements or conduct which conveyed to the claimants that the defendant was willing to assume personal responsibility for them. Lord Steyn held that reliance by the claimants on the assumption of responsibility is necessary to establish causation. However, the test is not whether, in fact, the claimant relied upon the assumption of responsibility, but whether it was reasonable to rely on the defendant to take personal responsibility in all the circumstances.

Thus it can be seen that recovery for pure economic loss arising from the negligent provision of services is now possible under English law. The *Hedley Byrne* test as applied to negligent misstatements has, by necessity, been adapted to apply more easily to the provision of services. For example, reliance by the claimant, as a question of fact, could not be established in many situations involving the provision of services.

The concept of 'assumption of responsibility' as the basis of liability
It was once thought that the 'assumption of responsibility' test was nothing more than a convenient phrase to describe the situation in which a duty of care would be recognised or imposed by the law. In *Caparo Industries Ltd plc* v *Dickman* (1990) Lord Oliver stated that 'it was not intended to be a test for the existence of the duty ... It tells us nothing about the circumstances from which such attribution arises.' However, as we have seen, there have been attempts to adapt the test as a criterion for liability in the recent cases concerning pure economic loss arising from the provision of services.

One criticism of the current concept of 'assumption of responsibility' as a test for liability is that it is too uncertain and imprecise to provide useful guidance to trial judges in future cases. As such, it could simply be used as a tool to justify a finding of liability when the court feels that the justice of the situation requires such a conclusion. This makes it hard for lawyers advising the parties to predict the outcome of a dispute, thus possibly necessitating expensive litigation.

There is evidence supporting the view that the concept might simply be used as a tool to justify liability in the authorities already discussed. In *White* v *Jones* Lord Goff openly admitted that he was motivated to achieve practical justice, because a lack of privity of contract would have denied the beneficiaries a claim. The testator's estate had suffered no loss and so a claim for breach of contract would not have been sustainable on the facts. The defendants would escape liability for their admitted negligence unless the court was prepared to impose a concurrent duty in tort.

The formulation of 'assumption of responsibility' by Lord Steyn in *Williams* is also unsatisfactory in that it cannot explain all the cases. For example, in *Smith* v *Eric S Bush (A Firm)* (1990) the defendant surveyors, instructed by a building society, had sought to avoid liability to the claimant house purchaser by the use of a disclaimer. Nonetheless, the claimant was held to be entitled to rely upon the valuer's report, even though the disclaimer said that the survey was prepared for the benefit of the building society and not the claimant. Surely, it could not be said that the surveyor had shown a willingness to assume a personal responsibility to the house purchaser by statements or conduct, given the clear wording of the disclaimer? Lord Steyn regarded *Smith* v *Bush* as an awkward case decided on special facts, which was very much based on the need to 'yield to practical justice'.

Perhaps a more coherent version of the 'assumption of responsibility' is that formulated by Lord Browne-Wilkinson in *White* v *Jones*. This would involve liability based upon 'a conscious assumption of responsibility for the task' which benefits the claimant, rather than 'a conscious assumption of legal responsibility to the plaintiff for its careful performance.' Such a formulation would avoid the difficulties associated with Lord Steyn's approach when it comes to explaining cases such as *Smith* v *Bush*. Alternatively, it has been suggested that the *Donoghue* v *Stevenson* (1932) conception of proximity, which asks whether the claimant was a person 'so closely and directly affected by my act that I ought reasonably to have them in contemplation', would provide a suitable alternative criterion in cases like these: see Cooke J, *Law of Tort* (4th edn, 1999).

SUGGESTED ANSWER TO QUESTION SEVEN

General Comment

This would have proved a popular question for candidates involving, as it did, consideration of the elements of the tort of negligence. Candidates should have appreciated that this was not a question concerning the duty of care owed by doctors to their patients. An analysis of the current authorities involving possible duties to prevent harm arising from the deliberate wrongful acts of third parties was required. Much of the discussion should have centred around the existence or otherwise of a duty of care, and related issues of causation and remoteness.

Key Points

- Primary liability of Juliet
- Did she owe a duty to safeguard the prescription forms to prevent them from falling into the wrong hands?
- Was there a breach of duty?
- Did the intervening criminal conduct of the thieves and/or Liam's own decision to use the prescription to obtain the drugs amount to a novus actus interveniens?
- Was Liam contributory negligent?
- Was Dale also liable in negligence (on similar grounds)?
- Vicarious liability
- Were the partners of the surgery liable for Juliet's wrongdoing?
- If Dale was negligent, who was his employer?

Suggested Answer

Primary liability of Juliet

The issue here is whether Juliet could be said to owe a duty to safeguard property in her control so that it could not be used to injure others. The establishment of such a duty of care, together with the further issue of whether, in law, Juliet could be said to have caused Liam's injuries, are fraught with difficulty.

Duty of care

Following the case of *Caparo Industries Ltd plc* v *Dickman* (1990) there is now a three-stage test in order to determine whether a duty of care arises in a novel situation.

1. The harm suffered by Liam must have been reasonably foreseeable. It is submitted that there is no great problem with this test. A reasonable person would surely have foreseen that the blank prescriptions might be the subject of a theft in an inner city area in which the incidence of crime necessitated the hiring of a security guard. It must also have been reasonably foreseeable that stolen prescriptions would inevitably fall into the wrong hands and be used to obtain supplies of drugs, the dangerous consequences of which are obvious.
2. There must have been a relationship of proximity between Juliet and Liam. The application of this test is far more problematic. There is no pre-existing relationship between Juliet and Liam. In addition, this is a case of non-feasance on the part of Juliet, ie a failure to safeguard property in her control so as to prevent it from falling into the wrong hands. It is unlikely that any positive duty to look after the prescription forms arises unless, possibly, she has been issued with guidelines as to their security. In the case of non-feasance, duties to prevent harm arising from the deliberate wrongful acts of third parties are only created in exceptional circumstances. There is no general common law duty to this effect.

   Lord Goff, in *Smith* v *Littlewoods Organisation Ltd* (1987), identified four situations in which such an exceptional duty might arise (although he conceded that there might be others) the most analogous of which are as follows.

   a) Where there is a special relationship between the defendant and the third parties who inflict damage by criminal activity. Such a duty was held to exist in *Home Office* v *Dorset Yacht Co Ltd* (1970) in which damage done by escaped inmates of a Borstal institution was held to be recoverable, the escape arising from the negligent supervision of the inmates by three Borstal officers. However, a special relationship only arose in that case as a result of the statutory duties placed on Borstal authorities to control their trainees. In this case Juliet clearly has no responsibility in respect of the two men who attacked the car, and therefore it is submitted that no liability arises for their wrongful act under this exception.

b) Where the defendant knows, or has the means to know, that a third party is creating a danger on his property and he fails to take reasonable steps to abate the danger. Thus in *Smith*, the defendants were not held liable in respect of their failure to prevent vandals from entering their unoccupied premises and starting a fire which spread to the plaintiff's property. Although their Lordships conceded that there is a general duty on occupiers to ensure that their premises are not a source of danger to neighbouring properties, this did not extend to preventing vandals from doing damage where a reasonable person would not have foreseen that steps were necessary to make the premises lockfast. In *Smith*, a reasonable person in the defendant's position would not have foreseen the need to secure the premises, as the defendant had no notice that vagrants were regularly in the building or that fires had previously been started there.

Lord Goff's approach was subsequently followed by the Court of Appeal in *Topp* v *London Country Bus (South West) Ltd* (1993) in which the defendant was held not to be liable for a hit and run incident caused by joyriders who stole the defendant's minibus, even though the vehicle had been left unlocked with the key in the ignition awaiting a relief driver. It could be argued that, since Juliet knew of the high incidence of attacks on doctors in the area, she failed to take reasonable steps to abate the danger, especially if the previous attacks were with a view to obtaining blank prescriptions. She might, for example, have taken a smaller number of prescription forms with her rather than a whole pad, and taken some extra steps to secure them, such as locking them away in the glove compartment or in the boot of the car.

3. It must be fair, just and reasonable for the court to impose a duty of care in all the circumstances of the case. This is, of course, difficult to assess. The court might be persuaded to extend the duty recognised in *Smith* to Juliet's circumstances as the facts are clearly analogous. Such an incremental development would not appear to fall foul of policy considerations, such as the need to prevent a flood of possible similar claims.

Breach

The factors relevant to whether Juliet's conduct fell below that to be expected of the reasonable person have been discussed above, when considering whether she failed to take reasonable steps to abate the danger.

Causation and remoteness

There is no doubt that Juliet's failure to safeguard the prescription forms was a factual cause of Liam's injuries. There is, however, a major issue as to whether, as a matter of law, she should be held liable for the damage which she has in fact caused. There are two possible intervening events (novus actus interveniens) which may serve to break the link between Juliet's possible negligence and Liam's injuries.

1. The intervening criminal conduct of the two men who stole the prescription forms. In *Home Office* v *Dorset Yacht Co Ltd* Lord Reid stated:

    > 'Where human action forms one of the links between the original wrongdoing and the loss suffered by the plaintiff, the action must at least have been something very likely to occur if not to be regarded as a novus actus interveniens.'

    This proposition is clearly closely related to the question of whether Juliet owed a duty to take reasonable steps to prevent the possibility of a theft, given her knowledge of the likelihood of attacks in the area. It is submitted that if Juliet owes a duty to Liam similar to that which was identified in *Smith*, then the damage caused by the third parties will not be regarded as too remote a consequence of a breach of that duty. The issues of duty, causation and remoteness are closely linked in situations such as these.

2. The intervening decision of Liam to use the stolen prescription form in order to obtain a supply of drugs. The unreasonable intervening conduct (going beyond a matter of pure contributory negligence) of the claimant will amount to a novus actus interveniens: *McKew* v *Holland & Hannen & Cubitts (Scotland) Ltd* (1969). It is submitted that Liam's actions fall well within the scope of this rule, and his loss will therefore be treated as too remote from any negligence on the part of Juliet to warrant recovery.

Defences

In the unlikely event that Juliet were to be held liable for Liam's injuries, Liam's damages would undoubtedly be substantially reduced having regard to his share in the responsibility for the loss: s1(1) Law Reform (Contributory Negligence) Act 1945. Clearly Liam was very much at fault in using the stolen prescription to obtain the drugs and in subsequently consuming them.

Primary liability of Dale

The basis for the possible liability of Dale will be very similar to that of Juliet, although some differences apply. It is submitted that a duty to safeguard property left in his control will only arise if Dale was aware of the presence of the prescription forms in the glove compartment. The fact that Dale remained in the car might indicate that Juliet had left him there for the purpose of guarding the forms rather than to provide personal protection for her upon entering the block of flats. On the other hand, the lapse in time before discovering that the forms had gone missing might indicate that Dale's attention hadn't been drawn to the presence of the forms in the first place.

If one of Dale's functions was to safeguard the prescription forms, then his failure to lock the passenger door whilst waiting in this particular neighbourhood would be an additional factor suggesting a breach of duty.

Vicarious liability

If Juliet has been negligent in failing to safeguard the forms, then the other partners in the Laburnam Street Surgery will liable to the same extent under the Partnership Act 1890.

Dale's employer will also be vicariously liable for any negligence on his part. The fact that he may have been discharging his duties in a negligent or careless manner will not take him outside the course of his employment: *Century Insurance Co v Northern Ireland Road Transport Board* (1942). The only question remaining is whether Dale is an employee of Owlish Security Services, the agency which supplied him, or of the Laburnum Street Surgery. The modern approach is for the courts to consider a range of factors in relation to each potential employer such as:

1. who provided Dale's wage or other remuneration?;
2. who paid his national insurance contributions?;
3. who directed Dale as to the mode of performance of his work to such a degree as to make the other his employer?;
4. who had the power to dismiss Dale?; and
5. how long has Dale worked for the Laburnum Street Surgery?

There is little evidence in the question as to Dale's true position, although the fact that he drives the doctor's car, rather than one supplied by Owlish Security, is some indication that he may be an employee of the surgery.

SUGGESTED ANSWER TO QUESTION EIGHT

General Comment

This question required considerable thought, and a detailed analysis of the facts, given the relative complexity of the question. Candidates needed to know the rules necessary to impose liability for economic loss caused by negligent advice and information, and had to be able to apply them to a set of rather awkward facts. Different approaches to structure were also possible here. Candidates should have made some observations about the different economic losses that arose in this case, and whether they were all recoverable, bearing in mind the general aim of damages in tort. Such discussion would normally be reserved until the end of a question. However, candidates could have set the scene by making it clear from the outset which losses Louisa might have been able to recover (if at all).

Key Points

*   Identify, in relation to the aims of damages in tort, which losses Louisa might be able to recover following her reliance on negligent information and advice
*   Discuss whether Louisa was owed a duty of care by The Dabbler in respect of economic losses caused by reliance on negligent investment advice (investigate whether a 'special relationship' existed between them and whether Louisa reasonably relied on their advice)

• Discuss whether Louisa was owed a duty of care by The Clarion in respect of economic losses caused by reliance on negligently provided information

Suggested Answer

This question concerns potential liability for economic loss caused by negligent advice and information. It is more difficult to impose liability for negligent statements than for negligent actions: careless words can spread rapidly resulting in a proliferation of claims and potentially unlimited financial losses. Therefore, policy considerations have led to the introduction of rules which limit the class of potential claimants in such cases. The mere foresight of harm arising from negligent advice is insufficient to establish a duty of care.

Which losses might Louisa be able to recover in negligent misstatement?

It should be noted from the outset that, even if duties of care can be established in this case, Louisa is unlikely to be able to claim for all the potential losses she has suffered. This is because the aim of damages in tort is to restore the claimant to the position she would have been in had the tort never been committed (the 'reliance' interest). There have been very few tort cases in which the claim resulted in an award of damages to protect the 'expectation' interest, ie by putting the claimant into the position she would have been in had the defendant properly carried out their obligation. One exceptional category of cases have arisen in relation to the negligent execution of a testator's instructions by a solicitor in the preparation of a will: see *Ross* v *Caunters* (1980) and *White* v *Jones* (1995). However, these cases appear to represent a very limited exception to the general rule.

The losses accruing to Louisa in this case seem to be as follows.

1. The loss of interest/investment income on the £80,000 which Louisa would have earned had she not withdrawn the funds to invest in Dentache plc shares.
2. The administration costs of buying (and possibly selling) the shares.
3. Any loss resulting from a fall in the value of Dentache plc shares. It should be noted that Louisa has not actually made a loss, since the price of these shares has recovered, and it is submitted that she may now be under a duty to mitigate her loss by selling the shares in order to prevent future loss from accruing (assuming she is to claim in negligent misstatement).
4. The failure to make an economic gain, ie a profit from the Dentache plc shares, which would have been made had the information quoted in The Dabbler been correct.

The loss in (4) above clearly relates to the expectation interest, and is not recoverable in negligent misstatement. The restoration of Louisa to the position she was in before any tort took place would require the courts to ensure that Louisa had suffered neither financial loss nor financial gain. It is submitted that it would not be fair, just and reasonable to expect the maker of a statement to be held responsible for a lack of financial gain arising from negligent advice. As a matter of policy, it might be thought that those who 'gamble' in the hope of making a profit should be expected to accept the risk of making a loss.

Is Louisa owed a duty of care by The Dabbler in respect of the (pure) economic losses arising from the negligent investment advice?

The development of this area of law has been heavily influenced by trends in judicial policy and therefore the decisions have not always been consistent. However, some common requirements can be deduced from the body of case law, starting with the House of Lord's decision in *Hedley Byrne & Co Ltd* v *Heller & Partners Ltd* (1964).

A duty of care arising from a negligent misstatement can only be established if the following two criteria apply.

1. There must have been a special relationship (of close proximity) between the claimant and the defendant. The existence of such a relationship is dependent upon a variety of factors. It has been suggested that a relationship 'equivalent to contract' must exist between the claimant and defendant before the defendant will be held to have voluntarily assumed responsibility to the claimant. See the judgements of Lord Devlin in *Hedley Byrne* and Lord Templeman in *Smith* v *Eric S Bush (A Firm)* (1990). In the instant case, it could be argued that such a relationship might exist between The Dabbler and those who purchase copies of it from a retailer. Whether such a relationship could be said to exist in respect of those who simply read the magazine in a public library is more difficult to say. In *Caparo Industries plc* v *Dickman* (1990), Lord Oliver defined the range of persons to whom a duty is owed in terms of the purpose for which the statement was made. He identified four necessary elements for the existence of a duty of care, as explained below.

   a) The advice must be required for a purpose which is either specified in detail or described in general terms, and this purpose must be expressly or inferentially made known to the advisor when the advice is given.

   The whole purpose of The Dabbler is to give investment advice to its readership, and this would of course have been known to the editorial staff. However, whether the purpose is simply to give general investment advice (to point readers in the right direction) or to give specific information about companies is unclear. It could be argued that the information concerning Dentache plc was very specific, and the fact that the magazine advised its readers to consider purchasing shares 'as soon as possible' might indicate that The Dabbler had voluntarily assumed responsibility to their readership in respect of the accuracy of this information.

   On the other hand, it could be argued that the advice being given was simply to 'consider' purchasing shares in Dentache plc, and therefore the purpose was to suggest that readers might make an investment after undertaking further research and possibly obtaining a second opinion. It must be remembered that the rules, as a matter of policy, are intended to reduce the potential class of claimants. The losses accruing to The Dabbler and other similar periodicals would potentially be unlimited if every reader were permitted to recover for financial losses following reliance on poor investment advice. In *James McNaughten Paper Group plc* v *Hicks Anderson & Co (A Firm)* (1991) Neill LJ identified, as an additional relevant factor, the size of any class of persons to which the advisee belongs. It is submitted that it is unlikely that the courts would impose a duty of care on The Dabbler in respect of the advice honestly given, as the potential class of claimants would be very large.

b) The advisor must know (expressly or inferentially) that the advice will be communicated to the claimant, either specifically or to a member of an ascertained class, in order that it should be used by the advisee for that purpose. It is submitted that The Dabbler must be aware that its potential readers are likely to include those who visit public libraries.

c) It must be expressly or inferentially known that the advice communicated is likely to be acted upon by the advisee for that purpose without independent enquiry (see below on 'reasonable' reliance).

d) The advice must be acted upon by the advisee to his detriment.

The advice given must be formal considered advice. 'Off the cuff' advice or 'passing comment' will not usually give rise to a special relationship. However, it is submitted that written advice contained in a magazine whose purpose it is to inform its readership of investment decisions must be regarded as formal considered advice. The person giving the advice must usually possess some special skill/knowledge: *Esso Petroleum Co Ltd* v *Mardon* (1976). It can be assumed that those who write for The Dabbler have some expertise in the field of investment decisions, or at least hold themselves out as doing so.

2. It must have been reasonable for the claimant to rely on the defendant's statement. Louisa clearly relied on the advice she had read, as she was influenced to invest on the strength of it. It is unlikely, however, that her reliance was reasonable. It has already been pointed out that the purpose of such a magazine might only have been to inform general investment decision-making by pointing readers in the right direction. It would seem unreasonable for Louisa to make such a large investment without undertaking further research or even seeking independent financial advice. This is particularly the case given that Louisa's decision was based upon her recollection of an article in a magazine which was published a week earlier. The price of shares in Dentache plc might already have increased following the earlier publicity and the investment might no longer be regarded as a good one.

It is submitted, therefore, that Louisa is not owed a duty of care by The Dabbler in respect of the advice given, in that no special relationship arose between them (the advice arguably not having been provided for the purpose of making specific investment decisions) and in any event, it would have been unreasonable for Louisa to rely on the advice in the circumstances.

Even if a duty was owed by The Dabbler to its readers, it could be argued that the duty was discharged by the printing of a correction in the first available issue, at least in respect of losses sustained after publication.

Is Louisa owed a duty of care by The Clarion in respect of the misprint?
The failure to correctly transpose the serial numbers of the winning premium bonds also gives rise to difficulty. In applying the criteria identified by Lord Oliver in *Caparo* it seems likely that a special relationship did arise between The Clarion and Louisa. The

newspaper knew that the information they gave would be used by readers for the purpose of checking their serial numbers. It is also clear that Louisa relied on this information to her detriment.

However, the main issue is whether it can be said that Louisa reasonably relied on the printed information. Surely the newspaper could reasonably expect Louisa to receive official confirmation of her win, or at least to confirm the numbers from another source, before relying on the information. There is also some authority to suggest that the courts may draw a distinction between the mere passing on of information and the giving of advice based upon that information: see the Privy Council case of *Royal Bank Trust Co (Trinidad) Ltd* v *Pampellonne* (1987). The mere printing of winning serial numbers might simply be regarded as the passing on of information, and therefore, would not give rise to any duty of care.

SUGGESTED ANSWER TO QUESTION NINE

General Comment

A general essay question on the principles of negligent misstatement after *Hedley Byrne*. Students must display a good knowledge of recent cases.

Key Points

- Duty of care situation in instances of negligent misstatement
- The principle enunciated in *Hedley Byrne*
- An examination of cases post *Hedley Byrne*
- Present status quo
- Particular focus involving situations where the giver of the advice is silent or does not speak

Suggested Answer

It has long been established that as regards careless acts the law will impose liability on the *Donoghue* v *Stevenson* (1932) principle, but it will not impose liability in respect of omissions. Liability in negligence is confined to misfeasance and not non-feasance: see, for example, the speech of Lord Goff in *Smith* v *Littlewoods Organisation* (1987), where his Lordship stated this general rule and identified four exceptions. By analogy, in negligent misstatement, one might assume that while liability may arise in respect of a negligent misstatement, no liability will arise from a failure to speak. Essentially, the statement from *Banque Financière* says that no liability will attach to a failure to speak subject to just one exception, namely where there has been a voluntary assumption of responsibility in the relevant sense and reliance on that assumption.

In *Candler* v *Crane Christmas* (1951) the courts were not prepared to extend duty of care to instances involving negligent misstatements. However, subsequently the position changed in *Hedley Byrne & Co Ltd* v *Heller & Partners Ltd* (1964) where it was held that in order to succeed the plaintiff must show that the defendant had particular knowledge or skill or expertise. Second, it must be proven that the defendant knew or ought to have known that the plaintiff would rely on the statement/s and that it was reasonable to do so. Finally, it must be demonstrated that there was a 'special relationship' (one which is akin to contract), without any disclaimer of liability.

A further point worh pursuing is what the Court of Appeal meant by the phrase 'voluntary assumption of responsibility' as in *Smith* v *Eric S Bush (A Firm)* (1990). In *Smith* it was stated that the phrase can only have any meaning if it is understood as referring to the circumstances in which the law will deem the maker of the statement to have assumed responsibility to the person who acts on the advice, which essentially has turned the test from a subjective to an objective one.

It is this interpretation which is of relevance in so far as the quotation in the instant question is concerned. Therefore, it is arguable that what was said in *Banque Financière de la Cité CA* v *Westgate Insurance* (1989) is susceptible to rephrasing; by saying that a failure to speak can give rise to liability only where the law will deem the non-speaking party to have assumed responsibility (voluntarily) to the other, ie a failure to speak will give rise to liability only where a duty to speak arises.

However, the Court of Appeal has decided in several recent cases that a duty can be owed in the absence of a voluntary assumption of responsibility. In *Banque Financière* itself the court held that in an appropriate case the court could hold that having regard to the special circumstances and the relationship between the parties, a defendant could be treated in law (even though not in fact) as having assumed a responsibility towards the plaintiff. This principle can be seen in cases such as *White* v *Jones* (1995) and *Welton* v *North Cornwall District Council* (1997). More recently the House of Lords in *Gorham* v *British Telecommunications plc* (2000) and *Grim* v *Newman and Another* (2003) reiterated the principle enunciated in *Hedley Byrne* and emphasised that the criteria for the imposition of a duty of care in situations where there is evidence of negligent misstatement are: a voluntary assumption, reasonable reliance and some element of a fiduciary based relationship.

It would seem, therefore, that the quotation in the question is incomplete to a certain degree, in that it makes no reference to those situations where the defendant is deemed to have assumed a duty or responsibility, unless one reads 'voluntary assumption of responsibility' to include these situations.

2

Breach of Duty

Introduction

Professor Fleming defined negligence as 'conduct falling below the standard demanded for the protection of others against unreasonable risk of harm'. The test is based on an objective standard known as the reasonable man's (person's) test as stated in *Blyth* v *Birmingham Waterworks* (1856). The reasonable man was defined in *Glasgow Corporation* v *Muir* (1943) and *Wilsher* v *Essex Area Health Authority* (1988). The following elements also play a role in determining the standard of care expected of defendants:

1. Foreseeability: *Roe* v *Minister of Health* (1954).
2. The magnitude of the risk: *Bolton* v *Stone* (1951), *Haley* v *London Electricity Board* (1965) and *Paris* v *Stepney London Borough Council* (1951). See also *Coxall* v *Goodyear Great Britain Ltd* (2002).
3. Utility of the defendant's activity: *Daborn* v *Bath Trainways* (1946) and *Watt* v *Hertfordshire County Council* (1954).
4. The practicality of precautions: *Latimer* v *AEC Ltd* (1953).
5. The common practice: *Lloyd's Bank* v *E B Savoury* (1933), *Brown* v *Rolls Royce* (1960) and *Knight* v *Home Office* (1990).
6. The standard of care of children: *Mullin* v *Richards* (1998).
7. The standard of care in sports: *Condon* v *Basi* (1985) and, recently, *McCord* v *Swansea City AFC Ltd* (1997).
8. The standard of care in emergencies: *Ng Chun Pui* v *Lee Chuen Tat* (1988).
9. The standard of care of professionals: *Bolam* v *Friern Hospital Management* (1957), *Bolitho* v *City and Hackney Health Authority* (1997) and *Sidaway* v *Bethlem Royal Hospital* (1985). More recently, see *Penney* v *East Kent Health Authority* (1999). See also *Shakoor* v *Situ* (2000) and *Parkinson* v *St James and Seacroft University Hospital NHS Trust* (2001).

Proof of the breach can also be adduced by involving s11(1) of the Civil Evidence Act 1968. See also *Wauchope* v *Mordecai* (1970) and *Pickford* v *ICI plc* (1998). Finally, the relevance of the age-old maxim 'res ipsa loquitur' also deserves mention. It simply means facts which speak for themselves. The classic definition was formulated in *Scott* v *London and St Katherine Docks Co* (1865). See also the latest case of *Widdowson* v *Newgate Meat Corporation* (1997) on the effect of the maxim. Other relevant cases include: *Barkway* v *South Wales Transport Co* (1950), *Henderson* v *Henry Jenkins* (1970) and *Ward* v *Tesco Stores Ltd* (1976).

Questions

INTERROGRAMS

1. What was the objective standard test given in *Blyth* v *Birmingham Waterworks* (1856)?
2. What is the standard of the reasonable man used? What are the characteristics of a reasonable man?
3. Is the standard of care reduced in the case of an emergency?
4. What is the standard of care demanded of a child?
5. What is meant by the term res ipsa loquitur?

QUESTION ONE

Peggy is aged 75 and disabled. The social services department of her local council, the Doomtown Borough Council, provides her with several forms of assistance, including its 'Meals on Wheels' service, which delivers a midday meal to her every day. Because she has very limited savings, these services are provided free of charge. The department knows that she suffers from diabetes and that it is therefore vital that she has meals at regular times. One day a new driver on the 'Meals on Wheels' service went to the wrong address and, receiving no reply, left the meal intended for Peggy outside. At 1.00pm Peggy telephoned the social services department to say that her meal had not been delivered. She left a message on the answering machine. The receptionist did not listen to the recorded messages until 3.30pm. By that time Peggy had collapsed. A neighbour heard the noise of her fall, but, because she had fallen immediately inside the front door of her flat, could not get in. There was a long delay in reaching Peggy and she lapsed into a coma, from which she is unlikely to recover.

Advise whether Peggy has a claim in tort.

University of London LLB Examination
(for external students) Law of Tort June 2001 Q3

QUESTION TWO

Mrs White was admitted to hospital with breathing difficulties. That evening Dr Green decided to perform an emergency operation and insert a device in her windpipe. She was then transferred to intensive care under Nurse Brown. Nurse Brown was a temporary nurse hired from the Florence Agency. The agency paid her remuneration and the hospital paid a fee to the agency. Nurse Brown was instructed to summon a doctor if there was any change in Mrs White's condition. She was a very experienced nurse who had previously worked in a specialist clinic where she had tended people in Mrs White's condition. When Mrs White's windpipe became temporarily obstructed, she attempted to clear it herself but was unsuccessful. Mrs White died.

Most doctors would not have performed surgery when Dr Green did but would have waited until it was clear that she was not responding to other treatment, but some would have acted as he did. It is not clear whether Mrs White would have recovered from the emergency if Nurse Brown had summoned help or if she would have died anyway.

Advise Mrs White's executors.

University of London LLB Examination
(for external students) Law of Tort June 1993 Q7

QUESTION THREE

In January Agnes was aged 85 and living in her own home which she owned. Her daughter Brenda thought that she was becoming too frail and forgetful to continue living on her own and wanted her to get a place in sheltered accommodation run by the local council. The council said that Agnes's condition would have to be independently assessed by the two doctors, one appointed by Brenda and one chosen by the council. The two doctors, Cyril (Brenda's nominee) and Daniel, visited Agnes. She was lively during the visit and the doctors reported that she was a fit and robust lady, in good condition for her age and well able to live on her own. She was refused a place in the sheltered housing.

Brenda immediately had expensive work done to adapt her own home so that her mother could come and live with her. However in April before she was able to move Agnes wandered out one night, could not find her way home and fell over in the darkness breaking both hips. She has been in hospital ever since and is unlikely to be well enough to go to live with Brenda.

Advise Agnes and Brenda.

University of London LLB Examination
(for external students) Law of Tort June 1994 Q3

QUESTION FOUR

Hettie was a patient at the Manpool Hospital. Ian, the junior doctor in her ward, decided that to combat an infection she should receive a daily course of injections. In entering the details in the computer he put the decimal point in the wrong place. When Jane, the newly qualified nurse in the ward, gave Hettie her injections, she was surprised by the dosage but was too shy to question it. She therefore gave Hettie the dose shown, which was ten times that which was appropriate. Within a few hours Hettie's face, arms and legs had become extremely painful, swollen and grotesquely disfigured. Hettie's brother, Kevin, came to visit her next day. He had not been told of her appearance and was extremely shocked. Both Jane and Kevin have suffered severe psychiatric damage.

Advise Hettie, Jane and Kevin.

University of London LLB Examination
(for external students) Law of Tort June 1997 Q1

Answers

ANSWERS TO INTERROGRAMS

1. The court defined negligence as 'the omission to do something which a reasonable man, guided upon those considerations which ordinarily regulate the conduct of human affairs, would do, or something which a prudent and reasonable man would not do.'

2. Lord Macmillan in the House of Lords' case *Glasgow Corporation* v *Muir* (1943) stated that the standard of foresight of the reasonable man is in one sense an impersonal test. It eliminates the personal equation and is independent of the idiosyncrasies of the particular person whose conduct is in question. Some persons are by nature unduly timorous and imagine every path beset with lions; others, of more robust temperament, fail to foresee or nonchalantly disregard even the most obvious dangers. The reasonable man is presumed to be free from both over-apprehension and from over-confidence.

3. As far as emergencies are concerned, the courts take the view that where a defendant acts in an emergency or in the heat of the moment, the standard of care is adjusted to take account of the dilemma in which the defendant is placed. In *Ng Chun Pui* v *Lee Chuen Tat* (1988) the court held that the decision taken by the defendant in such instances is a reasonable one and he will not be liable, even though, in hindsight, he would have adopted another course of action.

4. Normally the standard expected of a child would be the standard of a child of corresponding age.

5. The term means 'facts which speak for themselves'. Where the maxim applies the court is prepared to draw an inference that the defendant was negligent without hearing detailed evidence of what the defendant did or did not do. It eventually reverses the burden of proof from the plaintiff to the defendant (ie to disprove negligence).

SUGGESTED ANSWER TO QUESTION ONE

General Comment

This is a question on the breach of duty by a social services department. It raises a discussion of the broader area of breach of statutory duty. Although there aren't any specific cases on this type of responsibility assumed by the council, candidates should be able to draw a conclusion from comparable cases. Ultimately, is the council liable to Peggy?

Key Points

- Has the council assumed a duty of care towards Peggy?
- Did they know of Peggy's vulnerability?
- Have they discharged their duty of care?
- Breach of that duty
- Loss and damage
- Remedy

Suggested Answer

Lord Browne-Wilkinson in *X* v *Bedfordshire County Council* (1995) stated that a person who has suffered damage as a result of the breach of a statutory duty may have an action in tort. This has been described as 'an action for breach of statutory duty simpliciter'. As far as English law is concerned, this is a specific form of common law action which is distinct from the tort of negligence, even where the negligence action is based on a common law duty of care arising either from the imposition of a statutory duty, or from the performance of it. It must be remembered that a mere careless performance of a statutory duty, does not in itself give rise to any cause of action in the absence of either a 'right of action for breach of duty simpliciter' or a common law duty of care in negligence.

The question does not offer any information as to whether there is a specific statute involved which provides for the provision of a 'meals on wheels' service by the Doomtown Borough Council (although such a duty may be implied from the Local Government Acts). Hence a common law negligence approach is to be preferred in determining the issues: whether the council has in fact assumed a duty of care over Peggy, and whether Doomtown Borough Council is in breach of that duty, as a result of which Peggy has suffered serious injury.

From the facts, it is evident that the council has assumed a responsibility towards Peggy, aged 75, by agreeing to provide her with a midday meal every day. The council appears to have assessed Peggy's case and decided to provide her with this service free of charge: surely the council are exercising a discretion either under the auspices of a statute, or under the common law powers of a public authority in terms of the provision of services to deserving and entitled members of the public or community concerned. On the basis of this relationship, Doomtown Borough Council have assumed responsibility towards Peggy, and as such owe her a duty of care. Clearly they are aware of Peggy's history and medical condition and as such they should have appreciated her vulnerability. The principles of liability as established under *Caparo Industries plc* v *Dickman* (1990) appear to have been satisfied in this instance. There is reasonable foreseeability and there is a relationship of proximity. Surely then, it must be just, fair and reasonable to impose a duty of care under the circumstances. An examination of the relevant case law in this area is therefore essential before the issue can be conclusively determined.

In *X* v *Bedfordshire County Council* the court decided that where a statute imposes general administrative functions on public bodies, and involves the exercise of broad administrative discretion following subjective decisions, it was highly unlikely that Parliament intended to create a private law right of action. This, however, does not (it must be said) preclude an action for negligence. In *Geddis* v *Proprietors of the Bann Reservoir* (1878), it was stated that where a public authority acts in the exercise of a statutory power, then negligence may be held to be actionable and will defeat a defence of statutory authorisation.

Another interesting case is *Kent* v *Griffiths* (2000), where the Court had to decide whether the ambulance service owed a duty of care to an individual when the service was summoned to render assistance to that individual. The Court of Appeal held that the ambulance service does owe a duty of care to those to whom it is summoned for assistance. This duty arises once the service 'accepts the call' for assistance. Similarly, in *Barnett* v *Chelsea and Kensington Hospital Management Committee* (1969), the court observed that a hospital accident and emergency department owes a duty of care to those who seek its assistance, and cannot simply turn away patients without accepting responsibility in the tort of negligence.

In *Costello* v *Chief Constable of the Northumbria Police* (1999) the court held that a police inspector who witnessed an attack on a female police officer by a female prisoner owed that police officer a duty of care, as he had assumed a responsibility to her. Conversely, in *Leach* v *Chief Constable of Gloucestershire Constabulary* (1999) the Court of Appeal held that the police do not owe a duty of care to protect an 'appropriate adult' from mental or psychological harm.

As far as fire services are concerned, the case of *Capital and Counties plc* v *Hampshire County Council and Digital Equipment Co Ltd* (1997) bears significant relevance. In this case the Court of Appeal held that, except in a case where a fire service negligently increased the damage or caused additional damage, there is no proximity of relationship between the fire brigade and the building owner in respect of negligence in the tackling of a fire.

The keyword in all the cases discussed above is negligence. So long as negligence is established, the action is sustainable. In Peggy's case, there is a clear assumption of responsibility and there is sufficient evidence on the facts to support the argument that the council was in breach of its duty.

In relation to the neighbour, there is no liability accruing, as the neighbour had in no way assumed liability towards Peggy (either before the incident or even when he/she went to offer help). Peggy therefore can sue Doomtown Borough Council for negligence.

SUGGESTED ANSWER TO QUESTION TWO

General Comment

This is a fairly specific question on medical negligence which also covers issues concerning vicarious liability. Quite a technical question which requires the student to have a thorough knowledge of the law relating to both areas.

Key Points

- Medical negligence: the duty of care; the standard of care
- Negligence of nurse: breach and causation
- Vicarious liability

Suggested Answer

Dr Green has performed an emergency operation on Mrs White who subsequently dies. The first point to establish is the basis on which her executors can claim. Under the Law Reform (Miscellaneous Provisions) Act 1934 s1(1) all causes of action vested in a person on her death survive for the benefit of the estate and any damages recovered form part of the estate of the deceased.

Turning to Dr Green's actions, we are concerned with possible medical negligence. The duty of care of the medical practitioner has been considered in numerous cases. In *R v Bateman* (1925) it was said that 'he owes a duty to the patient to use diligence, care, knowledge, skill and caution in administering the treatment'. The standard of this care is that of the ordinary competent medical practitioner who is exercising the ordinary degree of professional skill: *Chin Keow v Government of Malaysia* (1967). Further, in *Bolam v Friern Hospital Management Committee* (1957), McNair J said that a practitioner was not guilty of negligence, 'if he acted in accordance with practice accepted as proper by a responsible body of medical men skilled in that particular art … merely because there was a body of opinion who would take a contrary view'.

Applying the law to the facts, we are told that most doctors would not have performed surgery when Dr Green did, although some would have done. Presuming this minority view is also held by a body of responsible medical practitioners, the fact that Dr Green has not followed the common practice will not be sufficient to show negligence. Indeed, it was held in *Maynard v West Midlands Regional Health Authority* (1984), in the House of Lords, that negligence ought not to be established by the judge having to choose between two bodies of respectable professional opinion. This was confirmed recently in *Bolitho v City and Hackney Health Authority* (1997).

The operation was an emergency, therefore it is most likely that Mrs White's consent could not be obtained. Impliedly, however, she consented to allow herself to be treated in consideration for a promise that Dr Green would exercise proper care and skill. Had her express consent been obtained, there would have been further issues as to the amount of information disclosed to her (per *Sidaway v Board of Governors of the Bethlem Royal Hospital* (1985)).

It would appear, then, that Dr Green has not acted in breach of his duty of care in carrying out the operation and has not been negligent. Even if that were not the case, one would still have to consider the questions of causation and remoteness, since Mrs White dies some time after the operation. Dr Green is not liable for the negligence of nurses at the hospital when they are not employed by him and it is submitted that, even if he were in breach of his duty of care, the actions of Nurse Brown may well act as an intervening cause to make Mrs White's death too remote.

If we now consider Nurse Brown's liability, we can ask the question, why did Mrs White die? There seem to be two linked answers. First, she may have died because Nurse Brown failed to summon a doctor to deal with the obstruction; second, she may have died as a result of Nurse Brown's failure to clear the obstruction herself. The omission to summon a doctor would have to be 'the omission to do something which a reasonable man … would do', to be in breach of the duty of care: *Blyth v Birmingham Waterworks Co* (1856). Certainly, there was an instruction to summon a doctor upon any change in the patient's condition and that is an important factor against Nurse Brown. But it may be that a reasonable nurse, judged by the standard of the reasonably competent nurse, would have considered this temporary obstruction too minor a change in the patient's condition to justify a doctor's attendance. Further, Nurse Brown's failure to clear the obstruction may not, in itself, be evidence of any negligence on her part. These are largely questions of fact and expert opinion.

We are also told that there is a chance that Mrs White would have died anyway. That being so, we may not be able to say that 'but for' Nurse Brown's negligence, Mrs White would not have died: *Barnett* v *Chelsea and Kensington Hospital Management Committee* (1969). It would be for the plaintiff executors to prove on the balance of probabilities that negligence was the cause of death. The test of causation was recently reviewed and reaffirmed in *Fairchild* v *Glenhaven Funeral Services Ltd* (2002).

Supposing that Nurse Brown is liable, she could be sued in her personal capacity. However, on the basis of suing 'the deepest pocket', the executors will want to know whether they can sue the Florence Agency and/or the hospital (ie whichever body manages the hospital). Nurse Brown is employed by the Florence Agency but works under the hospital's direction. Whether or not the agency remains vicariously liable for Nurse Brown's torts depends to an extent on the construction of the contract between the agency and the hospital. In *Mersey Docks and Harbour Board* v *Coggins and Griffith (Liverpool) Ltd* (1947) 1 it was held that if the servant when doing the negligent act, is merely exercising the discretion vested in him by the general employer and not obeying the specific directions given by the particular employer, he remains the servant of the general employer. It is difficult to draw the line on the facts of this case, but it is submitted that the general employer, the agency, may well remain vicariously liable.

However, while they can be sued by the executors, the hospital also owes a primary duty to its patients which it cannot delegate to employees or agencies: see *Gold* v *Essex County Council* (1942). If a nurse working in the hospital has been negligent, then the hospital is itself liable. On the issue of hospital liability, the following recent cases will compound the approach taken by the courts in earlier decisions: *Penney* v *East Kent Health Authority* (1999); *Nunnerly* v *Warrington Health Authority* (1999); and *McFarlane* v *Tayside Health Board* (1999).

A final point with regard to vicarious liability concerns the nature of Nurse Brown's act. If she has been merely careless or negligent then obviously the agency cannot avoid liability. However, if they can show that her actions were wilfully wrong, that may take her actions out of the course of her employment. In other words, she is employed to do X and if she does it carelessly, the agency is still liable. But if she does Y, which she has been specifically instructed not to do, that may extinguish liability. Case law has not been so straightforward, however, and, again, the dividing line is hard to draw (see, for example, *Twine* v *Bean's Express Ltd* (1946) and *Rose* v *Plenty* (1976)). On the facts of this case, it does not appear that her failure to obey an instruction was so much a wilful wrong as a considered judgment.

In conclusion, I would advise the executors that their action in negligence lies against the agency and the hospital, but that it is not at all clear that Nurse Brown has, in fact, acted negligently.

SUGGESTED ANSWER TO QUESTION THREE

General Comment

At first glance, this question may appear to be a professional negligence question. However, in reality it requires the student to address all the elements of the tort of negligence, namely duty, breach, causation and loss. It is framed in such a way as to raise doubts under each of these heads.

Key Points

- Did the council owe a duty of care? – if so, what is the extent of that duty and to what extent did the council fulfil its duty? – did the doctors owe a similar duty of care?
- Breach: did the council breach its duty? – did the doctors breach theirs?
- Causation: Agnes wandered out alone, could not find her way home and fell over in the darkness breaking her hips – was this series of events caused by any breach of duty by the council and/or the doctors?
- Loss: Agnes suffered physical injury – Brenda carried out expensive work on her home in preparation for her mother's arrival – that expense appears to have been wasted – was the injury to Agnes and/or the financial loss to Brenda foreseeable?

Suggested Answer

Agnes and her daughter Brenda first approached the council with a view to moving Agnes into council-run sheltered accommodation in January. Before the council would provide a place, they required an independent medical assessment of Agnes by two doctors, one appointed by Brenda, and one appointed by the council.

Following the assessment by the two doctors, opining that Agnes was fit and capable of living alone, the council refused to provide sheltered housing. Brenda immediately had expensive work done to adapt her home so that her mother could move in. Before Agnes could move in, however, she wandered out one night in April, could not find her way home, and fell over in the darkness, breaking her hips. It is now unlikely that Agnes will move into Brenda's house.

The facts outlined in the question suggest a possible claim in negligence against the council and/or the doctors. The tort of negligence has been defined by Winfield and Jolowicz (*The Law of Torts* (13th edition) p72) in the following terms:

'Negligence as a tort is the breach of a legal duty to take care which results in damage, undesired by the defendant, to the plaintiff.'

At this stage of my advice to Agnes and Brenda, it is necessary to consider whether the council, and/or the doctors owed any duty of care to either Agnes, and/or Brenda.

A duty of care is imposed on a party in the following terms, set out by Lord Atkin in the seminal case of *Donoghue* v *Stevenson* (1932):

'You must take reasonable care to avoid acts or omissions which you can reasonably foresee would be likely to injure your neighbour. Who, then, in law is my neighbour? The answer seems to be – persons who are closely and directly affected by my act that I ought reasonably to have them in contemplation as being so affected when I am directing my mind to the acts or omissions which are called in question.'

If a duty exists, it is necessary to define the extent of that duty. According to Lord Keith in the decision of the House of Lords in *Governors of Peabody Donation Fund* v *Sir Lindsay Parkinson & Co Ltd* (1984):

'The true question in each case is whether the particular defendant owed to the particular plaintiff a duty of care having the scope which is contended for, and whether he was in breach of that duty with consequent loss to the plaintiff.'

Brenda was obviously concerned about Agnes, and as a result she went to the council. In those circumstances, it would appear that the council was aware of Brenda's concerns, and owed a duty of care to both Agnes and Brenda, such duty being of the nature of ensuring that Agnes was offered sheltered accommodation if she needed it.

The council, in my opinion, discharged that duty by providing a system whereby two independent doctors, including one nominated by Brenda, were appointed to assess the need, if any, of Agnes. It is difficult to argue that the council could have done any more for Agnes and/or Brenda.

Having been appointed, the two doctors also owed a duty of care to Agnes and/or Brenda, to assess Agnes for the purpose of recommending whether or not she needed sheltered accommodation. The level of that duty was laid down by McNair J in *Bolam* v *Friern Hospital Management Committee* (1957) as follows:

'Where you get a situation which involves the use of some special skill or competence, then the test as to whether there has been negligence or not is not the test of the man on the top of the Clapham omnibus, because he has not got this special skill. The test is the standard of the ordinary skilled man exercising and professing to have that special skill ... he is not guilty of negligence if he has acted in accordance with a practice accepted as proper by a responsible body of medical men skilled in that particular act.'

Thus, in order to determine whether or not Cyril and Daniel (the doctors) breached their respective duties, it would be necessary to consider precisely what they did in purporting to assess Agnes, and whether or not their assessment technique complied with 'a practice accepted as proper by a responsible body of medical men'.

Even if it could be shown that the doctors, and either or both of them, acted negligently in assessing that Agnes was able to live alone, it would still be necessary to show that their breach of duty caused the loss and injury suffered by Agnes and Brenda.

Agnes wandered out of her home and fell over. These events took place only three months after Brenda first approached the council. It is not evident from the facts given in the question how quickly Agnes would have been re-housed if the assessment had recommended her move. If she would not have been moved in that short period of time in any event, the doctors' breach, if found, would not have caused her injury.

This is the 'but for' test as stated by Lord Denning in *Cork* v *Kirby MacLean Ltd* (1952) as follows:

'If the damage would not have happened but for a particular fault, then the fault is the cause of the damage; if it would have happened just the same, fault or no fault, the fault is not the cause of the damage.'

Equally, the doctors could argue that their acts or omissions caused Agnes to remain at home, but did not cause her to go out and get lost and/or injured. The level of Agnes' disability at the time of the assessment and the foreseeability of such an occurrence would determine whether or not the doctors' acts or omissions were causative of the injury.

Brenda's loss was immediate, in that she acted on the report of the doctors by adapting her home. If the doctors were negligent, they caused her loss. However, Brenda cannot be said to have relied upon the expertise of the doctors, in that her actions indicate that she did not agree with their assessment. Thus her expenditure does not fall into the *Hedley Byrne & Co Ltd* v *Heller & Partners Ltd* (1964) category of cases.

Brenda may still be able to claim for the expenditure by relying on *Ross* v *Caunters* (1980) pure economic loss. That case could not be accommodated within the Hedley Byrne doctrine because the plaintiff had not relied upon the skill of the defendant. But the plaintiff did suffer pure economic loss (as has Brenda) and in finding for the plaintiff Megarry VC relied upon the judgments of Mason and Gibbs JJ in *Caltex Oil (Australia) Pty Ltd* v *The Dredge 'Willemstad'* (1976).

The test which they posited was that the defendant should be held liable for economic loss caused by his negligent conduct when he can reasonably foresee that the specific plaintiff, as opposed to a general class of persons, will suffer financial loss as a result of his negligence.

Whether or not Brenda's financial expenditure could have been foreseen by the doctors will depend on their degree of knowledge of her relationship with Agnes, and her plans in the event of a refusal to re-house by the council.

The doctors might argue that even if the expenditure could be foreseen, the fact that it was wasted was not caused by their negligence. So, if Agnes' injuries were not caused by the doctor's negligence, nor could the fact of the wasted costs be caused by the doctors' negligence.

This brings the whole question of foreseeability into issue. A defendant is only liable for losses which directly result from his negligence in circumstances where some loss is foreseeable.

In Agnes' case the distinction between the tests laid down in *Re Polemis and Furness, Withy & Co* (1921) (directness of loss) and *Overseas Tankship (UK) Ltd* v *Morts Dock & Engineering Co, The Wagon Mound (No 1)* (1961) (reasonably foreseeable loss) is of importance.

The essential question is whether it could be foreseen that Agnes would suffer any physical damage if she was not placed in sheltered accommodation. If so, according to the Polemis test, if the doctors were negligent, they would be liable for her injuries if it was a direct result of their negligent assessment.

The *Wagon Mound (No 1)* test requires that the risk of loss suffered must be reasonably foreseeable to the reasonable man, and not a risk that the reasonable man would dismiss as being far-fetched.

Again, the question of foreseeability of physical injury caused by Agnes wandering out of her house is a question of fact, and would depend on the level of knowledge of the doctors regarding Agnes' tendency to wander and to get lost, and the likelihood of her falling down and becoming injured.

In conclusion, it is apparent that both Agnes and Brenda face a number of obstacles if they are to prove that the doctors in this case have been negligent. Even if negligence is established, they face similar difficulties in proving causation and foreseeability of the loss and damage they have suffered.

SUGGESTED ANSWER TO QUESTION FOUR

General Comment

This question requires a consideration of breach of duty and, in particular, the 'reasonable man' standard applicable to medical professionals. The effect of lack of experience, and the distinction between prognosis and treatment, should be discussed, as should the vicarious liability of the hospital authority. The question of nervous shock/psychiatric injury should be given reasonable prominence; in particular the sibling relationship and the time-scale/causative aspects.

Key Points

- Duty – breach of duty – the 'reasonable man' standard
- The *Bolam* test – prognosis and treatment – the duties owed by Ian and Jane
- Inexperience and the need to acquire expertise
- Nervous shock – primary and secondary victims
- Siblings as secondary victims/'mere bystanders'
- The time gap and causation
- Vicarious liability of the hospital

Suggested Answer

There is overwhelming authority for the proposition that a medical professional or a health authority will owe a duty of care to patients undergoing treatment; the necessary foreseeability, proximity and 'just, fair and reasonable' aspects of a duty are patently present. The real question is of the standard of care required to discharge the duty or, conversely, below which a breach of duty occurs. The case law has put a gloss upon a 'reasonable man' objective standard so that the test to apply to medical professionals is that of McNair J in *Bolam v Friern Hospital Management Committee* (1957), that of 'the ordinary skilled man exercising and professing to have that special skill'. This test has found great favour with the English courts and has been held to apply not simply to medical professionals but to other types of professional and, indeed, to any situation where one is exercising skill and expertise: see *Bolitho v City and Hackney Health Authority* (1997). This principle was recently reiterated in *Penney v East Kent Health Authority* (1999) by the Court of Appeal.

We are not told whether Ian has discussed the proposed injections with Hettie or not. This raises the point whether any failure to consult Hettie or to advise her about possible effects would, in itself, constitute negligence. *Sidaway v Board of Governors of the Bethlem Royal Hospital* (1985) shows that the same test should apply to giving advice about proposed treatment as to the standard required in giving treatment, ie the

Bolam test. Ian will be measured against this. On balance, in failing to spot a very significant error in time, he would be likely to be found to have fallen below the standards of any body of reasonably competent medical professionals and, as a consequence, to have breached his duty towards Hettie. The question of any duty owed to Kevin is dealt with below.

The same *Bolam* reasoning will apply to Jane as a nurse. The question might be raised as to whether the standard should be lowered to allow for her relative inexperience (or, indeed, that of Ian). This will not be a factor; this much is clear from *Wilsher* v *Essex Area Health Authority* (1988). There is no room for a sliding scale varying with experience.

The damage to both Jane and Kevin is psychological in nature and this can create problems because of restrictive judicial attitudes towards recovery for this type of damage. The first question is whether the sufferer is categorised as a primary victim, ie one who suffers psychiatric damage as a result of a sudden shock to the system caused by the negligence of the tortfeasor. Here, there is little problem for Hettie's recovery because there are no special restrictive mechanisms at work, and recovery is based upon simple *Donoghue* v *Stevenson* (1932) principles as in *Dulieu* v *White* (1901) and *Page* v *Smith* (1995). The test is one of reasonable foreseeability of any type of physical (including mental) damage to such victims. By contrast, where a sufferer is a secondary victim, ie one who suffers shock because of danger or harm caused to another by the negligence of the tortfeasor, the special restrictions imposed by *McLoughlin* v *O'Brian* (1983), as explained and extended by *Alcock* v *Chief Constable of South Yorkshire Police* (1991), come into play.

There are two problems raised by these cases in the situation in question. The first one is the categorisation of the victims. Hettie is arguably a primary victim, although we are not told of the precise means or process by which her condition arose. There would be no difficulties for her in the light of *Page* v *Smith* in that, provided some harm to her person was foreseeable, the precise type need not be foreseeable. Kevin can only, on the given facts, be a secondary victim. According to the House of Lords, such a victim must stand in such a relationship to the person harmed or in danger as would exhibit the sort of ties of love and affection to be found between spouses or between parents and children. This is a question of fact in the particular circumstances, according to *Alcock*. If the relationship is not this close, Kevin is likely to be equated with a 'mere bystander' and unable to recover: *McFarlane* v *E E Caledonia* (1994).

Jane is in a rather anomalous position. She is possibly to be considered as a 'mere bystander' but it is more likely that her damage results from her knowledge of involvement in Hettie's injury. She would find assistance from her employee status as equating to a 'professional rescuer' within *Frost* v *Chief Constable of South Yorkshire Police* (1997) and possibly from *Dooley* v *Cammell Laird & Co* (1951). This presumption, however, is now rebutted by the House of Lords decision in *White* v *Chief Constable of South Yorkshire Police* (1999) where their Lordships held that the employer-employee status does not convert their status from secondary to primary victims. Further, the equation with professional rescuers also failed because they had not objectively exposed themselves to danger or reasonably believed that they were doing so.

The second problem raised by the House of Lords cases is that of the closeness in time and space between the negligence giving rise to the shock-causing event and the time at which the secondary victim observes the result and is shocked. Where there is no subsequent negligence by the original tortfeasor, the passage of time beyond the 'immediate aftermath' tends to bar recovery as in *Alcock*; there are too many possibilities for novus actus interveniens. Here, there seems to be no such problem because the fact of permitting visitors (or any unprepared person) to see such a shocking sight is, arguably, a quite separate act of negligence in itself. There might be defence arguments of novus actus interveniens, if, for example, Kevin had sought Hettie out without notifying anyone of his presence.

The hospital, as employers of Ian and Jane, will almost certainly be vicariously liable for such torts as they have committed within the course of their employment. There is nothing here to suggest that they were acting otherwise than in the course of employment. If the hospital system was at fault in allowing Kevin to visit Hettie unprepared, its liability will be primary.

3

Causation and Remoteness

Introduction

CAUSATION

Once the plaintiff establishes that the defendant owed him a duty of care and was in breach of that duty, it must also be proven that it was the defendant's conduct which caused the plaintiff's loss or damage and that that damage is not too remote in law. Causation is decided by the invocation of the 'But For' test, as illustrated in *Cork v Kirby Maclean* (1952) and *Barnett v Chelsea and Kensington Hospital Management Committee* (1969). In determining the element of causation, the following factors are considered:

1. Pre-existing conditions: *Cutler v Vauxhall Motors* (1971) and *Performance Cars v Abraham* (1962).
2. Omissions: *McWilliams v Sir William Arrol* (1962). See also *Chester v Afshar* (2002).
3. Multiple causes: *Galoo v Bright Grahame Murray* (1994) and *Cook v Lewis* (1952).
4. Proof of causation: *McGhee v National Coal Board* (1973), *Wilsher v Essex Area Health Authority* (1987), *Hotson v East Berkshire Area Health Authority* (1987) and *Kay v Ayrshire and Arran Health Board* (1987). See also *Fairchild v Glenhaven Funeral Services* (2002).
5. Loss of a chance: *Allied Maples Group v Simmons & Simmons* (1995) and *Stovold v Barlows* (1995). See as well *Sharif v Garrett & Co* (2002).
6. Successive causes: *Baker v Willoughby* (1970), *Jobling v Associated Dairies* (1982) and *Beoco Ltd v Alfa Laval* (1994).

REMOTENESS

The plaintiff's loss must not be too remote in order to be recoverable. *Re Polemis* (1921) and the directness test governed the determining of remoteness until the advent of *The Wagon Mound (No 1)* (1961). Under the *Wagon Mound* test of foreseeability, although the type or kind of injury or damage which occurs must be foreseeable, neither the precise manner of its occurrence, nor its extent is relevant: see *Jolley v Sutton London Borough Council* (2000) on this point. For damages to the person: see *Bradford v Robinson Rentals* (1967), *Hughes v Lord Advocate* (1963) and *Robinson v Post Office* (1974). For damages to property: see *The Wagon Mound (No 2)* (1967) and *Vacwell Engineering v BDH Chemicals* (1971). One regard must also be given to the element of 'novus actus interveniens', ie intervening acts of the plaintiff (*McKew v Holland* (1969) and *Wieland v Cyril Lord Carpets* (1969)); intervening acts of nature (*Carslogie Steamship v Royal Norwegian Government* (1952)); and, finally, intervening acts of third parties: *Scott v Shepherd* (1733), *Knightley v Johns* (1982), *Rouse v Squires* (1973) and *Wright v Lodge and Shepherd* (1993). A recent illustration of what the court would accept as being too remote is provided by *Jolley* v *Sutton London Borough Council* (1998) (CA).

Questions

INTERROGRAMS

1. What is the 'but for' test?
2. What are the instances where the reasonable foreseeability test does not apply?
3. How does the test in *Re Polemis* differ from that of *The Wagon Mound (No 1)*?
4. What is meant by the phrase 'novus actus interveniens'?

QUESTION ONE

'Causation in tort should be a matter of common sense and not of philosophical theory.'
    Discuss.

University of London LLB Examination
(for external students) Law of Tort June 1998 Q5

QUESTION TWO

Theta invented a new computer game which he hoped would prove attractive in the lucrative Christmas trade for 1996. In May he approached Alphaline in the hope that they would be willing to market it in the United Kingdom. Alphaline showed considerable interest. Theta was however concerned about the financial stability of Alphaline and asked to see a copy of their most recent accounts. These had been prepared by Kappa. In the light of these accounts Theta decided that it would be too risky to give Alphaline the exclusive right to market the game. He then approached Betaline. Betaline commissioned a report from Sigma. Sigma sent Betaline an appraisal headed 'Confidential. For your information only.' It reported that the underlying concept of the game was too complicated and that it would have only very limited appeal. Betaline therefore refused to act for Theta. Disheartened Theta did not pursue the matter further.
    Alphaline is still a flourishing company in June 1997, the accounts prepared by Kappa presented an unduly gloomy picture. A game with a very similar concept to Theta's was developed in the United States and was extremely successful in the British market at Christmas 1996.
    Advise Theta.

University of London LLB Examination
(for external students) Law of Tort June 1997 Q7

QUESTION THREE

'Causation should be a matter of common sense and not of legal rules.'
    Discuss with reference to the law of tort.

University of London LLB Examination
(for external students) Law of Tort June 1996 Q5

QUESTION FOUR

'The maxim *res ipsa loquitur* makes it easier for a plaintiff to prove negligence; justice requires the creation of a similar rule for proof of causation.'
    Discuss.

University of London LLB Examination
(for external students) Law of Tort June 1994 Q5

QUESTION FIVE

'Where human action forms one of the links between the original wrongdoing of the defendant and the loss suffered by the plaintiff, that action must at least have been something very likely to happen if it is not to be regarded as novus actus interveniens breaking the chain of causation.' (*Home Office* v *Dorset Yacht Co Ltd* (1970), per Lord Reid).
    Discuss this proposition and explain how since 1970 the courts have dealt with the problem of intervening *deliberate* human conduct.

University of London LLB Examination
(for external students) Law of Tort June 1993 Q6

QUESTION SIX

Sam is a trainee fireman with the Waterside Fire Brigade. While undergoing instruction in driving a fire engine, he was ordered by his instructor Tom to drive at high speed along a country road with his blue lights flashing and bell sounding. Sam could see that the driver of the car ahead, Ursula, had become agitated, but he kept going. Ursula panicked in trying to make room for the fire engine and collided with a lamp post. Ursula received serious eye injuries but was released immediately. Her passenger Violet was trapped in the car. Ursula needed urgent medical treatment and was taken to a nearby hospital. However, there had been a major railway accident a short time earlier and the hospital was unable to admit other casualties. Ursula was therefore removed to another hospital six miles away; the hospital was unable to save her sight, but this would have been possible if she had been able to receive prompt treatment. Violet was released after two hours. She was not seriously hurt but was taken by ambulance to hospital for examination. On the way the ambulance was involved in a further accident (without negligence on anyone's part) and Violet sustained two broken legs.
    Advise Ursula and Violet.

University of London LLB Examination
(for external students) Law of Tort June 1990 Q8

Answers

ANSWERS TO INTERROGRAMS

1. This is where the court asks the question, 'If the damage would not have happened

but for a particular fault, then that fault is the cause of the damage.' In other words, 'but for' the defendant's act or omission, would the plaintiff have suffered a loss or damage?

2. Instances where the reasonable foreseeability test does not apply are: first, where the defendant intends to inflict harm on the plaintiff (*Doyle* v *Olby* (1969)); second, where there is strict liability under the rule in *Rylands* v *Fletcher* (1868); and, third, in cases of breach of statutory duty or where the Act of Parliament was intended to confer a benefit to the plaintiff.

3. Essentially, in *Re Polemis* (1921), it was held that the damage must be a direct result of the defendant's negligence, whereas in *The Wagon Mound (No 1)* the court held that the damage must be a reasonably foreseeable consequence of the defendant's negligence.

4. Basically it means intervening acts, whether they are the plaintiff's, third parties' or of nature. These acts are, or must be, capable of breaking the chain of causation so as to transfer liability to the intervenor. Whether the intervening act is that of nature, then no liability results from that point on.

SUGGESTED ANSWER TO QUESTION ONE

General Comment

It is unlikely that candidates will have had a detailed knowledge of any of the philosophical approaches to the issue of causation, and so what was required here was comment on the extent to which the rules could be said to reflect a commonsense approach to the imposition of liability. The focus was primarily on causation in fact. However, it would have been reasonable to include discussion on intervening cause, or even remoteness of damage.

Key Points

- Introduce by explaining briefly the function of the rules of causation in tort
- Causation in fact
- Explain and illustrate 'but-for' test
- Explain how the rule runs into difficulty in cases involving multiple and successive causes and how the courts have modified their approach to achieve a result which accords with common sense
- Causation in law
- Rules on intervening act
- Based on common sense?

Suggested Answer

One way in which the law reflects notions of individual responsibility is by ensuring that a link exists between the conduct of a defendant (an act or an omission) and some harmful consequence before liability can be imposed. It is this link which justifies fixing the defendant with liability and requiring him to pay compensation. The nature of the link has been the subject of some philosophical debate and a number of possible approaches have been identified. However, the law has required the adoption of a small number of practical commonsense approaches which can be readily understood and applied to a range of real life factual scenarios. It is these approaches, and the extent to which they accord with common sense, which is discussed below.

The question of causation in tort can be approached in two stages. The first involves asking whether, as a matter of fact, the defendant's negligence was a cause of the claimant's loss. It is this so-called 'causation in fact' test which has received the most attention from philosophers. The second stage involves a consideration of whether, as a matter of law, the defendant ought to be held liable for the damage which he has in fact caused. Winfield and Jolowicz (*Tort* (15th edn, 1998) at p196) point out that this second stage involves the consideration of issues of fairness and legal policy.

Causation in fact

This stage merely establishes a factual link between the defendant's act or omission and the claimant's loss. The test normally adopted is the so-called 'but-for' test. In *Cork* v *Kirby MacLean Ltd* (1952) Lord Denning stated:

> 'If the damage would not have happened but for a particular fault, then the fault is the cause of the damage; if it would have happened just the same, fault or no fault, the fault is not the cause of the damage.'

The case usually quoted to illustrate this point is *Barnett* v *Chelsea and Kensington Hospital Management Committee* (1969) in which the death of the plaintiff's husband was held not to have been caused by an employee doctor's refusal to examine and failure to diagnose arsenical poisoning. It was found that it would have been too late to have saved the deceased by the time he arrival at hospital in any event.

Whilst the 'but-for' test certainly represents a commonsense approach to establishing a factual link between claimant and defendant, it is nothing more than a preliminary test to eliminate truly irrelevant causes, and is almost always satisfied in practice. However, the test breaks down in cases where there is more than one cause of the harmful consequence, its application leading to a result which defies common sense. An example given by Professor Atiyah illustrates the point nicely: see Cane, Peter (ed), *Atiyah's Accidents, Compensation and the Law* (4th edn, 1987). Two fires started independently by A and B unite and spread to C's house which is destroyed. In applying the test 'but for A's negligence would C have suffered loss?' the answer would be yes, given that B's negligence would have caused the same loss in any event. The question would be resolved the same way in respect of B's negligence and thus neither party would be held liable for C's loss. However, the courts would almost certainly adopt a modified, commonsense approach in order to fix such defendants with liability. As Lord Wright said in *Yorkshire Dale Steamship Co Ltd* v *Minister of War Transport* (1942) 'causation is to be understood as the man in the street, and not as either the scientist or the metaphysician, would understand it.'

The approach of the courts has been to resolve cases involving multiple possible causes according to notions of the burden of proof. An initial case of difficulty was the House of Lord's decision in *McGhee* v *National Coal Board* (1973) in which an employee was allowed to recover compensation against his employer in negligence after having contracted dermatitis, possibly through the lack of proper washing facilities at his place of work. Although the medical evidence was insufficient to establish that the skin disease had been caused by prolonged exposure to sweat and grime, recovery was still possible as the defendant's breach of duty was said to have materially increased the risk of the employee contracting the disease. It seems that this 'robust and pragmatic' approach was influenced more by considerations of policy than logic, Lord Wilberforce pointing out that (given the evidential difficulties for the claimant in establishing causation in such cases):

> 'It is the creator of the risk who, ex hypothesi, must be taken to have foreseen the possibility of damage, who should bear its consequences.'

However, the current approach of the courts in cases of multiple possible cause is to require that the claimant prove the defendant's negligence was a probable cause, ie a more likely cause than the possible alternatives. Thus in *Hotson* v *East Berkshire Area Health Authority* (1987) the House of Lords disallowed a claim for serious disabilities arising after an accident in which a boy injured his hip joint. On the facts, there was a 25 per cent chance that the defendant's failure to promptly diagnose the condition resulted in permanent disability (and a 75 per cent chance that the condition would have developed anyway, even if the plaintiff had been properly treated) and so the plaintiff failed to prove his case. Similarly in *Wilsher* v *Essex Area Health Authority* (1988), conflicting medical evidence was such that the trial judge had failed to identify whether retinal damage sustained by a patient during birth was caused by the negligent administration of an excess of oxygen by the doctor, or by a number of alternative possible non-negligent causes. The case was sent for retrial on the causation issue, the claimant being required to prove his case on the balance of probabilities. Thus, it could be said that one commonsense approach adopted in *McGhee*, allowing a claimant to recover damages in the face of the evidential difficulties in proving causation, has given way to another commonsense approach which insists that all cases must be proved on the balance of probabilities, thereby creating consistency and certainty in the law.

Another problem with the 'but-for' test occurs where the claimant's injuries are attributable to successive causes, only the first of which is related to the defendant's negligence. In *Baker* v *Willoughby* (1970) the plaintiff suffered injury to his leg as a result of the defendant's negligence, resulting in ongoing pain and discomfort and a loss of earning capacity. The plaintiff took up a new job after the accident, but was shot in the same leg by armed robbers whilst at work, necessitating an amputation. The defendant argued that his liability should be limited to the loss suffered by the plaintiff before the date of the robbery. The argument was rejected by the House of Lords, because even if the robbers could be sued for damages, they would have taken their victim as they had found him and would only have had to compensate the plaintiff for the loss of a bad leg. This would be manifestly unjust as the plaintiff would have been left uncompensated following the robbery for the difference between a good and a bad leg. The House in *Baker* therefore adopted a commonsense approach in order to do justice to the claimant.

However, *Baker* was subsequently thrown into doubt by the decision of the House of Lords in *Jobling* v *Associated Dairies Ltd* (1982). The defendant's liability to pay compensation in respect of the back injury sustained by the plaintiff at work (arising through a breach of statutory duty) was cut short by the independent onset, before trial, of a naturally occurring back condition. This condition was such that it would, in itself, have rendered the plaintiff unable to work. The Lords in *Jobling* were critical of the decision in *Baker*. It was noted that damages are generally reduced to take account of the 'vicissitudes of life', ie the possibility that the plaintiff's working life might be cut short by future events such as early death or unemployment. Where such an event took place before trial, the defendant should not be forced to continue to pay damages for future loss of earnings, as to do so would be to place the claimant in a better position than he would otherwise have been in had the tort not been committed.

There is clearly a conflict between the decisions of *Baker* and *Jobling*, although it has been suggested that *Baker* will continue to apply in cases involving two successive tortious causes. The decision in *Baker* was driven by a commonsense approach which aimed to prevent the plaintiff from being under-compensated. The decision in *Jobling* was driven by an equally logical desire to prevent the plaintiff from being overcompensated. It is therefore submitted that the courts will adopt a pragmatic, case-by-case analysis of causation rather than applying a uniform philosophical approach, in order to reach decisions which may be regarded as a matter of common sense. However, as we have seen, the commonsense approach of one judge can differ from another, and it should not be supposed that consistency will be found in the authorities. As Lord Sumner pointed out in *Weld-Blundell* v *Stephens* (1920):

> 'The trial of an action for damages is not a scientific inquest into a mixed sequence of phenomena, or an historical investigation of the chapter of events … It is a practical enquiry.'

One final area worthy of mention relates to the second stage of enquiry, ie whether, as a matter of law, the defendant ought to be held responsible for the damage which he has, in fact, caused. The starting point here might be to consider the rules relating to remoteness of damage. However, for the purposes of this essay it is more instructive to consider those situations in which the damage suffered by the claimant cannot be recovered, even though the 'but-for' test is established, because the courts consider that an intervening act has broken the link between the defendant's negligence and the claimant's loss. It is submitted that these novus actus interveniens scenarios are all firmly based upon common sense, and a desire to do justice on the individual facts of each case.

The first category is where, following the negligence of the defendant, some unreasonable act of the claimant (going beyond mere contributory negligence) renders the injury suffered too remote from the original act or omission. In *McKew* v *Holland & Hannen & Cubitts (Scotland) Ltd* (1969) the plaintiff, having suffered mild injury to his leg as a result of the negligence of the defendants, suffered further injury when his leg gave away on a steep flight of stairs. It was held that the plaintiff was unable to recover further compensation, as his unreasonable act of descending the steep stairs with no handrail broke the chain of causation.

An intervening act of nature which is independent of the negligence of the defendant may also serve to break the chain of causation. Such was the case in *Carslogie Steamship Co v Royal Norwegian Government* (1952). Here the plaintiff's ship suffered extensive damage in a storm on a journey it would not otherwise have made, but for a delay caused by the defendant's negligence. The storm was treated as a supervening event, breaking the chain of causation and relieving the defendant of liability for the subsequent storm damage.

Finally, the unreasonable intervening act of a third party may break the chain of causation where it takes the form of a negligent or reckless independent cause. Thus, in *Knightley* v *Johns* (1982), a negligent defendant who caused an accident, blocking a tunnel, was not held liable for injuries sustained by a police motorcyclist who was negligently instructed by the officer in charge to drive back into the tunnel against the flow of traffic.

The courts have much more discretion to exercise their common sense in these cases, by allocating blame between the two defendants whose negligence contributed towards the claimant's loss. Thus in *Rouse* v *Squires* (1973), a negligent driver jack-knifed his lorry across the road, causing an accident. Several minutes later, the second defendant negligently collided with the vehicles involved in the first accident, causing the plaintiff's death. It was held that both defendants' actions were operative causes of the accident and liability was allocated to the first defendant in the proportion of 25 per cent.

SUGGESTED ANSWER TO QUESTION TWO

General Comment

In this situation, the nature of the loss indicates that Theta will be required to look at the area of *Hedley Byrne* liability as extended to the recent House of Lords cases. There are always problems with prospective lost profits recovery in negligence, and in Betaline's situation the problem is further complicated by the context of a specially commissioned report which indicates a contractual relationship. There are also considerable problems of causation and remoteness which should be examined.

Key Points

- Theta and Kappa accounts: the purpose of preparation and the scope of any duty owed – proximity
- Theta and the Sigma report – lack of proximity
- Theta and Betaline: whether Betaline advised Theta and whether there was justifiable reliance
- Theta/Betaline and Sigma: the contractual context – concurrent tort/contract liability – the heading to the appraisal – proximity
- The product developed in America: causation and remoteness

Suggested Answer

It is assumed, for present purposes, that Kappa and Sigma had been negligent in preparing the accounts and the appraisal, respectively. The accounts prepared by Kappa were, presumably, prepared for Alphaline only and there seems to be no reason why Kappa should have had Theta in mind when they prepared them. This is an important point because Theta is considering a potential loss of profits which can only be characterised as prospective pure economic loss. The only cause of action which suggests itself is negligent misstatement within the principle in *Hedley Byrne & Co Ltd* v *Heller & Partners Ltd* (1964). Because the scope for actions based on negligent words is potentially so wide the courts have insisted on a fairly narrow rule of proximity between the parties as in *Caparo Industries plc* v *Dickman* (1990). This would indicate that Kappa's duty of care would be unlikely to extend beyond Alphaline and its members, although had Kappa been asked or told about the further communication to Theta, a duty might then arise. Even if there were a duty, Theta would have severe problems in proving the nature and extent of his reliance and the causation of his damage in such circumstances.

Theta then is further frustrated in his plans by Betaline's refusal to act for him. It appears that Theta probably knew nothing of the Sigma report so it will be difficult for him to claim that he relied upon it to his detriment. If this is the case, any claim based upon negligent misstatement falls at the first hurdle because reliance is the whole basis of this area of obligation and there cannot be reliance without knowledge.

There is a possibility that Betaline may have gone further than a simple refusal to act and might have indicated their reasons. These are marketing specialists and there is a possibility that some liability might attach to loose words used by them if it is reasonably foreseeable that Theta might rely upon them. There is no need for the defendant to have specialised knowledge (*Howard Marine and Dredging Co* v *A Ogden and Sons (Excavations) Ltd* (1978)), but the more specialised a person is, and the less sophisticated the recipient of the statement, the more likely it is that a duty may arise: *Smith* v *Eric S Bush (A Firm)* (1990). There would, however, be a serious difficulty for Theta to overcome here. Betaline have indicated that they themselves will not proceed with Theta, but there are no indications that they have gone so far as to positively advise him against further investigation of marketing potential. Without this it seems unlikely that a claim will lie; a simple loss of enthusiasm after a rebuff would not be the sort of reliance exhibited in the case law. This would apply particularly where the advice took the shape of a refusal to enter a commercial arrangement.

Betaline have almost certainly entered into a contractual relationship in commissioning an appraisal from Sigma. There is a possibility that Sigma may feel that they are advising both partners to a prospective joint venture. This is a question of evidence and, if this is the case, Theta would almost certainly be able to pursue Sigma for breach of implied term in contract, absent a clear disclaimer. If Sigma had disclaimed, the possibility of a tort action remains but the courts are reluctant to allow a circumvention of the contract in this way (*Tai Hing Cotton Mill* v *Liu Chong Hing Bank* (1986)), although there is no doubt now that concurrent liability in tort and contract can exist: *Henderson* v *Merrett Syndicates Ltd* (1994).

If Sigma are clear that they are only advising Betaline, the heading to their appraisal seems to make clear an intention that the matters referred to should not be passed on to another, which should be enough to prevent a duty arising to persons other than Betaline. The use of the word 'information' may indicate that they seek to disclaim any liability for reliance along the lines seen in *Royal Bank Trust Co (Trinidad) Ltd* v *Pampellone* (1987), where a distinction was drawn between 'information' and 'advice'.

Any claim at all by Theta will meet great difficulties in quantifying the loss because of the great success of the American product on the British market in 1996. This raises complex arguments of causation in the sense of whether there would have been a market for Theta's product and of remoteness as to the extent of a potential market position for the future. Theta has very great problems in establishing any claim at all.

SUGGESTED ANSWER TO QUESTION THREE

General Comment

The question requires a discussion of the law relating to causation, an analysis of the scope of the 'but for' test and its application. Although there is no right answer to a question of this nature, it is suggested that the examinee avoid a general discussion on remoteness of damage, although the areas overlap considerably and analogies may be drawn.

Key Points

* But for test: acts and omissions
* Problems: multiple and successive causes – proof of causation

Suggested Answer

A defendant will not be liable in tort unless it can be shown that his tortious conduct was the cause of the damage suffered by the plaintiff. The classic definition of causation was given by Lord Denning in *Cork* v *Kirby Maclean Ltd* (1952):

> 'If the damage would not have happened but for a particular fault, then that fault is the cause of the damage; if it would have happened just the same, fault or no fault, the fault is not the cause of the damage.'

This is a clear legal principle which may often seem harsh in its application, eg in *Barnett* v *Chelsea and Kensington Hospital Management Committee* (1969), the plaintiff's husband was refused treatment at the casualty department of a hospital when he complained of vomiting. When the man subsequently died of poisoning it was held that the defendants were not liable, as the cause of death was poisoning, and the man would have died had the plaintiffs not been negligent.

Problems arise when pre-existing conditions aggravate or diminish the damage caused by a tortfeasor, eg in *Performance Cars Ltd* v *Abraham* (1962) the defendant crashed into and damaged a Rolls Royce car. The plaintiff's car had already been involved in another crash, and the plaintiff had been awarded the cost of a respray to his car in an earlier judgment. Because the plaintiff had already been awarded the cost of repairing the car, it was held that the defendant had caused no additional loss to the plaintiff. The 'but for' test here mitigates against double recovery by the plaintiff, but it has also been pointed out that the maxim that the tortfeasor takes his victim as he finds him will work in favour of the tortfeasor in such scenarios.

Another difficult area involves loss caused by an omission to act rather than an act. In *McWilliams* v *Sir William Arrol & Co Ltd* (1962) the plaintiff was killed in an industrial accident. Although the defendants, his employers, were in breach of their statutory duty to provide safety equipment, they were able to show that the defendant would have been unlikely to have used the equipment in any case and they were not liable. Further, Lord Keith argued in *Yuen Kun Yeu* v *Attorney-General of Hong Kong* (1988) that it was a principle of English law that no liability in negligence would attach to 'one who sees another about to walk over a cliff with his head in the air and forebears to shout a warning'. Lord Diplock added further in *Home Office* v *Dorset Yacht Company Ltd* (1970) that in the parable of the good Samaritan both the priest and the Levite who passed by on the other side of the road were guilty of an omission which was likely to cause damage to health, but added that no liability would attach to them under English law.

The problem here is not that the damage would not have occurred 'but for' the omission but that there were successive causes of damage, ie the damage to the Samaritan was initially caused by thieves, but exacerbated by the failure of anyone to help. The conduct of more than one defendant may pass the 'but for' test. This is an age-old philosophical question, well illustrated in Atiyah's *Accidents Compensation and the Law* 4th ed p99. The example provided is if two fires are started independently by A and B and these fires combine and destroy the property of C, who caused C's loss? A, B, both or neither? On a very strict application of the 'but for' test neither would be liable as the damage would have occurred without A's negligence, likewise without B's. It is in hard cases such as these that the law must contain an element of common sense. Although there is no relevant English authority on the point, in the Canadian case of *Cook* v *Lewis* (1952) it was held that each defendant was 50 per cent liable in a similar scenario.

Cook v *Lewis* leads into one of the thorniest problems in the law of causation, that of the standard of proof. In *McGhee* v *National Coal Board* (1973) an employer was held liable in negligence for an employee's contraction of dermatitis. The House of Lords held that the employer's failure to provide washing facilities had *increased the risk* of the employee contracting the disease. It was never established that the lack of facilities had actually caused the disease. This case was subsequently applied by the Court of Appeal both in *Wilsher* v *Essex Area Health Authority* (1987) and in *Fitzgerald* v *Lane* (1987). In both cases the defendants were held to be liable in negligence, and in both the plaintiff established only that the defendant's conduct had *increased the risk* of damage occurring (not that the conduct had actually caused the damage). Slade LJ referred in *Fitzgerald* to the fact that it would have been impossible in that case for the plaintiff to prove that the defendant actually caused the loss. The Court of Appeal seemed to be mitigating the harshness of the rules of causation, particularly in medical cases where it is often impossible to pinpoint the precise cause of a disease, the justification for this being 'broad justice'.

The tensions between the certainty of legal rules and the application of notions of fairness and justice in hard cases, or judicial discretion, is apparent in these decisions. The House of Lords has subsequently retreated from a liberal interpretation of *McGhee* in a line of cases including *Kay* v *Ayrshire and Arran Health Board* (1987) and *Hotson* v *East Berkshire Area Health Authority* (1987). The culmination of this process was the House of Lords' decision in the *Wilsher* appeal. This reversed the Court of Appeal decision and established firmly that in all cases the plaintiff bears the burden of proving on the balance of probabilities that his loss was caused by the defendant. Lord Bridge added that any attempt to use the decision in *McGhee* to modify this principle was 'fruitless'.

It would seem then that English law has adopted a rule-based approach to the issue of causation rather than a common-sense approach. This certainly has the advantage of certainty, however as technology advances it may become more and more difficult to establish liability against doctors, employers etc because proof of causation will become too difficult to obtain, and this may be a recipe for results which offend against common sense. The courts seem to have opted out of the debate, wishing to avoid a haphazard uneven development of the principles of law in this area. Perhaps this is a question which the legislature should consider.

SUGGESTED ANSWER TO QUESTION FOUR

General Comment

This is a question that involves discussing the basis for proving a charge of negligence and assessing, in particular, whether two aspects of the negligence equation require, or should require, different standards of proof.

Key Points

- Res ipsa loquitur
- Causation
- Negligence
- Proof
- Reform

Suggested Answer

It is generally understood that in negligence actions it is for the plaintiff to prove that the defendant owed him a legal duty, which by reason of an act or omission on the part of the defendant has not been effected. The question of proving that failure to discharge the duty owed is at the heart of discussing res ipsa loquitur and causation. The question boldly asserts that the former makes it easier to prove negligence. As the law stands res ipsa loquitur does not affect the burden of proving negligence; that remains at all times on the plaintiff. The presumption that is encapsulated within the maxim is a presumption of fact, rather than it being one of law. The question of the relative easiness of proving negligence must therefore depend on the factual circumstances that lie behind the substantive allegation. This being the position, it seems difficult to use res ipsa loquitur as a justification for changing a central plank of the burden of proof.

The essence of the phrase res ipsa loquitur is that *the thing speaks for itself*. At the most basic level, the court requires no proof of the negligence other than the incident at the heart of the action and does not concern itself with the specifics of what the defendant did or did not do. This indicates that rather than being a rule of substantive law, it is actually an evidential issue for the court. The maxim has three central components:

1. the defendant must be in control of the thing that causes the damage;
2. the accident must be such as would not ordinarily occur without the intervention of negligence;
3. there must be an absence of explanation for the accident.

If the circumstances arise in which these conditions are satisfied, it is then necessary to deal with the most important aspect of res ipsa loquitur: the consideration of what effect the maxim has on a particular situation. These considerations have given rise to considerable judicial discussion. There are, in fact, two schools of thought on this matter. One of these takes a broad view of the maxim that coincides with the interpretation placed on it in the question. If the plaintiff is able to show a prima facie case in negligence, it then falls on the defendant to prove that he was not negligent. This means that the burden of proof must shift, invoking a completely different basis for determining liability in negligence. In the case of *Henderson* v *Henry E Jenkins & Sons* (1970), the House of Lords considered, in response to the prima facie case of negligence raised by the plaintiff, the defendants had not managed to rebut that prima facie case. If this represented the true position in law, it would be possible to say that in having res ipsa loquitur at his disposal a plaintiff would have an easier task in proving negligence.

However, in *Ng Chun Pui* v *Lee Chuen Tat* (1988), the Privy Council looked again at the issue. It was Lord Griffiths, who said that:

> 'It is misleading to talk of the burden of proof shifting to the defendant in a res ipsa loquitur situation. The burden of proving negligence rests throughout the case on the plaintiff.'

This, then, represents not only the second school of thought, but also the current state of the law. If the defendant is in a position which enables him to rebut any inference that res ipsa loquitur raises, then the plaintiff has failed to prove that the defendant was negligent. This helps to put the maxim firmly in an understandable context. It shows that to consider that the maxim makes the plaintiff's task easier is to miss the point of it, and perhaps to give it an importance that it does not deserve.

This leaves the examination of the second part of the question in a state of crux. There is, in reality, no real difference between causation and res ipsa loquitur, insofar as they relate to what the plaintiff has to show in order to prove negligence. In both situations, the plaintiff has to show that his loss has been caused by the negligence of the defendant. In the circumstances that were present in the case of *Hotson* v *East Berkshire Area Health Authority* (1987), it was for the plaintiff to prove that the injury to his hip was caused by the negligence of the defendant. The House of Lords held that it was for the proof to be on the balance of probabilities, and in that case, on that standard, the injury was caused by the plaintiff falling out of a tree, rather than by any subsequent failures in medical treatment. The case is a prime example of the more restrictive test that is now in place in this area. At one point, it did seem that a liberal interpretation, which allowed an increase in the *risk* of damage to permit a successful claim, without proving actual damage (*McGhee* v *National Coal Board* (1973)), was to be followed. The retreat from this position was not very long in coming and reflects the widely held view, that it is not for the courts to dramatically alter the basis of tort liability. The desire is for certainty in this area, for a plaintiff to know that it is for him to prove, that on the balance of probabilities, the defendant's breach of duty was the cause of any subsequent loss. It is possible to consider more and more situations in which the plaintiff has a harder job proving causation. As technology increases and medical boundaries are broken, so the plaintiff has to deal with uncertainties that make the job of proving causation nigh on impossible. If Parliament was to decide that the causation aspect of considering negligence claims should evolve, it may, then, be appropriate to do away with it. However, it is difficult to imagine a set of circumstances where this would be feasible. Justice requires certainty and also that a case can be proved on the evidence before the court. To take causation out of the negligence equation, therefore, would probably necessitate a complete overhaul of the standards and burdens of proof.

It seems that the court has to tread a very fine line when it comes to consideration of both aspects under discussion. It further seems that it is the evidence before the court that will hold sway and it is hard to draw strict academic principles from what remains a subjective assessment of what is offered by both sides. The case of proving the causative link in negligence is a difficult one but there are certain solid foundations, in terms of burden and standard of proof, that all plaintiffs and defendants must work from.

SUGGESTED ANSWER TO QUESTION FIVE

General Comment

This is a difficult essay question which many students will wish to avoid. It requires not only an explanation of Lord Reid's dictum, but also a good knowledge of the case law on the subject.

Key Points

- Explanation of the proposition
- Case law since 1970: *Lamb* v *Camden* – *Ward* v *Cannock Chase* – *Rouse* v *Squires* – *Knightley* v *Johns* – *Smith* v *Littlewoods*
- Conclusion

Suggested Answer

'I feel bound to say with respect that what Lord Reid said in the *Dorset Yacht* case [*Home Office* v *Dorset Yacht Co Ltd* (1970)] does nothing to simplify the task of deciding for or against remoteness, especially where the fresh damage complained of has been caused by the intervening act of a third party': Watkins LJ in *Lamb* v *Camden London Borough Council* (1981).

Lord Reid's dictum in the *Dorset Yacht* case concerns the principle that the consequence is too remote if it follows a break in the chain of causation. This break in the chain of causation, or novus actus interveniens, could be as a result of a natural event (as in *Carslogie Steamship Co Ltd* v *Royal Norwegian Government* (1952)), the act or omission of the plaintiff (as in *McKew* v *Holland & Hannen & Cubitts (Scotland) Ltd* (1969)), or the act or omission of a third party. It is with this last that we are concerned.

In the leading case of *The Oropesa* (1943) – which pre-dates Lord Reid's dictum – it is said:

> '... to break the chain of causation it must be shown that there is something which I will call ultroneous, something unwarrantable, a new cause which disturbs the sequence of events, something which can be described as either unreasonable or extraneous or extrinsic' (per Lord Wright).

In other words, the defendant's breach of duty has been followed by the truly independent, but not necessarily tortious, act of a third party which causes the plaintiff's damage.

Lord Reid has restated the principle in this way: unless the act of the third party was something very likely to happen, it will break the chain of causation. Therefore something that was merely foreseeable would be seen as a novus actus interveniens. As Lord Reid went on to say later in the same judgment, 'I do not think that a mere foreseeable possibility is or should be sufficient'.

There have been a number of cases on this point since 1970, but briefly one should place the *Dorset Yacht* case in context. It was an attempt to broaden the scope of the 'neighbour principle' of *Donoghue* v *Stevenson* (1932) and Lord Reid suggested that the time had come to regard that principle as applicable in all cases where there was no justification or valid explanation for its exclusion. His obiter statement regarding third party interference was not reflected in the other speeches in that case.

However, if one turns to case law since 1970, one reaches the conclusion that it is very difficult to say where exactly the dividing line is drawn between those third party acts which terminate the defendant's liability and those which do not, but the test is essentially whether the intervening act is reasonably foreseeable.

In *Lamb* v *Camden London Borough Council* (above), the plaintiff's house was damaged through the defendant's negligence. The house became unoccupied and squatters moved in on two occasions, causing further damage. The Official Referee held that the squatting was a 'foreseeable' risk but not a likely one and, applying Lord Reid's speech in the *Dorset Yacht* case, he held that the damage they caused was too remote. However, whilst upholding this decision, the Court of Appeal was critical of Lord Reid's proposition, as has been noted above.

In contrast, in *Ward* v *Cannock Chase District Council* (1986), on similar facts, the defendants were held liable. The difference between the two may lie in the degree of wilful wrongdoing by the third party. A third party's negligence will be more foreseeable than its wilful conduct. But ultimately what the court is looking at is whether the reasonable man would foresee the intervening acts in question. While squatting may be foreseeable, the actual conduct of the squatters – particularly if it is wilfully wrong – is not a reasonably foreseeable consequence which can be attributed to the defendant's negligence.

To contrast two further cases which are factually similar: in *Rouse* v *Squires* (1973), a lorry jack-knifed across a motorway owing to the first defendant's negligent driving. A second lorry, also being driven negligently, crashed some minutes later into the pile-up, killing someone who was assisting at the scene. The first defendant's negligence was held to have caused his death, Cairns LJ saying that, having negligently created the danger to other road users, the first defendant was responsible for the further accident, despite the second lorry driver's negligence. Only if this latter had deliberately or recklessly driven into the obstruction would the chain of causation be broken.

In *Knightley* v *Johns* (1982), on the other hand, a subsequent collision was held too remote where the first defendant's negligent driving caused the blocking of a busy tunnel. A police inspector, who took charge, at first negligently failed to close the tunnel, but then sent a police motorcyclist (the plaintiff) the wrong way along the tunnel to close it. He collided with another motorist. This accident was too remote, because there had been so many errors between the initial negligence and the subsequent collision.

These cases suggest, therefore, that it is a question of fact where the line is precisely drawn, the need to draw a line and its general position being a question of policy, although policy based on common sense. As Oliver LJ said in *Lamb*: 'I confess that I find it inconceivable that the reasonable man, wielding his pick in the road in 1973, could be said reasonably to foresee that his puncturing of a water main would fill the plaintiff's house with uninvited guests in 1974.'

This passage from his judgment was endorsed by Lord Mackay in *Smith* v *Littlewoods Organisation Ltd* (1987) in the House of Lords. Referring also to the speech of Lord Reid, his Lordship concluded that the only way it would be possible to persuade a judge that an outcome was not only possible but reasonably foreseeable was to show that it was also highly likely. In other words something more than mere foreseeability would be required. Despite the criticism of Lord Reid, this does not seem far from what Lord Reid was saying. It is perhaps the perennial difficulty in tort, and particularly in negligence, of trying to reach a definition using indefinable terms.

Perhaps the last word should go to Lord Denning, who said in *Lamb*: 'The law has to draw a line somewhere. Sometimes it is done by limiting the range of persons to whom duty is owed ... At other times it is done by saying that the consequence is too remote to be a head of damage ... But ultimately it is a question of policy for the judges to decide.'

SUGGESTED ANSWER TO QUESTION SIX

General Comment

This question involves a consideration of breach of duty and causation in negligence, with particular reference to the possibility of a novus actus interveniens breaking the chain of causation. Finally the question of vicarious liability should also be considered.

Key Points

* Breach of duty – *Blyth* v *Birmingham Waterworks*
* Causation – *Knightley* v *Johns* and *Rouse* v *Squires*
* Foreseeability
* Novus actus interveniens
* Vicarious liability

Suggested Answer

It is well established law that Sam as a driver owes a duty of care to all other road users and would clearly be able to meet the latest formulation of the criteria laid down for the imposition of a duty of care in *Caparo Industries plc* v *Dickman* (1990). In carrying out this duty of care Sam must act as a reasonable man: *Blyth* v *Birmingham Waterworks* (1856); this is an objective test which means that the standard of care required of a trainee driver is the same standard as required of an experienced and competent driver: *Nettleship* v *Weston* (1971), and it is by this standard that Sam must be judged. When Sam drives at high speed along a country road he is prima facie in breach of his duty as a reasonable man would not act in this way. If Sam were en route to an emergency then his actions would be those of a reasonable man: *Watt* v *Hertfordshire County Council* (1954), but this is not the situation here. Ursula's collision is caused by Sam's breach of duty so prima facie Sam is liable for any injuries caused. Sam may seek to argue that Ursula did not make room for the fire engine to pass, but acted instead in a careless manner and that she caused her own injuries, ie that her panic and collision was a novus actus interveniens. As Ursula has been placed in an emergency or difficult situation by Sam's negligence however, the court is unlikely to make this finding if Ursula acted reasonably in the agony of the moment, even if with hindsight she could have avoided the accident: *Jones* v *Boyce* (1816). But it is open to the court to find contributory negligence on Ursula's part and to reduce any damages awarded by s1 Law Reform (Miscellaneous Provisions) Act 1945 having regard to Ursula's fault in causing the accident. All that Sam will have to show is that Ursula failed to look after herself properly: *Davies* v *Swan Motor Co* (1949).

Hence Sam is liable for the eye injury initially suffered by Ursula (subject to any reduction in damages); the question arises, however, is Sam liable for Ursula's subsequent loss of sight or is the earlier railway accident a novus actus interveniens? The new act (ie the railway accident) is an act of a third party and we must decide whether this act is the true cause of Ursula's loss of sight. From the facts of the problem it seems that the loss of Ursula's sight was caused only by the delay, and so Sam would not be liable for this additional damage: *Knightley* v *Johns* (1982). It is not a situation where the delay was a natural and probable consequence of the first accident and was foreseeable as in *Rouse* v *Squires* (1973); instead there has been a break in the chain of causation. Note that the question that must be decided here is one of causation and not foreseeability as Sam is liable for any personal injury that ensues in the accident as he need only foresee the kind of damage and not the extent: *Smith* v *Leech, Brain* (1962).

Similarly Sam will be liable for Violet's slight injuries suffered in the collision but not for her two broken legs, as the cause of the broken legs was a novus actus interveniens which was not a natural and probable consequence of the first collision (see above).

As we are told that Sam was undergoing instruction and is a trainee fireman, it is clear that Sam is an employee, the Waterside Fire Brigade (or the appropriate local authority) is his employer, and Sam was acting in the course of his employment. The fact that Sam was doing so in a negligent manner is irrelevant: *Century Insurance v Northern Ireland Road Transport Board* (1942).

Thus the Waterside Fire Brigade (or the appropriate local authority) will be responsible for Sam's actions and Ursula and Violet are advised to sue the Fire Brigade in respect of the injuries first suffered in the collision; as regards the later more serious injuries they are without a remedy. Ursula and Violet should also be advised that if they failed to wear seat belts and the wearing of a seat belt would have reduced their injuries that a reduction will be made for contributory negligence on their part: *Froom v Butcher* (1975).

4

Contributory Negligence and Volenti Non Fit Injuria

Introduction

CONTRIBUTORY NEGLIGENCE

This operates as a partial defence and has the effect of reducing the plaintiff's damages. The position is governed by the Law Reform (Contributory Negligence) Act 1945. The key points to note are:

1. Fault by the plaintiff: *Nance v British Columbia Electric Railway Co* (1951) and *Tremayne v Hill* (1987).
2. The standard of care element: *Davies v Swan Motor Co* (1949), *Jones v Livox Quarries* (1952) and, recently *Platform Home Loans Ltd v Oyston Shipways Ltd* (1999). Specific examples of concern:
   a) that of children: *Gough v Thorne* (1966), *Yachuk v Oliver Blais* (1949), *Morales v Eccleston* (1991) and *Mullin v Richards* (1998);
   b) that of workmen: *Caswell v Powell Duffryn Associated Colleries* (1940), *Pitts v Hunt* (1991) and *Bux v Slough Metals* (1974);
   c) that of rescuers: *Harrison v British Railways Board* (1981) and *Sayers v Harlow Urban District Council* (1958);
   d) emergencies: *Jones v Boyce* (1816).
3. Causation issues: *Froom v Butcher* (1976), *Stapley v Gypsum Mines* (1953) and *Capps v Miller* (1989).

The courts will reduce damages to such an extent as the court thinks just and equitable: *Pitts v Hunt* (1991) and *Fitzgerald v Lane* (1989). Apportionment is based on the Civil Liability (Contribution) Act 1978. See also the recent cases of *Reeves v Commissioner of Police of the Metropolis* (1999) and *Standard Chartered Bank v Pakistan National Shipping Corporation (No 2)* (2003).

VOLENTI NON FIT INJURIA

Unlike contributory negligence, volenti operates as a complete defence to the plaintiff's claim. It's when the defendant can prove that the plaintiff knew of the risk involved and had voluntarily submitted to that risk. It must be shown that the defendant had committed a tort. Voluntariness on the part of the plaintiff must be proven: *Bowater v Rowley Regis Corporation* (1944), *Smith v Baker* (1891), *ICI v Shatwell* (1965), *Haynes v Harwood* (1935) and *Chadwick v British Transport Commission* (1967). That the plaintiff accepts or agrees to accept the risk of injury must also be established: *Dann v*

Hamilton (1939) and *Nettleship* v *Weston* (1971). Finally, it must be shown that not only did the plaintiff know of the risk, but that he consented to the risk: *Smith* v *Austin Lifts* (1959). Note the relevance of s2(1) and (2) Unfair Contracts Term Act 1977 in relation to exclusion clauses and volenti.

However, recently the Court of Appeal in *Reeves* v *Commissioner of Police of the Metropolis* (1997) held that the volenti defence is inappropriate where the act relied on was the very act which the defendant was under a duty to prevent. This reasoning seems to be in line with *Kirkham* v *Chief Constable of Greater Manchester Police* (1990).

Questions

INTERROGRAMS

1. What needs to be proven for contributory negligence?
2. What was stated in *Nance* v *British Columbia* in 1951?
3. What needs to be shown for the defence of volenti to be successful?
4. Do spectators consent to injury?

QUESTION ONE

Fred is driving his sister Gail to the railway station on a dark evening so that she can catch an overnight train to Scotland for an important meeting. They have been held up in heavy traffic and Gail is convinced that she will be late. After they have waited at a red light for some time, Gail exclaims, 'You stupid fool. The lights have jammed. There's not a thing in sight. Get a move on.' Fred can see no traffic approaching and moves across the junction. He strikes a bicycle ridden at a fast speed by Harry, who is wearing black jeans and sweater. Gail is injured. Harry has unusually brittle bones and dies of his injuries.

Advise Gail and Harry's estate.

University of London LLB Examination
(for external students) Law of Tort June 1997 Q8

QUESTION TWO

Plodders Ltd are a firm which arranges light removals. Kieran works for them as a driver. Kieran uses his own van which he maintains himself and to which he attaches a sign reading, 'Plodders Ltd' when he is working for them. Plodders provide Kieran with overalls and with the equipment needed for loading and unloading goods. He is allowed to take someone with him to assist. On Sunday he was instructed that on the following day he was to travel to Rochester (some miles outside London) to pick up some furniture and bring it back to London. He was told not to go until the afternoon as there would be no-one at home until 2.00 pm. Kieran however decided to leave early so as to spend the morning visiting the cathedral and castle. He took his friend Patrick with him. As he drove into Rochester about 15 mph faster than permitted and rounded a curve in the road he had to brake suddenly to avoid a cyclist ahead of him. The van skidded off the road and down an embankment. Kieran and Patrick were trapped in the van. The cyclist, Camilla, a nurse, jumped over the railings at the edge of the road down to where the van had fallen. She landed on some broken glass which had been concealed by bushes. Kieran was uninjured, but Patrick suffered very serious injuries and Camilla was badly cut and off work for several weeks.

Advise Patrick and Camilla whether they have causes of action against (i) Kieran and (ii) Plodders Ltd.

University of London LLB Examination
(for external students) Law of Tort June 1995 Q8

Answers

ANSWERS TO INTERROGRAMS

1. The defendant must prove two things in order to succeed in the defence of contributory negligence. First, he must prove that the plaintiff was at fault, and, second, that the plaintiff's negligence was a cause of the damage he suffered. This is mirrored by s1(1) of the Law Reform (Contributory Negligence) Act 1945.

2. In *Nance* the court held that 'when contributory negligence is set up as a defence, its existence does not depend on any duty owed by the injured party to the party sued and all that is necessary is to prove to the satisfaction of the jury that the injured party did not in his own interest take reasonable care of himself, and, contributed, by this want of care, to his own injury.'

3. In order for the defence of volenti to be successfully invoked, the defendant has to prove three elements: first, that the plaintiff had knowledge of the risk involved; second, that the plaintiff voluntarily assumed the risk; and, third, that the plaintiff consented to the risk materialising.

4. This deals with the issue of the standard of care owed by competitors of a game to the spectator. The position is neatly summed up by Diplock LJ in *Wooldridge* v *Summer* (1963), wherein he states: 'The spectator takes the risk because such an act involves no breach of the duty of care owed by the participant to him. He does not take the risk by virtue of the doctrine expressed or obscured by the maxim volenti non fit injuria.'

SUGGESTED ANSWER TO QUESTION ONE

General Comment

This type of question calls for an exposition of the various defences to negligence, as well as some discussion of joint liability and the extent of the remedies involved. With so many points to cover, some degree of economy on detail is needed, and planning of the answers is particularly important.

Key Points

• Duty – breach – joint liability to Harry – contribution

- Gail's claim against Fred – defences: volenti, contributory negligence, ex turpi causa
- Harry's claim – defences
- Remoteness and the brittle bones
- The claim by the estate

Suggested Answer

The duty owed by one road user to another is so well established as to be beyond question. The real issues here are whether Gail will owe any duty towards Harry in addition to Fred, who obviously will, and whether there has been breach. Breach may be assumed because, even if the lights had broken down, it would have been prudent for Gail to get out of the car to have better visibility of other road users, but this would normally only show breach by Fred, as the driver. There is an argument here that Fred is acting in the furtherance of a common design in crossing the lights and this may be enough to bring down joint liability upon Gail for Fred's negligence as in *Brooke v Bool* (1928).

Alternatively, there may be an argument that Fred is acting as agent to Gail as principal and has committed a tort within his express authority, thus making her vicariously liable along the lines seen in *Ormrod v Crossville Motor Services Co Ltd* (1953). If this is the situation there would be nothing to prevent Fred's insurers (or the Motor Insurers Bureau if he were uninsured) seeking contribution against her under s1 Civil Liability (Contribution) Act 1978. A similar joint liability arose in *Scarsbrook v Mason* (1961), although the House of Lords in *Morgans v Launchbury* (1973) warned against too easy a recourse to agency principles in car cases where there was generally no fault on the part of the 'principal'. Here there seems to be primary fault on Gail's part.

Gail will be seeking recovery for her own injuries, probably against Fred and his insurers. Various defences may suggest themselves. Although the circumstances indicate that the absolute defence of volenti non fit injuria is in point, this defence is barred by s149(3) Road Traffic Act 1988 as against a passenger. This would not, of course, prevent a defence claim that Gail had contributed to her injuries by want of care for her own safety, and that the damages that she might be awarded should be reduced to reflect a just apportionment of her own blameworthiness under s1(1) Law Reform (Contributory Negligence) Act 1945. There might be a defence claim that, as the pair had agreed to do what is a criminal offence by the driver, her claim should be met by the defence of ex turpi causa non oritur actio. There is no doubt that injuries to, and torts against, the participants in illegal joint enterprises may sometimes be defended by ex turpi causa, but recent cases such as *Revill v Newberry* (1996) and *Pitts v Hunt* (1991) show that a very restrictive view is taken of this defence, particularly where illegality is simply in the mode of driving a vehicle.

As to Harry's claim, there may be a possibility of defences of volenti and contributory negligence. We are not told whether Harry had lights on his bicycle but, assuming that he did not, this might support a claim that he was contributorily negligent. He seems to have been travelling quickly which might be adding to an impression of want of care. In *Tremayne v Hill* (1987) a pedestrian, who failed to watch out for cars going through traffic lights on red, was held not to be contributorily negligent, but it is by no means certain that the same result would follow where a cyclist is going quickly, without lights, in dark clothes at night. All that needs to be established for contributory negligence is a want of care for one's own safety: *Nance* v *British Columbia Electric Railway Co Ltd* (1951). There seems little chance of establishing a volenti defence against Harry's claim because there must be some evidence that Harry was aware of the danger which was 'extreme and glaring' and, nevertheless, resolved to undertake the risk of it as in *Morris* v *Murray* (1991). There is nothing equivalent to that here except as referred to below.

It may be that had Harry not had such brittle bones, he might have survived the incident, possibly with minor injuries. In the normal run of matters, a defendant cannot be heard to raise such a defence because the governing principle is that the tortfeasor must 'take his victim as he finds him', ie with his weaknesses (*Dulieu* v *White and Sons* (1901)), and this principle extends liability to unexpected types of personal injury as in *Smith* v *Leech, Brain and Co* (1962), as well as to greater than expected degrees of damage. This must, of course, give way to the argument that if a person knows that he is extremely vulnerable to certain types of injury, this will, in a proper case, increase the possibility of a contributory negligence defence and, in a very extreme situation, the possible argument that he was volenti to an obvious, extreme and glaring risk.

The claim by Harry's estate will be brought under s1 Law Reform (Miscellaneous Provisions) Act 1934 on the same basis that he himself, had he survived, would have claimed for his personal injuries and damage to his bicycle, clothes, etc. The estate would not be able to claim for his 'lost years' earnings, but would be able to claim for funeral expenses (s1(2)(c)). The claim for his personal injuries would be along conventional lines and much would depend upon what pain, suffering and loss of amenity he suffered prior to his death, as well as lost earnings up to that time. Had Harry any surviving dependants, those persons could bring an action under the Fatal Accidents Act 1976 for bereavement, funeral expenses and actual and future pecuniary losses based upon the valuation of the lost dependency when taken over the period that such a dependency was likely to last. The basis of the calculation for a wage earner is usually the earnings up to the accident less whatever part which was spent by the deceased on his own upkeep. A suitable multiplier is then worked out by reference to the projected length of the dependency, and a suitable discount applied for accelerated receipt of the award, but this claim is for the benefit of the dependants and does not go to the estate.

SUGGESTED ANSWER TO QUESTION TWO

General Comment

This question deals with the liability of rescuers for contributory negligence and vicarious liability. Although the question is asked in two parts, because of the nature of the problem it is permissible to tackle all the issues in one essay rather than in two distinct parts as seems to be required, thus avoiding going over the same ground twice.

Key Points

- Introduction
- Contributory negligence

- Rescuers
- Vicarious liability
- Control test
- Multiple test
- Course of employment
- Conclusion

Suggested Answer

Patrick has suffered personal injuries as a result of Kieran's negligent driving. Whether he recovers damages against Kieran or Plodders Ltd depends upon the application of the rules of vicarious liability. The same rules apply in Camilla's case, although as a rescuer, she is in a special category of plaintiff.

Dealing first with Camilla's status as a rescuer, the reason this is relevant is that the defendant(s) may argue that she was contributorily negligent in jumping over the railings and therefore placing herself in a potentially dangerous situation. If a plaintiff is found to be guilty of contributory negligence then his damages are reduced accordingly under the Law Reform (Contributory Negligence) Act 1945. It is possible for a rescuer to be found guilty of contributory negligence, but it happens rarely. One such case was *Harrison* v *British Railways Board* (1981) in which a railway guard was injured whilst rescuing a passenger who had attempted to board a moving train. The court found that the guard was guilty of contributory negligence by virtue of the fact that he had failed to reduce the danger by not carrying out procedures required by the terms of his employment. However, in the vast majority of cases there will be no such finding. If a defendant creates a perilous situation, it is foreseeable that a brave passer-by will attempt a rescue. There are a number of cases which illustrate this principle. In *Brandon* v *Osborne, Garrett & Co* (1924) the plaintiff was injured by a sheet of falling glass when she attempted to pull her husband out of the way. It was held that she was not guilty of contributory negligence. In *Haynes* v *Harwood* (1935) the plaintiff, a policeman, was injured whilst trying to stop a bolting horse. The horse had been left unattended in the street and had been frightened by a child throwing a stone at it. It was held that the act of the child and the subsequent rescue attempt were both foreseeable and therefore the plaintiff was not guilty of contributory negligence. Applying these principles to Camilla's case it is highly likely that any award of damages she may receive will not be reduced because of contributory negligence.

Turning to the vicarious liability issue, in practice Patrick and Camilla would issue proceedings against both Kieran and Plodders Ltd in the alternative. As a matter of substantive law, however, certain tests need to be applied in order to determine which party is liable. The first point to establish is whether Kieran is an employee of Plodders Ltd in the traditional master and servant context, or an independent contractor, as the principles of liability are different.

It is often said that an employee is employed under a contract of service, whereas an independent contractor is employed under a contract for services. However, this simplistic approach does not explain the fundamental difference between the two types of contract. The courts have struggled to devise the definitive test and it seems that the different tests are all relevant but that each case will be decided upon its own facts. In *Ferguson* v *Dawson (John) and Partners (Contractors) Ltd* (1976) it was held that if the employer controls the type of work to be done and the manner in which it is to be done then it is likely to be a contract of service. This became known as the 'control test' but it has fallen out of favour in recent years with the rise of specialised and highly skilled areas of work in which the employee is left to decide how to carry out the work.

In *Ready Mixed Concrete (South East) Ltd* v *Minister of Pensions and National Insurance* (1968) a more precise test was developed. It was held that, for a contract of service, three conditions must be satisfied. First, the employee must agree to provide his work and skill for his employer in return for wages, second, he must agree to be under the control of his employer, and third, the terms of the contract must be consistent with it being a contract of service. The most comprehensive test, the multiple test, was that used in *Market Investigations Ltd* v *Minister of Social Security* (1969). This is a two-stage test in which the first question to ask is whether the worker is providing a service as a person in business on his own account. If so, then he is not an employee. The factors to be taken into account are whether the worker provides his own equipment, whether he is responsible for hiring his own helpers, his degree of financial risk, and his degree of responsibility for investment and management.

In Kieran's case, applying the above tests seems to suggest that he is an independent contractor working under a contract for services. This is borne out by the facts that he uses his own van, and that he chooses his own helpers. Against this is the fact that Plodders Ltd provide him with overalls and equipment. However, in the overall context, Kieran is highly likely to be found to be an independent contractor. If this is the case, then he will be liable in negligence to Patrick and Camilla, rather than Plodders Ltd, as it is trite law that an employer is not liable for the negligent acts of independent contractors.

If, on the other hand, the court finds that Kieran is an employee of Plodders Ltd then, prima facie, Plodders will be liable. For the employer to be liable the tort must be committed in the course of the employee's employment. This is a question of fact in each case, but the courts tend to adopt a somewhat liberal approach as a matter of public policy. The reason for this is that the employer is better able to pay damages as he is insured against such risks, whereas employees in the vast majority of cases are not. If, however, the employee's act is wholly unconnected to his employment, then he will be liable rather than his employer. In *Joel* v *Morrison* (1834) the court used the phrase 'was the employee on a frolic of his own?' to describe the situation where the employee acts outside the course of his employment. An example of such a case is *Beard* v *London General Omnibus Co* (1900) in which a bus conductor drove a bus in the absence of the driver and the employer was held not liable as he was clearly acting outside his employment. This can be contrasted with *Limpus* v *London General Omnibus Co* (1862) in which a bus driver who raced his employer's bus was held to be acting within his employment as he was still driving the bus, the task for which he was employed.

Applying these principles to the present case, if the court finds that Kieran is an employee of Plodders Ltd then he was acting within the course of his employment as he was doing what he was employed to do even though he was driving too fast. Accordingly, Plodders would be liable for Kieran's negligent driving.

Part II: General Concepts of Tortious Liability

5

Vicarious Liability

Introduction

The essence of this doctrine is to render X (the employer) liable to Z (a third party) for the tortious act of Y (X's employee). In order for liability to be imposed, three conditions must be satisfied:

1. there must be an emloyment relationship existing as between the employer and employee;
2. the employee must commit a tort (see *Dubai Aluminium Co Ltd* v *Salaam* (2002));
3. the tort must be committed in the course of employment: see *Lister* v *Hesley Hall Ltd* (2001).

Among the many rationales of this doctrine is one which states that since the employer benefits from the employee's work, it is only fair that he bears the burden too. There have been several tests propounded by the courts to define whether an employment relationship exists. They are: the control test (*Yewens* v *Noakes* (1880)); the business integration or organisation test: (*Stevenson, Jordan and Harrison* v *MacDonald* (1952)); and the 'label' test: *Market Investigations* v *Minister of Social Security* (1968). The issue of casual workers was settled by the Court of Appeal in *O'Kelly* v *Trusthouse Forte* (1983) when it stated that they were not employees. Consideration must also be had if the employee is seconded to another employer. Liability then rests on the employer having a high degree of control: *Mersey Docks and Harbour Board* v *Coggins & Griffith* (1947). A tort must be committed by the employee for liability to arise: *ICI* v *Shatwell* (1965). Finally, the tort must be committed by the employee in the course of employment. This means anything that is connected or related to the employment, ie either doing an authorised act in an unauthorised manner, or doing something prohibited, or doing something intentionally, negligently or recklessly. Acts done when the employee is on a frolic of his own will exonerate the employer from liability as that would be deeemed to be outside the course of employment. As a general rule, an employer will not be liable for the acts of his independent contractors unless there is a non-delegable duty in issue.

Joint and several liability exists and liability will be determined/apportioned on the basis of the Civil Liability (Contribution) Act 1978. See also the recent case of *Royal Brompton Hospital NHS Trust* v *Hammond* (2002) on this point. Also of relevance is the recent Limited Liability Partnerships Act 2000.

Questions

INTERROGRAMS

1. Why should the employer be liable for his employee's tort/s?
2. What is the distinction between ordinary and vicarious liability?
3. Would the employer be liable for a theft committed by an employee?
4. How would a court approach the definition of an employment relationship today?

QUESTION ONE

Jim is a lorry driver employed by Slapdash Carriers Ltd. His assistant was ill one day and he asked Kyle and Leo, two office boys, to load up his lorry as he had a lot of other things to attend to. All three of them know that office workers are forbidden by their employer to do so. Nevertheless they loaded some barrels on to the lorry and locked the tailgate. Jim had to deliver the load to the premises of International Thumbscrews plc. When he lowered the tailgate, a barrel rolled out and struck Melvyn, an employee of International Thumbscrews, who was waiting to unload the consignment.

Melvyn was permanently paralysed and will not be able to return to work. He has also had to give up his hobbies of snooker and cricket. He had been a valued employee and Thumbscrews provided him with a car and paid for adaptations to his flat. He became extremely irritable and aggressive as the result of his injuries and his girlfriend left him. His mother Noreen has, however, given up her job to care for him permanently.

Advise Melvyn (i) if he has a cause of action in tort and (ii), if so, how the damages will be assessed.

University of London LLB Examination
(for external students) Law of Tort June 2001 Q6

QUESTION TWO

Gina is a qualified word processor who is registered with Paperjam, a word processing agency. She is at present working at Macro & Merge Ltd, who have recruited her through Paperjam to cover for a member of staff on sick leave. On returning from lunch one day, she saw a man, whom she did not know, alone in the office loading computers onto a trolley. She struck him in the stomach, winding him and ran out locking the office door. The man was Hugo, who was employed by the maintenance department of Macro & Merge, and he was removing the computers in the course of his work. Hugo was known to his employers to suffer from asthma and to be prone to blackouts during which he sometimes needed assistance. Hugo had a very severe asthmatic attack and passed out. He has suffered permanent damage to his health.

Advise Hugo as to any claims in tort.

University of London LLB Examination
(for external students) Law of Tort June 1999 Q7

QUESTION THREE

Describe, and explain the purpose of, the concept of vicarious liability. Consider what, if any, development of the concept is appropriate now that the pattern of employment is changing and many people do not work for a single permanent employer.

University of London LLB Examination
(for external students) Law of Tort June 1997 Q2

QUESTION FOUR

Luke is unemployed but has enrolled on a government training scheme. He is sent three days each week for work experience to the offices of Newfield Industries plc. The office manager Matilda was sent to a conference one day in a town forty miles away and was told to take the company car. She asked Luke to go with her as part of his work experience. She also thought that she might be drinking and that Luke could then drive the car, but did not tell Luke this. Both Luke and Matilda knew that he was not allowed to drive the company car. On the way back Matilda stopped for a drink at a pub and asked Luke to take over the driving. Luke drove out of the pub car park without looking and caused Neil, a passing motor cyclist, to swerve. Neil struck a tree and was seriously injured.

Advise Neil as to any rights of action in tort.

University of London LLB Examination
(for external students) Law of Tort June 1994 Q8

QUESTION FIVE

'Neither the liability of an employer to an employee on the basis of breach of statutory duty, nor vicarious responsibility for fellow employees, adds much to the liability resulting from the employer's personal duty of care.'

Discuss.

Written by the Author

Answers

ANSWERS TO INTERROGRAMS

1. The justification of this doctrine is based on several factors. First, the employer has control over his employees, therefore he is responsible for the employee's acts. Second, the employer selects his employee and, if he chooses incompetent staff, he is responsible. Third, since the employer derives benefit from the services of the employee, so too should he bear the burden that accrues therefrom. Insurability is another element because the employer is in a better position to compensate the victim than the employee. Finally, it is to prevent recurrence and ensure that services are constantly improved.
2. For ordinary liability, three elements must be established. They are: first, the

existence of a duty of care; second, a breach of that duty; and, third, damage or loss resulting consequently. There need not be any type of relationship between the parties for ordinary liability. For vicarious liability an employment relationship must exist, a tort must be committed by the employee and, finally, it must be commited in the course of employment.

3. As far as theft is concerned, the position is this: if the theft is committed as part of a bona fide attempt to do the job or in the employer's interests, then it would fall within the scope of employment and would pin liability on the employer. However, if the crime is committed for the employee's own personal benefit or amusement, then no liability will befall the employer.

4. Although many tests exist in relation to defining an employment relationship, the courts would today look at several issues, such as: how the parties have described the legal relationship between themselves; whether the work done an integral part of the business, or incidental to it; who bears the risk of loss and the chance of profit; and who exercises control over the employee's performance of services.

SUGGESTED ANSWER TO QUESTION ONE

General Comment

This is a two part question. The first requires an analysis of the law on vicarious liability and the relevance of the concept of 'res ipsa loquitor' in relation to Melvyn. The second part of the question requires an assessment of damages under the various heads.

Key Points

*   The principles establishing liability under vicarious liability: the employer/employee relationship – the course of employment – the role of Kyle and Leo – the role of Jim – res ipsa loquitor
*   Assessment of damages: special damages – general damages

Suggested Answer

The most important and commonest example of vicarious liability can be found in the employer/employee relationship: an employer is liable for the torts committed by an employee who is acting in the course of his employment. An employer/employee relationship is thus essential and must therefore be primarily established.

On the facts of this question, it is clear that Jim is an employee of Slapdash Carriers and was employed as a lorry driver. Second, it must be established that the tort committed by Jim was done within the course of employment. This is also easily provable, as the question states that Melvyn suffered the injury when Jim went to unload the delivery from his lorry.

Therefore Melvyn, a third party, suffered an injury caused by Jim's negligence. This would implicate Jim's employer, Slapdash Carriers, on the basis of vicarious liability. However, what might arise as a potential problem is the fact that Slapdash Carriers may deny liability on the basis that, as Kyle and Leo were office boys and thus had no authority (express or implied) to load the barrels onto the lorry, that took them outside of the course of employment. In *Century Insurance Co v Northern Ireland Road Transport Board* (1942) it was stated that the employer will only escape liability if the employee goes outside the course of his employment, ie if the employee's act is not connected with the authorised act, as to be an independent act of the employee. Therefore, Slapdash Carriers may claim that Kyle and Leo were doing something other than that for which they had been employed. They were doing an unauthorised act. Whilst that argument may be acceptable in relation to Kyle and Leo, what about the role of Jim? It might be argued that Jim had improperly carried out his work by delegating the task of loading to Kyle and Leo. Jim was in fact doing something that he was authorised to do, but in a wrongful way: *Limpus v London General Omnibus Co* (1862). On this basis, Slapdash Carriers would most certainly be vicariously liable. There is no problem establishing negligence on the part of Kyle, Leo and Jim. The barrrels had been negligently loaded so as to roll out as soon as the tailgate was lowered. This raises the doctrine of 'res ipsa loquitor', otherwise known as 'the thing that speaks for itself'. If something is so obvious, there is no need to prove it: *Scott v London and St Katherine Docks Co* (1865).

Therefore, Melvyn would have no problem establishing a case under vicarious liability. If, on the other hand, Melvyn can establish that his employers have failed to provide him with a safe system of work, as in *Walker v Northumberland County Council* (1995), then Melvyn may have a case against his employers, International Thumbscrews, under employer's liability. But there is little on the facts of this case to suggest this possibility. The next issue to be considered is the various heads of damage that would be available to Melvyn in his personal injury claim. Melvyn has, as a result of the accident, become permanently paralysed.

Briefly, damages in personal injury claims are divided in two distinct groups. First, 'special damages'. This includes pecuniary loss up to the date of trial; it can also include costs of medical care, equipment, loss of earnings and other such expenses that the court might consider to be reasonable under the circumstances.

Second, 'general damages' or 'future damages'. This includes pecuniary loss such as future earnings, medical costs, costs of care, special facilities and costs of adapting the home. It also includes non-pecuniary loss, such as pain and suffering and loss of amenities. Non-pecuniary losses are difficult to quantify and awards are based entirely on arbitrary calculations. However, guidance is normally sought from authoritative works in the area, such as Kemp and Kemp, for instance. Loss of earnings are calculated by multiplying the multiplicand (the claimant's annual net loss) by a multiplier (a notional figure representing the number of years the court feels the award should cover).

Therefore, Melvyn would be able to recover all of the following:

1. the loss of earnings – both actual and future or prospective loss;
2. all medical and other expenses that have been reasonably incurred, such as travelling expenses, the cost of special equipment or of employing someone to carry out domestic duties which the claimant is no longer able to perform;
3. the loss of pension rights;
4. pain and suffering in respect of his injuries (permanent paralysis); and

5. loss of faculty and amenity, such as loss of job satisfaction, loss of leisure activities and hobbies and loss of family life (all are relevant in Melvyn's case).

Melvyn may also recover insofar as the car and the adaptations to his flat are concerned, but as this has been paid for by his 'compassionate' employers, the court will not allow double recovery (unless it is being claimed to reimburse his employers). Melvyn will not be able to claim for Nora's loss of earnings, but he would be able to claim for the cost of permanent care.

SUGGESTED ANSWER TO QUESTION TWO

General Comment

This is a relatively straightforward question for those students who are familiar with the torts of trespass to the person. In addition, it is always necessary to consider the possibility of employer's liability in negligence where injuries are sustained by an employee in the course of employment.

Key Points

- Discuss Gina's liability for claims in battery and false imprisonment
- Are Hugo's injuries too remote given his unusual physical susceptibility?
- Examine the defences of lawful arrest to a claim of false imprisonment and self-defence to a claim in battery
- If Gina has committed a tort against Hugo, are either Macro & Merge Ltd or Paperjam vicariously liable?
- Who was Gina employed by?
- Was her attack in the course of her employment?
- Are Macro & Merge Ltd liable in negligence on the basis of a breach of the duty to provide a safe system of work?
- Were Hugo's injuries too remote to recover for, given his unusual physical susceptibility?

Suggested Answer

Claims against Gina
Gina's liability in tort is relatively easy to establish in these circumstances. Hugo may have claims in battery and false imprisonment.

Battery
Battery is the intentional and direct application of unlawful force to another. The elements of battery are easily satisfied in this case. The contact with Hugo's stomach was a direct act on the part of Gina, ie a direct cause of her act of striking him. The act itself was intentional rather than merely accidental or negligent: *Letang v Cooper* (1965). The force used by Gina is certainly likely to be regarded as unlawful in that it was either hostile in the circumstances: *Wilson v Pringle* (1987) or without lawful excuse, lacking Hugo's consent: *Re F (Mental Patient: Sterilisation)* (1990). Battery, along with other

trespass related torts, is actionable per se, without the need to prove any injury to the claimant.

False imprisonment

This is the infliction of bodily restraint which is not expressly or impliedly authorised by law. Once again, the elements of false imprisonment appear to be present in the circumstances described. The confinement of the claimant must be such that his liberty is totally restrained: *Bird* v *Jones* (1845) with no reasonable means of escape. An issue here is whether Hugo was aware of his apparent confinement to the office after Gina's attack. Early authority appeared to suggest that false imprisonment is not committed where the claimant is unaware of any restriction placed upon his freedom: *Herring* v *Boyle* (1834). The modern approach, however, seems to be that a person can be falsely imprisoned whilst unconscious, although any award of damages will be purely nominal unless the claimant suffers some other form of harm as a result: *Murray* v *Ministry of Defence* (1988). It is submitted that Gina's intentional locking of the office door almost certainly gives rise to a claim for false imprisonment, and that Hugo is likely to be entitled to compensatory damages for any period of awareness of his confinement before he passed out, and possibly after he came to, and the fact that the harm he suffered following Gina's attack was aggravated by his on-going confinement without medical treatment.

Remoteness

Battery and false imprisonment are trespasses against the person, and as such are actionable per se without the need to prove any injury to the claimant. This means that Hugo can recover for all the injuries resulting from Gina's unlawful acts, whether or not they were foreseeable, including any direct harm caused by the impact to his stomach, the suffering caused by the winding and the subsequent asthma attack, and the injuries resulting in permanent damage to Hugo's health.

Defences

The main defence to a claim of false imprisonment is lawful arrest. Section 24(4) Police and Criminal Evidence Act 1984 allows anyone, including a private citizen, to make an arrest where they have reasonable grounds for suspecting that an arrestable offence is being committed (even if, in fact, there is no offence). It will be for Gina to justify any arrest on the balance of probabilities, unless she is to be found liable for false imprisonment. She will have to establish that she actually believed Hugo was in the course of committing a theft (an arrestable offence), and further, that she had reasonable grounds to suspect that he was doing so. It is this latter aspect which may cause problems for Gina. It could be argued that an objective observer would take the view that Gina's initial suspicion did not turn into a reasonable one, because she failed to challenge Hugo as to his presence in the office and to ask to see some identification. Macro & Merge Ltd appear to be a large employer, and Gina as a temporary member of staff clearly cannot expect to recognise everyone in the office. However, the question of reasonable suspicion is one which will have to be determined in all the circumstances of the case.

There is a further question as to the lawfulness of any arrest carried out by Gina, in that the provision of some information to the suspect upon arrest is normally necessary, unless the fact and grounds for arrest are obvious: *Christie* v *Leachinsky* (1947). In other cases, probably such as this, Gina would be required to give sufficient information to inform Hugo as to the factual and legal basis of the accusation against him. In the absence of such an explanation, there will be no valid lawful arrest.

It is unlikely that Gina will be able to raise self-defence to a claim of battery against Hugo. Gina would effectively have to establish the existence of a defence in tort of 'mistaken self-defence of the property of another', requiring considerable expansion of the existing authorities in this area.

Claims against Macro & Merge Ltd and Paperjam

Vicarious liability
Whilst Gina's liability in tort appears to be easily established, Hugo will want to claim against an organisation which is better placed to compensate him than a temporary employee. Gina's employer will almost certainly carry an insurance policy to meet such a claim. The two main issues that arise here relate to the identity of Gina's employer at the time of the incident and whether Gina was acting in the course of her employment when she attacked Hugo.

Who is the employer?
It is unclear whether Gina is employed on a temporary basis by Macro & Merge Ltd, or on an on-going basis by the agency that supplied her. The modern approach is for the courts to consider a range of factors and to examine all the circumstances of Gina's working relationship as against each potential employer. Such factors, none of which are conclusive on their own, will include the following.

1. Who paid Gina's wages and National Insurance contributions in return for her work and skill?
2. Who had the authority to exercise a sufficient degree of control over the manner in which Gina did her work?
3. Who could dismiss Gina?
4. How long was she hired out for?

Was Gina in the course of her employment when she attacked Hugo?
Assuming, for a moment, that Gina is an employee of Macro & Merge Ltd, she will be impliedly authorised (although not legally bound) to protect her employer's property, provided that her actions are not so outrageous that a reasonable employer would not have contemplated them as being within the scope of employment. For example, an employee was held to be acting in the course of his employment when he struck a boy whom he reasonably believed to be in the course of steeling goods belonging to his employer: *Poland* v *Parr & Sons* (1927). If the employee acts so excessively beyond what is necessary to deal with the emergency (eg were Gina to have shot Hugo) then the employee steps beyond the scope of his employment.

It is submitted, on this basis, that Gina is acting in the course of her employment with Macro & Merge Ltd. However, it may be one stage too far removed to suggest that she is acting in the course of any employment with Paperjam, the agency which supplied her, when acting to protect Macro & Merge Ltd's property against what she assumed was a theft.

Employers' liability

Macro & Merge Ltd may be liable in negligence for a breach of their non-delegable duty to devise and operate a safe system of work. Such a duty may arise in view of their knowledge of Hugo's asthmatic condition, his susceptibility to blackouts and his subsequent need for occasional assistance. The particular characteristics of a claimant are relevant in deciding how a reasonable employer ought to have discharged its duty. In *Paris* v *Stepney Borough Council* (1951) for example, an employer's failure to provide an employee, who was already blind in one eye, with safety goggles amounted to a breach of this duty due to the serious possible (and actual) consequences of the employee sustaining further eye injury. Thus it could be argued that Macro & Merge Ltd's failure to ensure that Hugo was accompanied at all times by another member of staff amounts to a breach of the duty to provide a safe system of work. Clearly, injury to Hugo was foreseeable as a result of the failure to provide adequate supervision, and so it does not matter that the extent of Hugo's injuries, and the precise way in which they occurred, could not have been foreseen: *Hughes* v *Lord Advocate* (1963).

SUGGESTED ANSWER TO QUESTION THREE

General Comment

In such a question, the narrative and descriptive of parts of the question should be dealt with fairly shortly. The essential points, such as necessary relationships and course of employment, judicial controls, etc, should be covered, but the candidate should take a vigorous approach to the real problems and possible solutions that follow from rapidly changing patterns of occupation. Consideration of alternative safeguards, such as statutory schemes, insurance, etc, might be discussed.

Key Points

- The origins and nature of vicarious liability
- The significance of employment situations as distinct from independent contractor situations
- The social and economic arguments involved
- Changes in working patterns and the implications for vicarious liability
- Suggested changes and developments to the doctrine – legislative intervention and insurance arrangements

Suggested Answer

The modern doctrine of vicarious liability has its historical roots in the idea that the master should be liable for the torts of his servant, if committed 'within the course of employment'. This pattern of liability to third parties within a close and well-known relationship has remained to modern times, and vicarious liability will still arise only in such relationships as employer/employee or principal/agent. There remains also the requirement that the tort should be committed within the course of employment or, with agents, within some express or implied or ostensible authority: *Storey* v *Ashton* (1869) (employees); *Lloyd* v *Grace, Smith & Co* (1912) (agency). The question of just what distinguishes an employee from some other form of contractor has occupied the courts to a very considerable extent and, after several attempts at a satisfactory rationale, such as the 'control test' (*Yewens* v *Noakes* (1880)) and the 'in business on own account' test from *Market Investigations Ltd* v *Minister of Social Security* (1969) (still used for taxation purposes), the modern view seems to prefer the three-stage approach favoured by MacKenna J in *Ready Mixed Concrete (South East) Ltd* v *Minister of Pensions* (1968) as being more appropriate to the question of vicarious liability for torts.

The question of 'course of employment' can be seen from the cases as being one that the courts consider a matter for decision by them rather than one which is dictated by the employer and the terms of employment. This is highlighted by cases on the effect of express prohibitions, such as the contrasting cases of *Twine* v *Bean's Express Ltd* (1946) and *Rose* v *Plenty* (1976). It is clear that the court will be the final arbiter of what is an 'unauthorised act' so as to take the matter outside the course of employment, preferring, on occasion, to find that the matter is an 'unauthorised mode of doing an authorised act' as in *Limpus* v *London General Omnibus Co Ltd* (1862).

A finding that an employment relationship subsists is usually much more advantageous to the third party victim of a tort because the alternative, that the tortfeasor is an independent contractor, means that the general vicarious liability of the employer for torts within the course of employment is replaced by an altogether narrower range of liabilities under which one independent contractor is, by way of exception to the general rule, liable for torts committed by an independent contractor employed by him. If the tort falls outside this narrower band of exceptional situations, the victim will only have a remedy against the direct tortfeasor who may sometimes be unable to satisfy a judgment.

The legal rationale for vicarious liability seems, at bottom, to come down to a matter of 'social convenience and rough justice': per Lord Pearce in *Imperial Chemical Industries Ltd* v *Shatwell* (1965). It seems logical that liability should fall jointly upon the primary tortfeasor and the person best able to profit from the other's labours and who, as employer, is in an infinitely better position to obtain insurance cover at sensible rates; the employer will be the one best able to assess the range of risk, scale of damage and the quality of employee required for the employment.

The doctrine of vicarious liability arose over a period in which the distinction between employee and self-employed was obvious and clear. Over the last few decades, patterns of business and occupation have changed to an unprecedented degree, with a large part of the adult working population becoming increasingly involved in part-time and short-period engagements. In combination with the business attractiveness of reducing employed labour forces this has led to many situations where the true working relationship is often extremely unclear. Examples of this can be seen in the *Ready Mixed Concrete* and *Market Investigations* cases. In many cases, the very reason for these changes is to restrict the liabilities to others, including third parties. Clearly, as matters stand, this will reduce the possibilities for vicarious liability, especially where the use of individual independent contractors replaces an employee workforce. This has gone hand-in-hand with a perceived increase in the use of the so-called 'masters indemnity' against the tortfeasor employee as seen in *Lister v Romford Ice and Cold Storage Co Ltd* (1957), probably at the instance of the insurers.

Is there, then, anything that can be done to help the third party in such circumstances? A possibility might be to extend the liability for the torts of independent contractors to the situation where, if the damage to a third party were reasonably foreseeable had it been caused by an employee, the fact that an independent contractor is used will not prevent a joint liability arising. This might be combined with a statutorily implied term into any such contract that, in the event that the parties had not agreed upon which party provides third-party cover, the liability will be deemed to be joint. In any event, the matter would require legislation; short of this, matters will have to progress naturally and only time will show how useful vicarious liability will be in the future.

SUGGESTED ANSWER TO QUESTION FOUR

General Comment

This is a question that involves a consideration of the relationship between employer and employee, and the way in which tortious acts fit into that relationship.

Key Points

- Negligence
- Vicarious liability
- Employer/employee
- Course of employment

Suggested Answer

It is possible from a consideration of the parties mentioned in the question to discern a number of people who, on face value, could be considered responsible for Neil's accident. These range from Luke, the obvious cause of the accident, through to Newfield Industries, the party most likely to be able to bear any costs, and even to an external body, like the Motor Insurance Bureau.

It seems appropriate to begin with Luke, as the driver of the car that caused the accident. The central difficulty with Neil initiating proceedings against any individual defendant is that they will either be impecunious or certainly not in a financial position to meet any claim. So, the issue of culpability becomes submerged in the reality of the economic situation and highlights that this problem involves discussion of practicalities as well as academic points. In the light of Luke's unemployed status, it seems unlikely that he will be able to compensate Neil. It seems probable that the same will apply to Matilda who, although she is in employment, is not likely to be in a position to pay the sorts of sums that can be involved in serious personal injury actions.

It then falls to consider Newfield Industries plc, who would be in a much better position to meet the claim, if not through any insurance they may have, then certainly through their position to pass on any losses. This, in essence, is the heart of the problem, namely whether Newfield Industries can be held vicariously liable for the actions of Luke and of Matilda. In order for the courts to find in favour of Neil, there are certain hurdles that such a claim must surmount. First, Newfield Industries will only be held responsible if a wrongful act has been committed by another person. There must have been a tortious act. It is difficult to see that there is any other interpretation to place on the incident in the light of the facts given in the question.

Second, Newfield Industries will only be responsible if it is possible to show a special relationship existing between them and the wrongdoer. This relationship has to be one recognised by law, and in reality this limb of liability only relates to the relationship between employer and employee. Matilda would obviously fall into the category of employee on the factual situation under discussion. There are, however, problems in relation to Luke and whether he is an employee of Newfield Industries. It seems probable that they would try to argue that any responsibility for Luke does not lie with them because he is on work experience as part of his government training scheme. In general terms, where an employer (A) 'lends' an employee to another employer (B), if that employee then commits a tortious act, it is difficult for A to shift any responsibility onto the temporary employer (B). It remains, however, a question of fact and it appears that the circumstances in this case would not allow Newfield Industries to deny that they controlled Luke. This being the case it seems undeniable that Luke would be seen as operating within the necessary special relationship.

The final hurdle will, in this case, prove the most difficult for Neil to establish, namely that Newfield Industries should be held vicariously liable for the actions of Luke. Neil needs to establish that Luke was acting in the course of his employment and so found a connection between Luke's act and his special relationship with Newfield Industries. This involves considering a mixed question of law and of fact and considering whether, at the time of the accident, Luke and Matilda were undertaking unauthorised deviations from their work. It was in *Joel* v *Morrisson* (1834) that the courts considered that a 'master' will not be liable for a 'servant's' actions, if the servant is on a frolic of his own. It is therefore for the courts to establish what is meant by a 'frolic of his own'. There is a suggestion in *Williams* v *A & W Hemphill Ltd* (1966), a Scottish case, that the actions must be solely for the selfish purposes of the employee. It therefore seems that stopping for a drink at the pub could not be seen as incidental to the journey and doing so takes the detour outside the course of their employment. It would also appear that the intentionally wrongful act by both Luke and Matilda, in allowing Luke to drive while knowing he was not permitted to do so, would take their actions outside the course of employment. Therefore, Neil appears not to have any recourse against Newfield Industries plc. However, mention should be made of *Ilkiw* v *Samuels* (1963), where a lorry driver allowed a third party to move his lorry without ensuring that he was able and insured to do it. The employers were vicariously liable because the lorry driver was employed not only to drive the lorry but to be in charge of it. Likewise, it might be possible to argue that Matilda was in a similar position. The potential scope of an action against Newfield Industries would be limited but in advising Neil on a purely practical basis, it may be worth, at the very least, initiating proceedings.

Finally, for the sake of completeness and bearing in mind the difficulties that Neil would face in tackling Newfield Industries plc, mention must be made of the Motor Insurers' Bureau (MIB). Neil may find that in the event of his failing to succeed in levelling the blame for his accident at Newfield Industries, the MIB may meet the unsatisfied judgment, if Luke was not insured to drive the car that caused the accident.

SUGGESTED ANSWER TO QUESTION FIVE

General Comment

Quite a widely drafted general question that covers employers' personal duties, employers' breaches of statutory duties and employers' vicarious liability for torts of employees during the course of employment. Hence a well-rounded approach to the answer is necessary.

Key Points

*   Employers' liability at common law – non-delegable nature
*   Breaches of statutory duties – non-delegable nature and extent of such duties
*   Vicarious liability
*   Implications of the Law Reform (Personal Injuries) Act 1948 – recent case law

Suggested Answer

At common law, an employer's personal duty of care to an employee comprises a 'threefold obligation', namely the provision of competent staff, adequate equipment and a safe system of work: *Wilsons and Clyde Coal Co* v *English* (1938).

This definition is not exhaustive and has been extended to cover a duty to warn a prospective employee of the risks, or inherent risks, involved in the work prior to the employee accepting employment: *White* v *Holbrook Precision Castings* (1985).

The burden, as dictated by convention, is on the employee to prove that the employer either deliberately or negligently breached the personal duty of care and that as a result the employee suffered loss and damage. The vital point here is that the personal duty of care is non-delegable in nature.

The injured employee may also be able to rely on two other forms of employer's liability which overlap, but which do not necessarily or precisely coincide with the employer's personal duty. These are breach of statutory duty and vicarious liability. It must be noted that for vicarious liability the employee must be shown to have been acting in the course of employment. This principle was recently the subject of judicial attention in *Lister* v *Hesley Hall Ltd* (2001).

With regard to statutory duties, it will be a matter of construction whether the particular duty was in fact intended by Parliament to be strict, such as in the case of the duty to fence dangerous machinery. If the duty is strict, the employee is relieved of the burden of proving fault although he must still prove breach of statutory duty and consequent damage, as in *Groves* v *Wimborne* (1898). In *London Passenger Transport Board* v *Upson* (1949) Lord Wright emphasised the importance of conceptual distinction between employers' personal and statutory duties. A statutory duty of the strict kind is, however, similar to the personal duty in being non-delegable in character.

The statutory duty may be interpreted to include a duty to protect the employee from suffering pure economic loss, if that kind of loss is within the ambit or scope of the relevant statute. For example, an Act to protect the performing rights of film actors could protect correlative financial interests. By contrast, the employer's personal duty of care does not extend to protect his employee from such loss because common law regards their relationship as being insufficiently proximate, with no assumption of special responsibility by the employer. This is consistent with recent common law hostility to the imposition of tortious duties to prevent pure economic loss, especially where a contract exists between the parties which may either expressly or impliedly deal with such loss in a more satisfactory manner than the law of tort. In *Reid* v *Rush & Tompkins* (1990) the Court of Appeal held that there was no duty to insure an employee or to warn him of the wisdom of self-insurance in a case where the employee was being sent to work overseas. This, of course, must be distinguished from the situations encompassed by the Employers' Liability (Compulsory Insurance) Act 1969.

With regard to vicarious liability, there was a considerable expansion in the scope of such liability following the passage of the Law Reform (Personal Injuries) Act 1948. Before the Act the employer had a defence called common employment which prevented an employee suing him for the torts of a fellow employee. The 1948 Act abolished this defence so that where the employee can prove fault by a fellow employee, a claim under the principles of vicarious liability will succeed. Nevertheless, the continued existence of the employer's personal duty to provide competent staff may still be of relevance, such as where the injured employee cannot prove fault but can establish that the other employee was not suitably qualified or experienced to perform the job in question.

Further, there may be one area where the personal duty is wider in scope than vicarious liability. That area covers dishonest conduct by an employee. As a general rule, an employer is not vicariously liable for such conduct even though he may have placed the dishonest employee in a position where he had the opportunity to steal from fellow employees, unless it was a special position of trust akin to an agency, as was the case in *Armagas* v *Mundagos SA, The Ocean Frost* (1986). However, an employer may be held liable for breach of his personal duty if he had knowingly employed a dishonest servant.

Finally, the personal duty is non-delegable and therefore constitutes an important exception to the principles of vicarious liability under which there is no liability for the acts of an independent contractor. For example, in *McDermid* v *Nash Dredging and Reclamation Co Ltd* (1987), where the defendant employer had put the plaintiff employee under the control of a tugmaster who operated an unsafe system of work on the tug, it was held that the defendant was liable for not providing a safe system of work. The House of Lords made it clear that the threefold obligation of the employer's personal duty was non-delegable in all of its three parts. This was recently reaffirmed in *Royal Brompton Hospital NHS Trust* v *Hammond* (2002).

6

Occupiers' Liability

Introduction

This is a specialised aspect of common law negligence. The primary distinction is that it is wholly governed by statute, ie the Occupiers' Liability Act 1957 which concerns the liability of an occupier of premises to his/her various classes of visitors and the Occupiers' Liability Act 1984 which concerns the occupier's liability to trespassers. As this area is governed wholly by statute, it is thus necessary to give close attention to the exact words used by Parliament, as they would set out the limits to the ambit of liability. The following must be defined:

1. An occupier – one who has sufficient degree of control over premises. The Act does not require the occupier to be living in the premises to owe a duty of care: *Cavalier v Pope* (1906) and *Wheat v Lacon* (1966).
2. A 'lawful visitor' – a person who enters with the express or implied permission of the occupier or those who have a contractual right of entry.

THE SCOPE OF THE OCCUPIERS' LIABILITY ACT 1957

- Section 1 defines the parameters of liability.
- Section 2 defines the extent of the occupier's ordinary duty.
- Section 2(1) and (2) sets out the common duty of care.
- Section 2(3)(a) governs duty owed to children: *Glasgow Corporation v Taylor* (1922) and *Phipps v Rochester Corporation* (1955).
- Section 2(3)(b) deals with the issue of common calling: *Roles v Nathan* (1963) and *Ogwo v Taylor* (1988).
- Section 2(4)(a) imposes the need for warnings of danger: *Roles v Nathan* (1963) and *Staples v West Dorset County Council* (1995).
- Section 2(4)(b) relates to liability in relation to independent contractors: *Haseldine v Daw* (1941) and *Woodward v Mayor of Hastings* (1945). See also the recent case of *Waddingtons plc v Leeds City Council* (1999).
- Section 2(5) provides the defence of 'volenti non fit injuria': *Simms v Leigh Rugby FC* (1969).
- Section 3 relates to the effect of contract on occupier's liability to third party.
- Section 5 deals with implied terms in contracts.

THE SCOPE OF THE OCCUPIERS' LIABILITY ACT 1984

The applicability of this Act is illustrated by s1(3)(a) and (b) which sets out the two-stage approach in discerning the duty of care to trespassers:

- Section 1(3)(a): *White v St Albans City and District Council* (1990).

- Section 1(3)(b): *Revill* v *Newberry* (1996).

See also, in general, *Addie* v *Dumbreck* (1929) which was subsequently overruled by the House of Lords in *British Railways Board* v *Herrington* (1972). The standard of care imposed is to take reasonable care to see that the trespasser does not suffer any injury while on the premises. The element of foreseeability must be present: *Jolley* v *Sutton London Borough Council* (2000) and *Tomlinson* v *Congleton Borough Council and Another* (2003).

Questions

INTERROGRAMS

1. What is an occupier for the purposes of the 1957 Act?
2. Who is a visitor for the purposes of the 1957 Act?
3. Who is a trespasser for the purposes of the 1984 Act?
4. Is it possible to exclude the duty of care imposed on the occupier under the 1957 and 1984 Acts?

QUESTION ONE

Satanic Industries occupy factory premises. They engaged Demon Constructors to carry out substantial construction work on the ground floor, including the reception area. Satanic erected notices at the entrance saying: 'Please take care. Construction work in progress'. Lily, a sales representative, visited the reception area: she had her pet dog, Boxer, with her. While she was talking to Satanic's purchasing officer, Boxer wandered off and fell through a thin sheet of plywood covering a hole in the floor and down a shaft. Lily was unable to reach him, but Matthew, who was an apprentice employed by Demon Constructors and was of very slim build, tried to lean down while Lily held on to his leg. More of the floor gave way and both Lily and Matthew fell into the shaft and were badly hurt. Boxer was so badly injured that he had to be destroyed.

Advise Lily and Matthew as to any claims in tort.

University of London LLB Examination
(for external students) Law of Tort June 2001 Q5

QUESTION TWO

Until June 1999 Jeff worked as an engineer at Megabyte, manufacturers of electrical equipment. He is now a sales representative for another firm. In March 2000 he had to visit Megabyte's factory in the course of his new job. He waved to the receptionist and went through the door behind her into the workshop to speak to some of his old friends. There is a notice on the door leading into the workshop which states: 'Workshop employees only. No admittance to visitors'. As he chatted, Jeff leant against a piece of heavy equipment, which toppled over on top of him. Kevin, the engineer to whom he was talking, tried to lift the equipment but was unable to hold it and had to let it fall back. Jeff suffered serious crushing injuries. Kevin damaged his back permanently and has had to seek a lighter job.

Megabyte had had the equipment inspected regularly by a specialist firm, which had failed to notice that it had come loose from its moorings.

Advise Megabyte as to its possible liability.

University of London LLB Examination
(for external students) Law of Tort June 2000 Q4

QUESTION THREE

Veronique works as an au pair with the Brown family. One evening when the Browns are out, she invites her friend Lucille to visit her. Lucille works as an au pair with another family. Lucille mentions that she has been unable to find a spare part for her old motor scooter. Veronique says that she is sure Mr Brown may have something in his workshop in the garden and that he will not mind if she has a look. Veronique takes Lucille out to the workshop. A substantial quantity of oil has been spilled on the floor of the workshop and Lucille falls over and cuts her arm very badly. Veronique takes Lucille to the local hospital in her car. On the way there is an accident caused by the negligent driving of Giles. Lucille suffers serious leg injuries. The arm injury does not respond to treatment and it has to be amputated.

Advise Lucille.

University of London LLB Examination
(for external students) Law of Tort June 1999 Q5

QUESTION FOUR

Belinda went to Mugshots, a firm of photographers, to obtain passport photographs. She was accompanied by her six-year-old son Craig, who is very deaf. Mugshots was having new shelving installed by Derek in a room adjoining the waiting area. Derek worked for the local council, but was doing the work for Mugshots in his own time in the evenings and at weekends. There was a swing door through from the waiting area to the area where Derek was working. Belinda was called into the booth to have her photographs taken, and told Craig to wait reading his comic. Craig however wandered off and pushed the swing doors. Ethel, the receptionist, shouted to him to come back, but he did not hear and went through the door. Derek had left a stepladder leaning against some half-finished shelving. Craig knocked against the ladder. The shelving fell on him, causing him a broken arm and leg. Belinda went running to him when she heard his screams. She has suffered from severe depression since the incident.

Advise Belinda and Craig.

University of London LLB Examination
(for external students) Law of Tort June 1998 Q4

QUESTION FIVE

Sally, aged ten and a very promising pianist, went to the Grungetown funfair with her mother. She took a ride on the children's chair-o'-plane. While she was on the ride, some pieces of metal broke off. Sally was struck in the arm. The ride was stopped immediately by an automatic safety mechanism and Sally was left trapped in her chair at the top of the ride. Tom, a visitor to the funfair, told staff that he was a steel erector and accustomed to working at heights, and that he was therefore willing to climb up and attend to Sally before the emergency services arrived. Tom had almost reached Sally when he lost his footing and fell to the ground. Sally was released after half an hour, but her arm was permanently disabled. Tom broke his back in the fall and is permanently paralysed and unable to find work.

Advise Sally and Tom as to their entitlement to damages and the principles on which any damages are assessed.

University of London LLB Examination
(for external students) Law of Tort June 1997 Q3

QUESTION SIX

Vick's hobby was jogging. He went for a long jog in the Essex countryside. He did not take a detailed map with him and as a result he got lost. He saw a road in the distance and, to get to it, he climbed over a locked farm gate and started to cross a farm field. There was a notice on the gate which stated: 'Private Property – No Trespassers. Warning: the farmland is dangerous. No liability accepted for any injuries.' Halfway across the field, Vick fell into a five-foot deep hole which was hidden by grass and branches. The owner of the farm, Cedric, had dug this hole two years ago when he was thinking of building a silo. Cedric had abandoned the silo project but forgotten to close the hole. Vick broke his back in the fall.

Advise Vick if he has any rights against Cedric.

Written by the Author

Answers

ANSWERS TO INTERROGRAMS

1. Section 1(2) of the OLA 1957 provides that an occupier is a person who would have been treated as such at common law, although it does not attempt to give a statutory definition. The House of Lords in *Wheat* v *Lacon* (1966) held that an occupier is a person who has a sufficient degree of control over the premises such that he/she ought to be under a duty of care to those who come lawfully onto the premises.
2. Again, the Act does not define visitors, but provides in s1(2) that a visitor is a person who would at common law have been treated as an invitee or licensee. This includes all those who enter with the express or implied permission of the occupier.
3. The 1984 Act defines the duty owed by the occupier to 'persons other than visitors'. Hence, it is more wide. It does not only refer to trespassers, it would also apply to people exercising private rights of way as in *Holden* v *White* (1982) and those exercising rights under the National Parks and Access to the Countryside Act 1949. It does not extend to those using the highway: see s1(7) of the OLA 1984.

4. As far as the 1957 Act is concerned, s2(1) specifically allows an occupier 'to extend, restrict, modify or exclude his duty to any visitor ... by agreement or otherwise', but this is subject to the application of the Unfair Contract Terms Act 1977. With the 1984 Act the position is less certain, though it is arguable that the 1984 Act provides an irreducible minimum duty which cannot be excluded as against trespassers or visitors for that matter.

SUGGESTED ANSWER TO QUESTION ONE

General Comment

Primarily the issues raised by this question revolve around occupiers' liability. There might possibly be some confusion caused by Boxer, the dog. Boxer is Lily's property and much will depend therefore on Lily's status in relation to her claim for physical injury and property damage. Matthew's situation deserves consideration from two perspectives: as an employee and also as a rescuer.

Key Points

* Lily: is she a visitor for the purpose of the Occupiers' Liability Act 1957? – Boxer's status – the efficacy of the warning
* Liability of independent contractors
* The occupier's liability
* Matthew's status: against whom does his claim lie?

Suggested Answer

In a question on occupiers' liability, certain preliminary issues must first be determined. First, the question of who the occupier is; second, whether the claimant can properly be defined as a visitor; and third, the requirement of premises.

There is no problem with establishing who the occupier is from the facts of the question. We are informed that Satanic Industries occupy the factory premises. Therefore, on the basis of *Wheat v E Lacon & Co Ltd* (1966), Satanic Industries may properly be described as the occupier. The factory premises would obviously satisfy s1(3)(a) Occupiers' Liability Act (OLA) 1957, which defines what is meant by premises. Finally, the issue of the visitor, which in this case is Lily and her pet dog Boxer. Can they be properly identified as visitors?

The question states that Lily is a sales representative and is therefore at the premises of Satanic Industries in the course of her employment. Hence, Lily would be a visitor for the purposes of the Occupiers' Liability Act (OLA) 1957, but what about her pet dog, Boxer? As Boxer is Lily's property in law, her status would obviously be relevant in relation to Boxer. On this basis, Boxer's presence at Satanic Industries is justified on the premise that as Lily is lawfully a visitor, her property also attains the same status. The next issue is to determine liability.

The duty owed by the occupier is the common duty of care as per s2(1) OLA 1957, which he may extend, restrict, modify or exclude insofar as he is free to. By virtue of s2(2) OLA 1957, the occupier must take such care as is reasonable 'in all the circumstances of the case to see that the visitor will be reasonably safe in using the premises for the purposes for which he is invited or permitted by the occupier to be there'. It must be noted that the emphasis is on the visitor, who must be reasonably safe, and not the premises. The duty in this respect is therefore similar to that in negligence.

Whilst Lily was engaged in a conversation with Satanic's purchasing officer, Boxer, her dog, wandered off and fell through a thin sheet of plywood covering a hole in the floor and down a shaft. In trying to rescue the dog, both Lily and Matthew, an apprentice employed by Demon Constructors, also fell into the shaft and were badly hurt. Boxer's injury was so bad that he had to be destroyed.

Is Satanic Industries responsible or could the blame be directed towards the independent contractors, namely Demon Constructors? Have Satanic Industries satisfied the requirements of s2(2) OLA 1957?

First, the issue of whether the notices erected at the entrance sufficiently warned visitors of any risk or danger must be determined. The notice itself does not say much except to say that construction work is in progress and that care should be taken. Section 2(4)(a) OLA 1957 provides that a warning may discharge the duty of care, providing that in all the circumstances of the case it is enough to enable the visitor to be reasonably safe: *Rae* v *Mars UK* (1989) and *Roles* v *Nathan* (1963). If the danger is so obvious, then there is no need for a warning: *Staples* v *West Dorset District Council* (1995).

It is certainly possible that the notice was insufficient to enable a human visitor to be reasonably safe, if there was construction work in the area being visited. It is arguable that the warning could have been more strongly worded. Second, the purchasing officer never stopped Lily or her dog Boxer, or reinforced the warning notices in any way. Lily could also find herself contributorily negligent for not realising that there might be a risk to the dog and not keeping it out of mischief.

Section 2(4)(b) OLA 1957 provides that the occupier is not liable for the fault of an independent contractor if he acted reasonably in entrusting the work to an independent contractor and took reasonable steps to see that the contractor was competent and the work was properly done. *Haseldine* v *Daw* (1941) provides a useful illustration of what steps need to be taken by the occupier to ensure that s2(4)(b) OLA 1957 is properly discharged. Since Demon Constructors have been contracted to carry out substantial construction work on the ground floor, obviously Satanic Industries may lack the technical expertise to ensure that the work is competently done, but surely minimal supervision is possible to ensure that the premises is left reasonably safe for the passage of visitors. On this basis, Satanic Industries would remain liable to Lily for her personal injury and for the loss of her property, Boxer. However, assuming Satanic Industries have discharged the duty as to supervision, then liability might lie directly with Demon Constructors.

In any event, both Satanic Industries and/or Demon Constructors may adduce the personal defence of contributory negligence on the part of Lily in allowing Boxer to roam in a potentially dangerous area.

As Matthew is an apprentice employed by Demon Constructors, surely the standard of care imposed by s2(3)(b) OLA 1957 cannot be applied. An apprentice does not, arguably, possess any special skill so that he may be expected to guard against special risks ordinarily incidental to the exercise of his calling: *Salmon* v *Seafarer Restaurants Ltd* (1983). On this basis, his employers, Demon Constructors, may be liable under employers' liability principles in failing to provide a safe place of work and a safe system of work for Matthew: *Latimer* v *AEC Ltd* (1953). There is also the possibility of a claim against Satanic Industries, as well as Lily for creating the dangerous situation that has consequently been the cause of Matthew's injury. Whilst he may be entitled to name all three parties as potential defendants, ultimately the court may apportion liability as they see fit as per the Civil Liability (Contribution) Act 1978.

However, in trying to rescue the dog Boxer, Matthew becomes a rescuer, but was he negligent in the manner in which he tried to rescue Boxer? When dealing with emergencies, the court normally does not expect the same standard of care expected of reasonable, prudent people: *Ng Chun Pui* v *Lee Chuen Tat* (1988). Therefore, under the circumstances Matthew will be able to recover damages for his injuries.

SUGGESTED ANSWER TO QUESTION TWO

General Comment

This is a question that requires consideration of the principles relating to occupiers' liability and not just the general principles of the tort of negligence. Issues concerning employers' liability are also relevant: therefore, the student should not merely discuss negligence.

Key Points

- The position of Jeff: is he a visitor or a trespasser? – Occupiers' Liability Act (OLA) 1957 if he is a visitor – Occupiers' Liability Act 1984 if he is a trespasser
- Was there an implied permission to enter into the workshop?
- Section 2(4)(b) OLA 1957 independent contractors
- The position of Kevin: principles of employers' liability in relation to rescuers – the role of independent contractors

Suggested Answer

Although touching on the area of negligence, this question is primarily concerned with the principles of occupiers' liability. Occupiers' liability is a specialised aspect of common law negligence. The primary distinction is that it is wholly governed by statute, ie the Occupiers' Liability Act (OLA) 1957, which concerns the liability of an occupier of premises to his or her visitors, and the Occupiers' Liability Act 1984, which concerns an occupier's liability to trespassers. As the issues are governed wholly by statute, it is necessary to give close attention to the exact words used by Parliament, simply because they will set out the limits to the ambit of liability.

Before considering the positions of Jeff and Kevin in relation to Megabyte individually, some common issues may be addressed. First, does Megabyte qualify as an occupier? In *Wheat* v *E Lacon & Co Ltd* (1966) an occupier was defined as: 'a person who exercises a sufficient degree of control over premises that he/she ought to realise that any failure on their part to take care may result in injury to a person coming lawfully there'. On this premise, Megabyte is an occupier. Second, the issue of premises must be addressed, which is covered by s1(3)(a) OLA 1957, which in turn states that 'any fixed or moveable structure' will be deemed to be premises: *Wheeler* v *Copas* (1981). Third, the issue of whether Jeff and Kevin were lawful visitors must be analysed. Visitors include invitees and licensees. This is stated by s1(2) OLA 1957, which requires such a person to have had the occupier's express or implied permission to come on to the premises, and includes those exercising a contractual right of entry. There is no problem with Kevin, who is an employee of Megabyte. He is clearly a visitor. Moreover, Megabyte will also be responsible on the basis of the principles of employers' liability. However, there might be a small problem with Jeff.

Jeff is a former employee of Megabyte but now works as a sales representative for another firm. On the particular day, he had visited Megabyte officially in the course of his new job. This may raise the issue of implied permission. However, it must be borne in mind that the occupier may limit the permission he gives to a visitor to enter the premises as regards space (*The Calgarth* (1927)), or the purpose of the visitor's visit (*R* v *Smith and Jones* (1976)), or as regards the time of the visit: *Stone* v *Taffe* (1974). Jeff went into the workshop notwithstanding the notice on the door leading into the workshop. The notice read: 'Workshop employees only. No admittance to visitors'. This notice clearly prohibits visitors from entering the workshop. Be that as it may, did Jeff go into the workshop in pursuance of his job? This is unlikely, given the fact that the question states that he went into the workshop to speak to some of his old friends. This would clearly subject Jeff to the notice. However, Jeff had waved to the receptionist and only then had he gone through the door behind her into the workshop. Therefore, as the receptionist was placed before the door, and as she had allowed Jeff to go into the workshop, was there acquiescence on her part? It would appear that there was an implied permission, as Jeff was not prevented from entering into the workshop. Clearly, the receptionist had authority to stop Jeff and she did not. Also, it is quite common for employers generally to allow former employees some liberty to move around the premises. On this basis, it is submitted that Jeff was a lawful visitor.

Was Megabyte in breach of its duty of care? By virtue of s2(1) OLA 1957, the duty owed by the occupier is the common law duty of care in respect of all visitors on their premises. Section 2(2) OLA 1957 states that the occupier must 'take such care as in all the circumstances of the case is reasonable to see that the visitor will be reasonably safe in using the premises for the purposes for which he is invited or permitted by the occupier to be there'. This means that the premises must be in good order or safe keep so as to ensure the visitor's safety. Fairly recently in *Jolley* v *Sutton London Borough Council* (2000) the House of Lords held that if damage is foreseeable, then there is liability, even if the way in which it is caused is not foreseeable. Clearly, the heavy equipment had not been safely secured to the ground. Thus it topples over on top of Jeff, who had leant against it. It could have been any employee in Jeff's position. Surely, on this basis, Megabyte ought to be responsible or liable for Jeff's injury. Perhaps if

Megabyte had put up a warning, as required by s2(4)(a) OLA 1957, to warn the visitor of any possible danger, then Megabyte may have discharged the duty of care: *Roles* v *Nathan* (1963). Megabyte had not put up any such warning. There is also the possibility that Megabyte may find itself falling foul of s28(1) Factories Act 1961, which imposes a duty to keep the premises safe so far as is reasonably practicable. The important issue here is whether Megabyte could escape liability on the basis that there was a specialist firm of independent contractors who were contracted to regularly inspect the machinery. It is evident that the firm concerned had failed to notice that the machine had come loose from its moorings. This clearly shows negligence on their part.

Section 2(4)(b) OLA 1957 provides that an occupier is not liable for the fault of an independent contractor if he had acted reasonably in entrusting the work to an independent contractor, and took reasonable steps to check that the contractor was competent and that the work was properly executed. Megabyte had clearly employed the services of a specialist firm. Therefore, they have discharged their duty under s2(4)(b) OLA 1957. But is there any failure of supervision on the part of Megabyte? Could they have discovered that the machine had come loose from its moorings on a reasonable, plain and non-technical inspection? If the answer is yes, then Megabyte are liable on the basis of *Woodward* v *Mayor of Hastings* (1945). If, on the other hand, the defect could not have been discovered on a reasonable inspection, then Megabyte are not liable to Jeff, but the independent contractors would be on the basis of *Haseldine* v *Daw* (1941).

As far as Kevin is concerned, an employer owes certain common law duties to an employee, such as the provision of a safe place of work, a safe system of work, proper plant and equipment and competent staff. These duties also overlap under a number of statutes, such as the Factories Act 1961 and the Employers' Liability (Defective Equipment) Act 1969. The issue here is whether or not there was properly maintained plant and equipment: *Smith* v *Baker* (1891). This in turn raises the question of a safe place of work: *Latimer* v *AEC Ltd* (1953). The duty on the employer is not absolute, but merely to take reasonable steps to provide a safe place of work. Again, by entrusting maintenance to a competent firm of specialists, Megabyte has arguably discharged their common law duties. Similar arguments to those used in Jeff's case with regard to the independent contractors may be adduced here. Whilst the employer's duty to his employees is personal and non-delegable, certain special or technical duties may be delegated, in which case the employer will not be held responsible for the negligent performance of those duties, particularly where independent contractors are involved: *Wilsons and Clyde Coal Co* v *English* (1938). On this basis, Kevin would be advised to pursue an action against the firm of independent contractors for negligence.

SUGGESTED ANSWER TO QUESTION THREE

General Comment

This question concerns the liability of an occupier of defective premises for loss or injury sustained by those who come onto those premises. Any such case should be dealt with as a statutory claim under the Occupiers' Liability Acts, rather than in common law negligence. Always consider whether the person suffering loss/injury was a visitor or a trespasser at the time of the accident and in the specific part of the premises on which the accident occurred. Occupiers' liability is a specialised aspect of common law negligence, and so it is relevant to consider the concepts of causation and remoteness of damages as they would apply to mainstream negligence claims where they are in issue.

Key Points

- Explain and identify who is the 'occupier' of the premises concerned
- Discuss whether Lucille is a visitor or trespasser when she enters the garden workshop
- Identify the relevant Occupiers' Liability Act
- Discuss whether the occupier owed Lucille a duty of care, and if so, whether such a duty was broken
- Are Lucille's injuries too remote to recover damages for as against the occupier?

Suggested Answer

The question concerns the liability of an occupier of premises for damage done to those who come onto the premises. The law relating to such liability is largely to be found in the Occupiers' Liability Act (OLA) 1957 as regards visitors, and the Occupiers' Liability Act (OLA) 1984 as regards non-visitors, ie trespassers.

The occupier of the premises

It is vital in all cases to correctly identify the occupier, as it is against this person or persons that a claim for loss/damage arises. Under s1(2) OLA 1957 and s1(2) OLA 1984 the definition of 'occupier' remains the same as at common law. The current test is to be found in the judgement of Lord Denning in the House of Lords case *Wheat* v *E Lacon and Co Ltd* (1966) which defines the occupier as a person who 'has a sufficient degree of control over premises that he ought to realise that any failure on his part to use care may result in injury.'

In this case it is clear that the Browns are the occupiers of the premises, as it is they who exercise sufficient control over the garden workshop in which the accident occurred. Veronique, as an au pair, cannot be said to be an occupier of either the garden workshop or the whole house, although it is possible that she has the necessary degree of control to be regarded as the occupier of her own room.

Is Lucille a visitor or trespasser when she enters the garden workshop?

It is necessary to decide whether Lucille enters the garden workshop as visitor or non-visitor in relation to the Browns in order to determine which Occupiers' Liability Act to apply to her circumstances. This is important, because the existence and scope of any duty owed by the occupier varies according to the status of the person who comes onto the premises.

Section 1(2) OLA 1957 states that a lawful visitor is, for the purposes of the Act, either an invitee or a licensee. This requires such a person to have had the occupier's express or implied permission to come onto the premises. On the other hand, the term 'trespasser' was defined by Lord Dunedin in *Addie (Robert) and Sons (Collieries) Ltd* v *Dumbreck* (1929) as a person 'who goes onto the land without invitation of any sort and whose presence is either unknown to the proprietor or, if known, is practically objected to.'

It is clear that Lucille lacks the Browns' express permission to enter the garden workshop, the invitation coming instead from Veronique. The question as to whether Lucille had the Browns' implied permission to enter seems to depend upon whether Veronique, as the au pair, had the Browns' actual or apparent (ostensible) authority to invite a private guest into the workshop in their absence. On this point, see *Ferguson* v *Welsh* (1987), an analogous case on multiple occupation in which the majority of the House of Lords held that a contractor licensed to enter the occupier's premises to do work was clothed with ostensible authority to invite a subcontractor and their employees onto the land.

Ultimately, each case turns on its particular facts; however, it seems reasonable to expect that Veronique may have been permitted to receive guests in the house, but highly unlikely that such permission would have extended to a search in the workshop for spare parts to a motor scooter. Such an activity surely would have required Mr Brown's express permission. It is therefore submitted that Lucille was a trespasser when she entered the garden workshop, and that any duty owed to her by the Browns would be defined according to the requirements of OLA 1984.

Did the Browns owe Lucille a duty of care under OLA 1984 and, if so, was such a duty broken?

Under s1(3) OLA 1984 the occupier will owe the non-visitor a duty of care provided the following apply.

1. He is aware of the danger or has reasonable grounds to believe it exists. Provided, as seems likely, that Mr Brown was aware of the oil spillage, it follows that at the very least, he must have had reasonable grounds to believe that someone might slip and fall over.
2. He knows or has reasonable grounds to believe that the other (Lucille) is in the vicinity of the danger concerned, or that he may come into the vicinity of the danger (in either case, whether the other has lawful authority for being in that vicinity or not). This requirement is clearly much more difficult to satisfy in the circumstances described, as there is nothing to suggest that Mr Brown might have anticipated that anyone would enter the workshop other than himself. However, it might be argued that if Mr Brown knows that Veronique is to receive a private guest with an interest in mechanics, he might reasonably infer that the guest might be tempted to take a look in the workshop.
3. The risk is one against which, in all the circumstances of the case, he may reasonably be expected to offer the other some protection. A substantial spillage of oil could reasonably be expected to be cleaned up, or alternatively, the door to the garden workshop might easily have been locked (if applicable) and the key removed. These observations also support the argument that, provided a duty is owed by the Browns to Lucille, the duty has been broken. Section 1(4) OLA 1984 provides that the duty is 'to take such care as is reasonable in all the circumstances of the case to see that [the

non-visitor] does not suffer injury on the premises by reason of the danger concerned.'

Lucille's main problem will be in establishing that a duty of care is owed to her under OLA 1984, particularly under part (2) of the three part-test above.

Assuming the Browns are in breach of a duty of care owed under OLA 1984 can they be said to have caused the loss suffered by Lucille, namely the amputated arm and the serious injuries to her leg?

Provided that Lucille satisfies the requirements of OLA 1984, she will be able to recover damages for personal injury (s1(9) OLA 1984), but not in respect of loss or damage to property; eg ripped or oil-stained clothing: s1(8) OLA 1984.

It is well established that injury to the person resulting from a breach of duty is recoverable in tort. This remains the position, even though the extent of the damage and the precise manner of its occurrence may not have been foreseeable: *Hughes v Lord Advocate* (1963). Physical injury is entirely foreseeable where surfaces are slippery, and Lucille will be able to recover compensation for the loss of her arm.

The final question is whether Lucille could claim against the Browns for the injuries to her leg. A defendant is not liable unless the claimant's loss has been caused by the negligence of the defendant, both in fact and in law. The injuries to Lucille's leg have resulted, albeit indirectly, from the original injury to her arm: 'but for' the accident in the workshop, Lucille would not have been in Veronique's car when the second accident occurred: *Barnett v Chelsea and Kensington Hospital Management Committee* (1969). However, it is suggested that Giles' negligent driving amounts to a new and independent intervening act by a third party (novus actus interveniens), making the leg injury too remote a consequence of any breach of OLA 1984 on the part of the Browns. In other words, it was the act of a third party (Giles) which was the true cause of the injury subsequently suffered by Lucille, an event which was completely independent of the defendant's negligence. In the words of Lord Wright in *The Oropesa* (1943) the second accident was 'a new cause which disturbs the sequence of events, something which can be described as either unreasonable or extraneous or extrinsic.'

SUGGESTED ANSWER TO QUESTION FOUR

General Comment

This is a question involving loss or injury to someone who comes onto another person's premises, resulting from a defect in the premises. Any such case should be dealt with as a statutory claim under the Occupiers' Liability Acts, rather than in common law negligence. The suggested solution given below is a very full answer to this question, and in an examination it would be permissible to deal only very briefly with the elements of occupiers' liability which are not really in issue, eg 'occupier', 'premises' and Craig's status as a visitor.

Key Points

*   Explain and identify the 'occupier' of the premises concerned –

- Discuss whether Craig is a visitor or trespasser when he enters the room adjacent to the waiting area
- Identify the relevant Occupiers' Liability Act
- Discuss whether the occupier owed Craig a duty of care, and if so, whether such a duty was broken
- Did Mugshots discharge their duty to Craig by providing a sufficient warning, or by the proper selection and supervision of an independent contractor?
- Can Belinda claim for her 'nervous shock' as a secondary victim of the accident?

Suggested Solution

The question concerns the liability of an occupier of premises for damage done to those who come onto the premises. The law relating to such liability is largely to be found in the Occupiers' Liability Act (OLA) 1957 as regards visitors to premises.

The occupier of the premises

Under s1(2) OLA 1957 the definition of 'occupier' remains the same as at common law. In this scenario, the occupier of the building in which the accident occurred is clearly Mugshots, as it is they who had a 'sufficient degree of control over the premises' and 'ought to have realised that any failure on their part to use care may result in injury': *Wheat v E Lacon and Co Ltd* (1966).

However, it is possible for there to be more than one occupier of premises at the same time. Multiple occupation was contemplated as a possibility by Lord Denning in Wheat (above) and was held to exist in *AMF International Ltd* v *Magnet Bowling Ltd* (1968). The question may arise as to whether Derek could be regarded as an occupier of the room adjoining the waiting area: even though he is not present during normal opening hours, he presumably has some ongoing control over the work area and the state in which it is left. Whilst every case turns upon its own facts, it was held in *Page v Read* (1984) that the degree of control associated with the presence and activities of a decorator painting a house was insufficient to give rise to a duty as an occupier. It is therefore submitted that the sole occupier(s) of the business premises in this scenario are likely to be the partners of Mugshots.

This does not prevent Derek from being held liable for Craig's injuries as a non-occupier under ordinary negligence principles, and it has been noted that there is little difference between the standards of care required in ordinary common law negligence compared to those required under OLA 1957. However, ultimately Craig would be best advised to pursue the defendant with the deepest pockets, and this will require a claim against Mugshots under OLA 1957, who are the most likely defendant to carry public liability insurance.

Premises

The room adjacent to the waiting area and the shelving are clearly premises within the meaning of OLA 1957, with s1(3)(a) of the Act referring to 'any fixed or moveable structure'. Even a ladder could be regarded as 'premises' provided it remains in control of the occupier when the accident occurs: *Wheeler v Copas* (1981).

Is Craig a visitor or trespasser?

Section 1(2) OLA 1957 states that a lawful visitor is, for the purposes of the Act, either an invitee or a licensee. This requires such a person to have had the occupier's express or implied permission to come on to the premises. Craig is a visitor to Mugshots' premises: his presence is known to the occupier (or its agents) and this presence is not objected to.

A limitation on the permission of visitors to enter some parts of the premises and not others can render the entrant a trespasser upon entry to the restricted area, provided proper steps have been taken to bring the limitation to the visitor's attention: *Gould* v *McAuliffe* (1941). However, it is submitted that the shouting of a warning to 'come back' directed at a deaf child was insufficient to achieve any such limitation, and therefore Craig should be regarded as a visitor when he enters the room adjoining the waiting area.

Are Mugshots in breach of the 'common duty of care'?

Section 2(1) OLA 1957 imposes a common duty of care on occupiers in respect of all visitors to their premises. Section 2(2) states that the duty is:

> '… to take such care as in all the circumstances of the case is reasonable to see that the visitor will be reasonably safe in using the premises for the purposes for which he is invited or permitted by the occupier to be there.'

In deciding how much care Mugshots should reasonably have taken to ensure that Craig was reasonably safe on their premises, a number of factors will be taken into account, such as the nature of the danger, the steps necessary to remove it and the likelihood of injury resulting. In addition, s2(3)(a) OLA 1957 expressly provides that 'an occupier must be prepared for children to be less careful than adults.'

In order to exercise a reasonable degree of care in supervising Derek, it could be argued that Mugshots should have supervised Derek more carefully, ensuring that the shelving was properly secured whilst Derek was absent from the premises. Mugshots might also have closed off the work area by rendering the swing doors inoperable, assuming access to the room could have been avoided during normal business hours. It could be further argued that the oral warning was not enough to allow Craig to be reasonably safe (under s2(4)(a) OLA 1957), in that it failed to identify a specific danger in a specific place, and because Mugshots either knew, or ought to have realised (on the basis of what they had seen of Belinda and Craig) that Craig was deaf. It is possible that shouting a warning to a small boy is inadequate in any event.

Mugshots will undoubtedly attempt to argue that their warning (via their 'agent' employee, Ethel) was enough, in all the circumstances, to enable Craig to be reasonably safe (s2(4)(a) OLA 1957), and that their duty towards him was thereby discharged. In addition, Mugshots might argue that they were entitled to assume that a reasonable mother would not permit her very young child to be allowed to remain in the waiting area alone, especially if very deaf. At the very least, Belinda could have asked the receptionist to supervise her child, and in addition, warned her of Craig's deafness. Alternatively, Belinda might reasonably have been expected to satisfy herself that there were no immediate dangers facing Craig whilst she left him to have her photograph taken. In short, Mugshots would argue that they could not have foreseen that the unsecured shelving in the work area would be a danger to Craig, given Belinda's responsibility for her child's safety. On this point see *Phipps* v *Rochester Corporation*

(1955), a case in which the occupier of land was held not to have broken any duty of care in respect of a child of five years of age who was not accompanied by an adult.

If this last argument were to succeed, the view appears to be that Belinda herself would be liable as a joint tortfeasor to Craig in common law negligence. Mugshots would primarily be fully liable to Craig, but would have a right to recover a contribution from Belinda under the Civil Liability (Contribution) Act 1978: see Winfield and Jolowicz (*Tort* (15th edn, 1998) at p301).

Have Mugshots discharged their duty to take reasonable care by adequate selection and supervision of an independent contractor under s2(4)(b) OLA 1957?
Mugshots will not be answerable to Craig under this provision if the following criteria are all satisfied.

1. There must have been 'faulty execution of any work of construction ... by an independent contractor employed by the occupier'. In practice, these words are given a broad and purposeful construction and it is submitted that they are wide enough to cover dangerously unguarded and unsecured work-in-progress, such as the shelving in the instant case.
2. Mugshots must have acted reasonably in entrusting the work to an independent contractor. It is submitted that it is most probably common commercial practice to engage an independent contractor to put up shelving, even if the job could probably have been undertaken by anyone in the firm with basic DIY skills. Thus, it is probably the case that Mugshots acted reasonably in hiring someone to carry out the work for them.
3. Mugshots must have taken reasonable care to ensure that Derek was competent to carry out the work. This will depend upon the reasons why Mugshots selected Derek to do the work in the first place, and whether they took steps to satisfy themselves that he had sufficient experience to do the job properly. It is clearly relevant to know whether Derek's job on the council involves work of a similar nature.
4. Mugshots must have taken reasonable care to check, if appropriate, that the 'work had been properly done'. Mugshots clearly failed to check that the shelving had been properly secured. Given that the work was not of a particularly technical nature, it is submitted that it would have been reasonable for them to have done so.

Thus it would appear from (4) above that Mugshots may remain answerable to Craig under OLA 1957, assuming that they are in breach of their common duty of care.

Liability in respect of Belinda's 'nervous shock'.
Assuming that Mugshots are liable to Craig under OLA 1957, or that Derek is liable as a non-occupier in negligence, Belinda may be able to claim as a secondary victim, ie one who was not personally involved in the accident nor placed in fear of suffering injury, but nonetheless perceived the consequences of a tort, suffering psychiatric illness as a result.

Two initial requirements which are immediately satisfied on the facts are as follows:

1. Belinda suffered a medically recognised psychiatric illness, ie severe depression: *Chadwick* v *British Transport Commission* (1967); and

2. the illness resulted from a sudden shock.

There are a number of criteria which must be met if Belinda is to succeed in her claim. These criteria were first established by the House of Lords in *McLoughlin* v *O'Brian* (1983) and subsequently refined in *Alcock* v *Chief Constable of South Yorkshire Police* (1992). These criteria all seem to apply to Belinda, and can be summarised as follows.

1. It was reasonably foreseeable that Belinda would suffer psychiatric illness, as her relationship with the primary victim (Craig) was sufficiently close. In *McLoughlin* it was held that the relationship between parent and child was sufficiently proximate to recover.
2. Belinda's proximity to the accident or its 'immediate aftermath' was sufficiently close in both space and time. Belinda was in the same building as Craig when the accident occurred and she immediately ran to him when she heard his screams.
3. Belinda suffered psychiatric illness through hearing the accident and seeing its immediate aftermath.

It must be remembered that Belinda may be held partly responsible for Craig's accident and, if so, she may suffer a reduction in compensation on a finding that she was contributory negligent under the Law Reform (Contributory Negligence) Act 1945.

SUGGESTED ANSWER TO QUESTION FIVE

General Comment

This question raises a wide range of issues so the planning of the answers is vital. Some attempt must be made to deal with Sally's cause(s) of action arising from the original impact and the delay in reaching safety and receiving attention; and the causative effects of the safety mechanism as well as the legal basis and extent of her recovery should be discussed. As for Tom, it will be necessary to consider his position both as visitor and as rescuer, possible defences based upon volenti non fit injuria and contributory negligence, and the basis and extent of his recovery.

Key Points

- Sally's possible causes of action: negligence, under Occupiers' Liability Act 1957 – *Rylands* v *Fletcher* – breach of statutory duty
- The automatic safety device – the half-hour delay – possible multiple causation and possible novus actus interveniens
- Sally's basis of recovery – loss of amenity and her musical prospects – remoteness of damage
- Tom as visitor: possible defences
- Tom as rescuer: possible defences
- Tom's basis of recovery

Suggested Solution

We are not told the precise cause of the metal fracture. The evidence on this may affect the causes of action relied upon by Sally, but the various possibilities that suggest themselves are: negligence simpliciter based on a failure to maintain or inspect; breach of the common duty of care owed to lawful visitors by the funfair as occupiers under the Occupiers' Liability Act (OLA) 1957; and there might be an 'escape' within the meaning attached to that phrase under the principle in *Rylands* v *Fletcher* (1868); there might, indeed, be a breach of statutory duty involved as a great deal of fairground machinery is affected by such duties, particularly where safety fencing of moving machinery is involved.

To examine possible difficulties within such a range of potential causes of action is not possible in the time available so, for present purposes, it is assumed that the damage was reasonably foreseeable and that Sally will have a good cause of action based on common law negligence and under the OLA 1957. The next question is whether Sally's injury was in any way affected by the half-hour delay caused by the automatic safety mechanism. If there is no particular additional damage caused by the delay, the situation between Sally and the funfair remains unchanged; if there was reasonable foreseeability of the metal fracture there was also likely to be reasonable foreseeability of the delay in reaching the ground. If, by contrast, the delay has caused some identifiable increase in damage, such as might occur with splintered bones or severed nerves, there is a possible defence argument that the automatic safety system has interfered with the causative process as a possible novus actus interveniens. This would be a complex argument and would probably turn on the question of how foreseeable the consequence was, and how practicable it was to get emergency access and egress. If there were real problems with causation, the court would adopt a commonsense approach: *Yorkshire Dale Steamship Co Ltd* v *Minister of War Transport* (1942).

Sally's recovery for her personal injuries will be along conventional lines, in that she would receive special damages for provable losses to the date of trial, such as damaged clothes, wasted school fees or tuition fees, extra travelling costs, etc. She will also recover for general damages under several heads. She would be able to recover for pecuniary loss in respect of future loss of earning potential, which would be likely to be estimated on an annual percentage sum below the national adult average earnings at the time of trial (the 'multiplicand') multiplied by a number of 'years purchase' representing her working lifetime (the 'multiplier'), which would be considerably reduced to allow for 'accelerated receipt'. The effect of taxation and national insurance contributions on earnings would be allowed for: *British Transport Commission* v *Gourley* (1956). Any additional prospective expenses, such as adaptation of home or chattels, might be claimed for, as well as prospective medical expenses. Sally will also, under general damages, recover for pain, suffering and loss of amenity in line with similar injury awards as evidenced by works such as Kemp and Kemp, but there may be a very considerable argument as to whether she will be able to recover for the devastating loss of amenity in being unable to pursue her musical interests and, possibly, a career. The speculative aspects of much of this with a plaintiff aged ten may well restrict recovery to something nearer to what a healthy non-musician might have recovered. Much will turn on the evidence as to her promise as a musician; the process is analogous to remoteness of damage considerations.

Tom might claim as a visitor under the OLA 1957, on the basis that the funfair staff permitted him to attempt a rescue. He may well fare better under this if there is any defence claim of unnecessary rescue or volenti than if he claims under common law as a rescuer. The fairground will be unable to raise the 'special risks, ordinary incident' defence in s2(3)(b) OLA 1957 because he is not exercising his calling but, instead, is there as their permitted rescuer, although they may raise a volenti non fit injuria defence against him under s2(5). If volenti is raised, the same principles will apply as if Tom proceeded as a rescuer of Sally on ordinary negligence grounds. He is unlikely to be seen as volenti (*Baker* v *T E Hopkins and Sons Ltd* (1959)) unless the rescue was seen to be 'wanton' as in *Cutler* v *United Dairies Ltd* (1933).

Tom's basis of recovery is similar to that of Sally, except that his loss of earning capacity will be much easier quantified, and there will be heavy existing and prospective costs for attendance and nursing care, again worked out on a multiplicand/multiplier basis.

SUGGESTED ANSWER TO QUESTION SIX

General Comment

Whilst there is a general theme relating to occupiers' liability, the facts clearly incline specifically towards the Occupiers' Liability Act 1984. Hence, discussion should focus on the liability of an occupier towards trespassers and *not* visitors, although a brief reference to the 1957 Act is useful to bring out the distinctions between the two statutes. Of relevance also is the Unfair Contract Terms Act 1977 and its non-application to the 1984 Act.

Key Points

- Occupiers' Liability Act 1984: duties owed by an occupier towards trespassers – the application of s1(3) and its subsections – the exclusion of liability and the effect of s1(5)
- A brief comparison with the Occupiers' Liability Act 1957 and the questionable applicability of Unfair Contract Terms Act 1977
- Defence of volenti and contributory negligence, if any

Suggested Answer

Clearly, the main issue is whether Vick can sue Cedric for compensation for breach of the occupier's statutory duty of care owed to a trespasser. Under the Occupiers' Liability Act (OLA) 1984 the liability of an occupier towards trespassers is defined by s1(3) which states that for a duty of care to arise:

1. the occupier is aware of the danger or has reasonable grounds to believe that it exists;
2. the occupier knows or has reasonable grounds to believe that the non-visitor is in the vicinity of the danger or may come into the vicinity of the danger; and

3. the risk is one against which, in all the circumstances, the occupier may reasonably be expected to offer the non-visitor some protection.

In the present problem the danger was a five-foot deep hole which Cedric himself had dug two years ago and which he had forgotten to fill in or close. Consequently, it would be difficult for Cedric to deny knowledge of this hazard. Further, he must have been aware of the risk of trespass because he had put up a notice discouraging it. Since no effective security measures were taken to prevent trespass (such as an electric fence), the possibility that a trespasser might ignore Cedric's notice and come onto the land within the vicinity of the hole is one that cannot be excluded, and Cedric should have been aware of it. Also, from a practical point of view, since it would take comparatively little effort and resources to fill in the hole or to fence it adequately, Cedric would have been expected to provide such protection against this particular danger, and one which posed a serious threat of injury to any potential trespasser.

Hence, it would appear that all three elements required for the imposition of liability on an occupier under s1(3) of the 1984 Act are present, despite the fact that Vick clearly falls within the definition of a trespasser as provided in *Addie v Dumbreck* (1929) and subsequently reaffirmed by the House of Lords in *British Railways Board v Herrington* (1972).

Under the OLA 1984, s1(5) permits an occupier to be excluded from his duty by giving adequate warning of the danger to the trespasser, or by otherwise discouraging trespassers from incurring risk. It would appear that the warning need not be such as to make the place reasonably safe for the trespasser to enter, in contrast to the duty owed by the occupier to visitors under s2(4)(a) of the OLA 1957, as illustrated by *Roles v Nathan* (1963). Hence, it is arguable that Cedric's general warning notice on the gate may be sufficient to exempt him from liability, although the court will have regard to all the circumstances of the case. It is noteworthy that because the hole was a potential risk to Cedric's visitors (despite the warning which was general in nature), the warning may be seen as inadequate to exonerate Cedric from liability. For a more recent decision on the effect of 'warnings', see the House of Lords' case of *Tomlinson v Congleton Borough Council and Another* (2003). Here, the warning provided by the occupier was held to be sufficient in order to indemnify the occupier of any liability towards potential trespassers.

Be that as it may, it also appears that although Cedric's liability is clear on the basis of the test laid down in *White v St Albans City and District Council* (1990), the OLA 1984 may not be subject to the provisions of the Unfair Contract Terms Act 1977 which specifically applies to the tort of negligence and the duty of care owed under the OLA 1957. Hence, it is open to Cedric to exclude liability for personal injury sustained by trespassers on his land, despite the injury being one which satisfies the remoteness test, as illustrated in *Jolley v Sutton London Borough Council* (2000).

The defence of volenti as provided by s1(6) OLA 1984 would not be available to Cedric because although Vick voluntarily entered the land which knew, by virtue of the notice, might be dangerous, he was acting under the pressure of being lost and the need to find the nearest road; in a sense he was rescuing himself and hence could not have been truly consenting to run the risk of injury. The defence of contributory negligence under the Law Reform (Contributory Negligence) Act 1945 would not be of any use to Cedric because the fact that Vick was to blame for getting himself lost in the first place is not sufficiently proximate to the incident of falling down into the hole to be regarded as contributory negligence. However, Vick's decision to ignore the warning notice might count as contributory negligence so as to justify a reduction in the award of damages by the court.

7

Defamation

Introduction

The tort of defamation is designed to protect the reputation of a person. Therefore, it is the publication of a statement which reflects on a person's reputation and tends to lower him in the estimation of right-thinking members of society and generally tends to make them shun/avoid that person. There must be publication. Therefore, the tort is not committed if nobody else saw or heard of the defamation. There is no legal aid available for defamation actions and it remains one of the rare civil actions tried by jury.

Defamation can be classified into two categories. First, libel, which is usually written. It is material in a permanent form or nature and is visible to the naked eye. Second, slander, which is usually oral. It is material in a transient form (temporary and audible). Whilst libel is actionable per se, slander is only actionable on proof of special damages. A recent case in the High Court, *Western Provident v Norwich Union* (1997), concerned defamation by e-mail.

- Examples of libel are writing, painting, signs, pictures, statutes, waxworks, broadcasting, television theatre, etc: *Monson v Tussauds* (1894).
- Example of slander: see *Youssoupoff v Metro-Goldwyn-Mayer* (1934).

In order for an action in defamation to succeed, three elements must be established. First, the material complained about must be defamatory: *Sim v Stretch* (1936), *Cassidy v Daily Mirror* (1929), *Tolley v J S Fry* (1931) and *Lewis v Daily Telegraph* (1964). Second, that the material referred to the complainant: *Morgan v Odhams Press* (1971), *Knupffer v London Express* (1944) and *Newstead v London Express Newspapers Ltd* (1940). Third, that it was published to a third party: *Theaker v Richardson* (1962), *Slipper v BBC* (1991) and *Cutler v McPhail* (1962). The recent case of *Godfrey v Demon Internet Ltd* (1999) offers an interesting illustration on the issue of publication. See also the recent cases of *McManus v Beckham* (2002), *Baldwin v Rushbridger* (2001) and *Loutchansky v Times Newspapers* (2001). Once these are established, the onus then shifts onto the defendant. It would be a defence if the defendant proves that the imputation was true (*Hellwig v Mitchell* (1910) and *Jones v Jones* (1916)), that it was made on a privileged (whether absolute or qualified) occasion. For a recent case on qualified privilege: see the House of Lords' decision in *Reynolds v Times Newspapers Ltd* (1999). See also *Kearns v General Council of the Bar* (2002), *Branson v Bower* (2001) and *Hamilton v Al Fayed* (2001). On absolute privilege, the recent House of Lords decision in *Taylor and Others v Serious Fraud Office and Others* (1998) and the Court of Appeal case of *Waple v Surrey County Council* (1998) provide useful examples. See also *Mahon v Rahn (No 2)* (2000). Third, that it was fair comment or justified on a matter of public policy. See also *Grobbelaar v News Group Newspapers* (2002). Other available defences include: innocent defamation (s1 Defamation Act 1996), consent

(*Chapman* v *Lord Ellesmere* (1932)), apology as under the Libel Act 1843, unintentional defamation (ss2–4 Defamation Act 1996 – offer to make amends) (see the recent case of *Milne* v *Express Newspapers* (2003)) and limitation period (one year – s5 Defamation Act 1996). Remedies are awarded in the form of damages and/or injunctions (in some cases). For an illustration of how damages are awarded for malicious falsehood: see the recent Court of Appeal decision of *Khodoparast* v *Shad* (1999). Sections 8 and 9 of the Defamation Act 1996 now provide new summary procedures for cases where the defence has no realistic prospect of success (particularly where damages do not exceed £10,000). See also the relevance of s8 of the Courts and Legal Services Act 1990 and *Rantzen* v *Mirror Group Newspapers* (1993) and *John* v *Mirror Group Newspaper* (1996). A recent case on this point is *Kiam* v *MGN Ltd* (2002). In *Goldsmith* v *Bhoyrul* (1997) the High Court held that a political party could not sue in defamation as it would be contrary to public interest.

Questions

INTERROGRAMS

1. Is there a right balance between what the law of defamation seeks to protect and the freedom of speech?
2. Is it libel or slander if one was to merely read out a libellous statement to a third party?
3. Can a dead person be defamed?
4. What are the elements of malicious falsehood?

QUESTION ONE

'My conclusion is that the established common law approach to misstatements of fact remains essentially sound ... The elasticity of the common law principle enables interference with freedom of speech to be confined to what is necessary in the circumstances of the case. This elasticity enables the court to give appropriate weight, in today's conditions, to the importance of freedom of expression by the media on all matters of public concern.' (*Reynolds* v *Times Newspapers Ltd*, per Lord Nicholls of Birkenhead.)

Discuss.

University of London LLB Examination
(for external students) Law of Tort June 2001 Q1

QUESTION TWO

A parliamentary by-election is taking place soon in the constituency of Barsetshire North. The *Barsetshire Chronicle* carried the following item on its front page about the candidates: 'What a motley crew are on offer for the good voters of Barsetshire North! First there's Maisie Mazda. Like all politicians, she likes to pass herself off as something she is not. She may look the glamourous granny, but we know it's not nature but the surgeon's knife which gave her the face and figure she always seems so anxious to flaunt. Then there's Tom Toyota. No orator he! His hackneyed phrases and turgid delivery must make him a prime candidate for "most boring politician of 2000". And if you don't like them, you're left with Horace Honda. Just what is Horace whispering into the ear of the lovely girl who calls him "daddy" but isn't his daughter (see photo left). For full by-election coverage, see page seven'.

Maisie Mazda had once had cosmetic surgery to remove a small mole from her cheek. The coverage on page seven explains that the girl in the photograph is Horace's niece, Jackie, whom he and his wife brought up after her parents were killed in an air crash when she was aged eight.

Advise as to any possible claims in defamation.

University of London LLB Examination
(for external students) Law of Tort June 2000 Q3

QUESTION THREE

'We do not for an instant doubt that the common convenience and welfare of a modern plural democracy such as ours are best served by an ample flow of information to the public concerning, and by vigorous public discussion of, matters of public interest to the community.' (*Reynolds* v *Times Newspapers* (1998).)

Discuss. To what extent is the English law of defamation consistent with that view?

University of London LLB Examination
(for external students) Law of Tort June 1999 Q1

QUESTION FOUR

Chill and Douche, two members of the building inspections team in the Loamshire Fire Brigade, carried out an inspection of the engineering building at Loamshire University. They reported that the notice boards were a fire hazard and that, if notices continued to be displayed anywhere in the corridors and staircases other than in specially constructed glass cases, they would seek a court order closing the building. At a meeting with student representatives a few days later, Flame, the Dean of Engineering, remarked that because of 'the Hitlerite tendency' of the local fire brigade, he had to prohibit students from displaying any notices advertising their societies. The next issue of the Student Union newspaper carried a banner headline reading, ' "FIRE INSPECTORS ARE FASCIST SCUM", SAYS DEAN.' Copies of this newspaper are handed out to students on the campus, and are also prominently on sale in local newsagents.

Advise the parties as to any possible claims in defamation.

University of London LLB Examination
(for external students) Law of Tort June 1998 Q7

QUESTION FIVE

Evaluate the changes made by the Defamation Act 1996. Are there any other changes to the law of defamation which you would like to see?

University of London LLB Examination
(for external students) Law of Tort June 1997 Q6

QUESTION SIX

At a recent meeting of Chinatown City Council it was decided that the fee charged for licences to operate taxis and minicabs in the city was to be increased threefold. In response to this, an emergency meeting was convened by the local Taxi and Minicab Drivers' Association wherein it was agreed that they would not undertake any work for the council or accept as passengers any councillors or senior officers of the council. Bob does not approve of such action and has renewed the contract for his company to take councillors and officials home from late night meetings of the council. Jack took a neighbour, who is a councillor, to hospital in his taxi after the neighbour had fallen and injured himself in his bathroom, but did not accept a fare for the journey. William is a taxi driver who has taken part in the boycott.

The monthly newsletter of the Taxi and Minicab Drivers' Association, which is circulated to all drivers, contains the following: 'Councillors have been seen riding in Chinatown taxis. We can only conclude that some of us put profits before comradeship.' No names are mentioned but the article is decorated with caricatures that remotely resemble Bob, Jake and William. A copy of the newsletter is displayed for a week in the window of the offices of Safety Taxis.

Advise Bob, Jake and William whether they can succeed in an action for defamation.

Written by the Author

Answers

ANSWERS TO INTERROGRAMS

1. Since we have no constitutionally protected freedom of speech in this country, the courts do not expressly consider the freedom of speech implications of a ruling in a defamation case. The law of defamation does however attempt to balance the protection of an individual's reputation and the freedom of speech. It must be noted that not all defamatory statements are on matters of public interest and so worthy of protection, but it should be remembered that the easier it is for the plaintiff to succeed in a defamation action, the more likely it is that significant inroads will be made into the protection of freedom of speech.
2. One of the elements of defamation is publication. So long as the complainant is able to establish that the defamatory material was published to a third party and which said material referred to him, he will be successful in his claim. It is the complainant's reputation in the eyes of others which is protected and therefore there need not be a direct communication between the maker of the statement and the third party.

3. It is only a living person who can bring an action in defamation. A dead person cannot be defamed, no matter how distressing the defendant's statement is to the deceased's relatives. Corporations, however, whether trading or non-trading, have personality for this purpose so that they can sue for defamatory statements made affecting their corporate reputation: see recent House of Lords' decision in *Derbyshire County Council* v *Times Newspapers Ltd* (1993). Also note that, recently, the High Court in *Goldsmith* v *Bhoyrul* (1997) held that a political party could not sue in defamation in the public interest.

4. The tort of malicious falsehood is largely aimed at protecting business interests and it requires proof of express malice. Be that as it may, there is no reason why it cannot be utilised to protect personal reputation: see *Joyce* v *Sengupta* (1993). It is imperative that the plaintiff in an action of this nature establish a financial loss of some kind: see the recent Court of Appeal case of *Khodaparast* v *Shad* (1999) for an illustration.

SUGGESTED ANSWER TO QUESTION ONE

This question deserves careful reading, as the hasty candidate may find himself discussing the law on negligent misstatements instead of the specific issues within the law of defamation on which the question focuses. The question also raises the issue of whether the law of defamation draws a balance with freedom of expression.

Key Points

- The general principle required for establishing an action for defamation
- The need to protect an individual's reputation
- The need for freedom of expression
- Is there a balance between the two?
- Was this issue addressed in *Reynolds* v *Times Newspapers Ltd*?
- The defence of privilege – justification
- Final analysis

Suggested Answer

Essentially the question raises an analysis of two moral rights, ie protection of privacy and protection of reputation. There is certainly a link in practice between the right to privacy and the right to reputation, although this link is not recognised by English law in any formal sense. In French law, for example, there are distinct categories of 'préjudice matériel' and 'préjudice morale' to cover those harms which respectively can and cannot be reduced to mere financial loss. In the UK, however, both the freedom of speech and the protection of reputation have developed separately. Hence the unawareness that each right does in fact protect an aspect of personal integrity and dignity. An examination of this distinct and yet overlapping feature is thus necessary. Perhaps this is what Lord Nicholls meant by the elasticity of common law in *Reynolds* v *Times Newspapers Ltd* (1999).

Defamation occurs where the defendant publishes a statement about the claimant which reflects on the claimant's reputation so as to lower him in the estimation of right thinking members of society, or which tends to cause the claimant to be shunned or avoided: Jones, *Torts* (7th edn, 2000).

Freedom of expression, on the other hand, is a public law concept that has developed as a form of residual right, insofar as civil liberties are concerned, alongside the right to assemble and associate. As to whether there is a balance between these two conflicting rights, it is a subjective issue which requires an objective assessment. Certainly, the advent of the Human Rights Act 1998 has undoubtedly affected the balance by introducing both a positive right to privacy (art 8 of the European Convention on Human Rights) and a right to freedom of expression (art 10 of the European Convention on Human Rights). In Europe considerable weight is given to the latter, especially, but not only, in relation to political and public affairs, including criticism of those in the public domain. This is also evident from the decisions and attitude of the European Court of Human Rights. Comparatively speaking, our existing strong bias towards the protection of a claimant's reputation may not adequately protect freedom of speech.

In *Reynolds* v *Times Newspapers Ltd* Lord Nicholls underlined the importance of personal reputation and commented:

> 'It is in the public interest that the reputation of public figures should not be debased falsely. In the political field, in order to make an informed choice, the electorate needs to be able to identify the good as well as the bad.'

In providing a right of redress to those who have unjustifiably suffered damage to their reputations by the publication of defamatory material, the law does, however, seek to balance individual interests against the general interests of a democratic society by ensuring free speech. The law achieves such a balance in two ways. First, by preventing some types of potential claimant from bringing actions in defamation, as was the case in *Derbyshire County Council* v *Times Newspapers Ltd* (1992), where the House of Lords held that local authorities, as democratically elected government bodies, and actual government departments which are statutory corporations, must be open to uninhibited public criticism, and are therefore not entitled to bring a claim in defamation. This decision clearly upholds the principle of freedom of expression as regards actions (or the lack of action) taken by local authorities and central government departments.

Second, a balance is struck by the law by providing a range of defences to those who are alleged to have published defamatory material. These defences are, first, justification, second, fair comment, and third, privilege which is categorised into two: absolute and qualified. Each of these will now be briefly dealt with. Defences have also been developed at common law which allow for honest opinions to be expressed on matters of public interest.

Justification is a full defence and if the defendant can prove that the substance of the defamatory statement is true, then he has defeated the claimant's action. This is so even if the defendant was acting spitefully in publishing the statement: *Alexander* v *North Eastern Railway Co* (1865).

The defence of fair comment is frequently invoked by the courts, especially by the press, and along with qualified privilege is one of the defences which is important in establishing the limits of free speech in this country. Indeed, Lord Nicholls in *Reynolds* stated that: 'the freedom of expression protected by this defence has long been regarded by the common law as a basic right, long before the emergence of the human rights Convention'. The defendant must show that the matter to which the statement referred was one of public interest, that his comment was an opinion based upon true facts (which were impliedly or expressly identified in the publication), that the comment was fair and that it was free of malice. In *London Artists Ltd* v *Littler* (1969) Lord Denning defined public interest as: '... that which is such so as to affect people at large, so that they may legitimately be interested in, or concerned with, what is going on; or what may happen to them or others'. Public interest therefore is a question of fact that the court has to determine.

In the recent case of *Mahon v Rahn (No 2)* (2000), the Court of Appeal reaffirmed that no action will lie for any defamatory statement, no matter how false or malicious, made in the following instances as a result of the defence of absolute privilege:

1. parliamentary proceedings, although MPs and peers can waive this privilege to pursue a defamation action (s13 Defamation Act 1996);
2. official reports in parliamentary proceedings;
3. matters of state communications;
4. judicial proceedings;
5. fair, accurate and contemporaneous reports of judicial proceedings in the UK and Europe (s14 Defamation Act 1996);
6. reports of the Parliamentary Commissioner;
7. communications between husband and wife.

This defence therefore recognises that, in certain circumstances, it is particularly important to encourage the free and uninhibited communication of particular information from particular sources. The court in *Adam* v *Ward* (1917) stated that the categories of privileged occasions are never closed.

The occasions on which a qualified privilege may arise are potentially wide, such as the fair and accurate reports of judicial and parliamentary proceedings, and there will be freedom of expression in these circumstances unless the publisher of the statement was actuated by malice. The burden of proof falls upon the claimant on these occasions to prove that the defendant was malicious. Such a burden will be difficult to discharge, and will involve proving that the defendant had no honest belief in the truth of his statement, or that the defendant used the occasion for some reason other than that for which the privilege existed: *Horrocks* v *Lowe* (1975).

Some common law jurisdictions have gone so far as to recognise a generic category of qualified privilege in respect of political discussion. Such recognition tips the balance in favour of the freedom of expression, as there is no initial presumption of defamation in the case of a politician who has been the subject of a widespread or adverse comment in the media.

In conclusion, it is submitted that the decision of the House of Lords in *Reynolds* is consistent with s12 Human Rights Act 1998, which requires the court to pay particular regard to the importance of freedom of expression. Indeed, the common law shows an elasticity to put both these rights on a scale which is just, fair and equitable.

SUGGESTED ANSWER TO QUESTION TWO

General Comment

This is a relatively straightforward question requiring specific application of the principles of defamation to the given scenario. Students should be vigilant not to merely provide a general survey of the rules governing defamation.

Key Points

- In respect of each party named, Maisie, Tom and Horace: analyse whether the statements are defamatory – does the statement refer to the party named? – publication – are there any defences available?
- What is the position of Jackie?

Suggested Answer

The principal aim of the law of defamation is the protection of individual reputation. Defamation occurs, therefore, where the defendant publishes a statement about the claimant which reflects on the claimant's reputation so as to lower him in the estimation of right thinking members of society, or which tends to cause the claimant to be shunned or avoided. The central problem is how to reconcile this purpose with the conflicting demands of free speech. It is undeniable that both are highly valued in our society, the one as perhaps the most dearly prized attribute of civilised man, the other the very foundation of a democratic community.

This question involves the publication of certain statements in relation to three candidates, Maisie, Tom and Horace, by the *Barsetshire Chronicle* in respect of a parliamentary by-election. Defamation can occur in one of two ways. The first amounts to libel and the second amounts to slander. Libel is usually written. It is material in a permanent form or nature and is visible to the naked eye: *Monson* v *Tussauds Ltd* (1894). Therefore, the statement published by the Barsetshire Chronicle clearly amounts to libel. Libel is actionable per se and involves the following elements which must be proven by the plaintiff. First, the statement is defamatory; second, the statement referred to the plaintiff; and third, the statement was published to a third party. We will now examine the position of Maisie, Tom and Horace individually to see if an action for defamation is sustainable on the facts.

Maisie Mazda and the Barsetshire Chronicle

1. Is there a defamatory statement? There are two statements which are relevant to Maisie. One is the fact that she likes to pass herself off as something she is not, and the other is that she has had cosmetic surgery to make her look glamourous. The issue here is: are these statements defamatory in nature? The test is: do these statements tend to lower the plaintiff in the estimation of right thinking members of society generally (*Sim* v *Stretch* (1936)), or do they expose the plaintiff (Maisie) to hatred, ridicule or contempt: *Parmiter* v *Coupland and Another* (1840)? Recently, in *Berkoff* v *Burchill* (1996), the court held that a statement which left the plaintiff subject to contempt, scorn or ridicule, or tended to exclude him from society, could

be defamatory even though it did not impute disgraceful conduct or lack of professional skill. The standard here is objective, ie what would right thinking members of society think, and not the plaintiff's friends: *Byrne v Dean* (1937).

On the face of it, the statements made by the *Barsetshire Chronicle* do appear to be defamatory in nature, as they imply that, if Maisie has not disclosed that she has had cosmetic surgery, she may be inclined not to disclose other matters too, thus implying a characteristic lack of candour.

2. Do the statements refer to Maisie? The statement in question must be a direct reference to the plaintiff (this is decided by the judge), and be understood as being a direct reference to the plaintiff by reasonable people (this is decided by the jury). Be that as it may, in *Morgan v Odhams Press Ltd* (1971) the court made it clear that there is no requirement that the defendant expressly refer to the plaintiff. On the facts, Maisie would have no problems establishing that the statements expressly referred to her.

3. Has there been a publication to a third party? No problem here, as the statements were published in a newspaper: *Sodgrove v Hole* (1901). Maisie, therefore, has a sufficiently strong case in defamation. The issue now is whether the *Barsetshire Chronicle* are entitled to rely on any defences.

4. Defence of justification? As the statements are assertions of fact, they have to be justified in substance, and the fact that Maisie did have cosmetic surgery to remove a small mole from her cheek would not sufficiently meet the charge: *Lucas-Box v News Group Newspapers Ltd* (1986).

5. Defence of qualified privilege? This defence applies to fair and accurate reports of judicial or parliamentary proceedings: *Turkington and Others v Times Newspapers* (2000). This defence has also been raised within the context of public interest. Since the statements made by the Barsetshire Chronicle are matters of opinion based on a substratum of fact, there is argument for the defence of qualified privilege to apply as the public are entitled to know facts about people whom they might elect as their representatives. However, this must be balanced with the decision in *Baldwin v Rushbridger* (2001), wherein the Court of Appeal stated that this defence should not be extended to journalists. This follows the view taken by the House of Lords in *Reynolds v Times Newspapers Ltd* (1999) where their Lordships felt that the media does not have an unfettered right to publish what they believe to be in public interest.

Tom Toyota and the Barsetshire Chronicle

1. Is there a defamatory statement? The newspaper called him 'the most boring politician of 2000' and said that his hackneyed phrases and turgid delivery make him a poor orator (a qualification which is essential for politicians). In *Hartt v Newspaper Publishing plc* (1989), the Court of Appeal held that in determining the meaning of the words, the approach adopted should be that of a hypothetical ordinary reader who was neither naive nor unduly suspicious, but who might read between the lines and be capable of loose thinking. On this basis, the statement might influence the voters (and others!) to conclude that Tom does not possess the requisite qualifications and character of a politician, which may influence their decision to

vote, or not vote, for him in the election. So, it does amount to a defamatory statement.

2. Does the statement refer to Tom? Yes, undoubtedly, Tom has been clearly identified by the article: *Cassidy* v *Daily Mirror Newspapers Ltd* (1929).
3. Has there been a publication to a third party? Yes, the newspaper article!
4. Defence of fair comment? There may be the defence of fair comment. That is, the statement is fair comment based on true facts made in good faith on a matter of public interest. On the basis of *Derbyshire County Council* v *Times Newspapers* (1993), it is accepted that politicians must be subjected to some scrutiny or criticism in the public interest. So long as the defendant is not actuated by any malice and honestly believed in the opinion expressed, the defence would be available: *Slim* v *Daily Telegraph Ltd* (1968).
5. Defence of qualified privilege? Again, similar arguments as those put forward in Maisie's case (above) might be relevant.

Horace Honda and the Barsetshire Chronicle

Is there a defamatory statement? There is no doubt that the comments in the newspaper would lead all its readers to imply that Horace is having an affair with a young woman. If the statement is not prima facie defamatory, but only by implication, then the plaintiff will have to plead an innuendo. Whilst a true innuendo involves the existence of extraneous facts which the plaintiff must prove: *Tolley* v *JS Fry & Sons Ltd* (1931), a false innuendo arises where the words have a secondary meaning, either because the words have several meanings or a slang meaning: *Allsop* v *Church of England Newspaper* (1972).

Therefore, Horace would be judged as having an affair, but only by those who merely read the headlines and not the full coverage. On the basis of *Charleston* v *News Group Newspapers* (1995), whether the statement would amount to defamation deserves closer scrutiny. In *Charleston*, a case which bore similar facts, the House of Lords held that the statement or article must be considered in its entirety, and not by simply looking at the part of the article (the headlines) instead of the whole article (ie the full coverage on page seven). The full coverage does explain the true position. I am inclined to believe that the court will follow the rationale of *Charleston* and will thus find that the statement relating to Horace Honda is not sufficiently defamatory.

Could Jackie sue for defamation?

If Jackie succeeds in establishing the elements of defamation then she might possibly have a case against the *Barsetshire Chronicle*, but on the basis that there was/were no defamatory statements (only her photo was published, and the full coverage on page seven provided an explanation), she would be unsuccessful. The *Charleston* arguments would once again prevail.

SUGGESTED ANSWER TO QUESTION THREE

General Comment

Candidates should have avoided a general discussion of the elements of defamation in this question, instead concentrating on the conflict between the need for freedom of expression and the need for the law to protect individual reputations. Discussion concerning the extent to which the law of defamation protects free speech should have concentrated on the defences to an action in defamation, including that of qualified privilege which was the subject of the appeal in the *Reynolds* case. Since this question was set, *Reynolds* has been the subject of a further appeal to the House of Lords, and it is that judgement which is subject to analysis and comment below. The judgment of Lord Nicholls in particular is essential reading for candidates in this area.

Key Points

- Explain that the question is about the conflicting interests of free expression and the need to protect individual reputations
- Briefly discuss the tort of defamation as a prima facie restriction on the freedom of expression
- Explain how the law seeks to redress the balance, ie by placing restrictions upon those who can sue and the defences available in a defamation action, those being justification, fair comment and privilege (explain the defences with particular reference to the promotion of free speech)
- Explain the approach adopted in other jurisdictions to whether political discussion enjoys qualified privilege
- Discuss the *Reynolds* case and the extent to which the decision upholds freedom of expression, making reference to the position under the European Convention and the Human Rights Act 1998

Suggested Answer

The quote refers to the need for freedom of expression, and in the context of the House of Lord's decision in *Reynolds* v *Times Newspapers Ltd* (1999) it was the expression and communication of information concerning political matters which was in issue.

The tort of defamation represents a restriction on the freedom of expression by recognising the need to protect individual reputations in certain circumstances. The publication of a statement which adversely affects a person's reputation is a defamation, and may be subject to civil proceedings. The claimant need not prove that the allegations were false. Nor must he prove that he suffered damage, provided that the publication was in written or permanent form. However, it should not be supposed that the need to protect individual reputations is a matter of merely personal interest. In *Reynolds*, Lord Nicholls underlined the importance of personal reputation and commented:

'It is in the public interest that the reputation of public figures should not be debased falsely. In the political field, in order to make an informed choice, the electorate needs to be able to identify the good as well as the bad.'

In providing a right of redress to those who have unjustifiably suffered damage to their reputations by the publication of defamatory material, the law does, however, seek to balance individual interests against the general interests of a democratic society by ensuring free speech. The law achieves such a balance in two ways: by preventing some types of potential claimant from bringing actions in defamation, and by providing a range of defences to those who are alleged to have published defamatory material. Each of these will be dealt with in turn.

Restrictions upon those who may bring actions in defamation
In *Derbyshire County Council* v *Times Newspapers Ltd* (1993) the House of Lords held that local authorities, as democratically elected government bodies, and central government departments, which are statutory corporations, must be open to uninhibited public criticism, and are therefore not entitled to bring a claim in defamation. Individual councillors who have been defamed may bring actions in their own name, but the only legitimate response of a local council which is subject to public criticism is to defend itself by public utterances and by debate in the local council chamber.

This decision clearly upholds the principle of freedom of expression as regards actions (or lack of action) taken by local authorities and central government departments.

Defences
A range of defences exist to protect defendants from defamation actions in certain circumstances, thus in theory upholding and encouraging the principle of freedom of expression. The defendant may, of course, establish that the allegations were true. However, this alone is not enough to encourage free speech: the difficulties of proving the truth of every allegation, and the fear and uncertainty of expensive litigation, would have a chilling effect, discouraging the publication of potentially important material. Thus, defences have also been developed at common law which allow for honest opinions to be expressed on matters of public interest, and for statements to be made on privileged occasions, even though honest factual mistakes were made.

Justification
If the defendant can prove that the substance of the statement was true, then he has a complete defence (*Alexander* v *North Eastern Railway Co* (1865)), even if he was acting spitefully in publishing the statement.

Fair comment
The defence of fair comment is frequently invoked by the courts, especially by the press, and along with qualified privilege is one of the defences which is important in establishing the limits of free speech in this country. Indeed, Lord Nicholls in *Reynolds* stated that 'the freedom of expression protected by this defence has long been regarded by the common law as a basic right, long before the emergence of human rights Conventions.' The defendant must show that the matter to which the statement referred was one of public interest, that his comment was an opinion based upon true facts (which were explicitly or implicitly identified in the publication, at least in general terms), that the comment was fair and that it was made without malice.

That freedom of expression is promoted by this defence may be illustrated by reference to the broad manner in which some of the elements are defined. A matter is said to be in the public interest whenever it 'is such as to affect people at large, so that they may legitimately be interested in, or concerned at, what is going on; or what may happen to them or others': *London Artists Ltd* v *Littler* (1969) per Lord Denning.

As to whether the comment is 'fair' Lord Nicholls in *Reynolds* stated:

'Judges have emphasised the latitude to be applied in interpreting this standard. So much so that the time has come to recognise that in this context the epithet "fair" is now meaningless and misleading ... the basis of our public life is that the crank, the enthusiast, may say what he honestly thinks as much as the reasonable person who sits on a jury. The true test is whether the opinion, however exaggerated, obstinate or prejudiced, was honestly held by the person expressing it.'

Privilege

This defence recognises that, in certain circumstances, it is particularly important to encourage the free and uninhibited communication of particular information from particular sources. This is achieved either by providing a blanket immunity from things published on particular occasions (absolute privilege), eg statements made in Parliament, or by judges, counsel, parties or witnesses during judicial proceedings, or by protecting what is published from liability unless the claimant can prove that the defendant was actuated by malice (qualified privilege).

A number of occasions benefiting from qualified privilege have been identified by the courts and by Parliament. For example, fair and accurate reporting of the public proceedings of legislatures, courts and public enquiries worldwide are subject to qualified privilege under the Defamation Act 1996.

However, the courts do not regard these categories of 'occasions' as being closed. In *Adam* v *Ward* (1917) Lord Atkinson stated:

'... a privileged occasion is ... an occasion where the person who makes a communication has an interest or a duty, legal, social or moral, to make it to the person to whom it is made, and the person to whom it is made has a corresponding interest or duty to receive it. This reciprocity is essential.'

The occasions on which a qualified privilege may arise are therefore potentially wide, and there will be freedom of expression in these circumstances unless the publisher of the statement was actuated by malice. The burden of proof falls upon the claimant on these occasions to prove that the defendant was malicious. Such a burden will often be difficult to discharge, and will involve proving that the defendant had no honest belief in the truth of his statement, or that the defendant used the occasion for some reason other than that for which the privileged existed: *Horrocks* v *Lowe* (1975).

Qualified privilege and the publication of political discussion in the media

Some common law jurisdictions have gone so far as to recognise a generic category of qualified privilege in respect of political discussion. Such recognition tips the balance in favour of the freedom of expression, as there is no initial presumption of defamation in the case of a politician who has been the subject of adverse comment in the media. This might be thought unfair given that the widespread dissemination of defamatory material is potentially extremely damaging to those in the public eye.

In the United States, recognition of a 'public figure' defence occurred in the case of *New York Times Co* v *Sullivan* (1964). A public official cannot recover damages for defamation relating to his official conduct unless he proves that the statement was knowingly false or made with reckless disregard as to its accuracy. A plaintiff is entitled to a pre-trial inquiry into a newspaper's sources and the editorial decision-making process.

In Australia, the High Court in *Lange* v *Australian Broadcasting Corporation* (1997) held that qualified privilege automatically exists in respect of the dissemination of information, opinions and arguments concerning government and political matters, subject only to a requirement of due care. Precise guidelines were laid down as to the steps required of publishers to satisfy the requirements of due care. A publisher must not only believe that the imputation was true, but must also take reasonable steps to verify the accuracy of the information and must seek and publish a response from the individual defamed, where practicable.

Reynolds *v* Times Newspapers Ltd

This case was brought by the former Irish Prime Minister, Albert Reynolds, following his resignation on the collapse of the coalition government in 1994. An article in the *Sunday Times* alleged that he had lied to the Irish Parliament and to his coalition colleagues. The story was of interest to a British readership, as Reynolds had been one of the chief architects of the Northern Ireland peace agreement. The article proved to be factually false even though it had been honestly made. The main issue before the House of Lords was whether the newspaper were entitled to rely on the defence of qualified privilege. Counsel for Times Newspapers invited the House to consider developing a new category of qualified privilege to cover the publication of political information, in line with the approach adopted in Australia.

Consequences for the protection of personal reputation

The leading judgment was that of Lord Nicholls, who underlined the importance of personal reputation:

> 'Reputation is an integral and important part of the dignity of the individual. It also forms the basis of many decisions in a democratic society which are fundamental to its well-being: whom to employ or work for, whom to promote, whom to do business with or to vote for. Once besmirched by an unfounded allegation in a national newspaper, a reputation can be damaged forever, especially if there is no opportunity to vindicate one's reputation.'

Their Lordships refused to establish a new generic category of qualified privilege based upon the publication of political information, as it was thought that this would not provide adequate protection for the reputation of politicians: it would be extremely difficult for a political figure to prove malice without discovering the newspaper's sources, which are largely protected by s10 Contempt of Court Act 1981. Contrast this with the position in the US, where a public figure is entitled to a pre-trial enquiry to discover sources and details of the editorial decision-making process. Their Lordships also pointed out that it was inconsistent to provide protection as regards political discussion but not in respect of other matters of serious public concern, given that certain non-political public figures exercise great practical influence.

A recurring theme throughout the judgments was the suspicion that any blanket privilege would be subject to abuse by the press given the commercial pressures to publish scoops and the temptation to exaggerate or distort facts to excite the interest of readers. Lord Nicholls in particular noted that the self-regulation of the press had not always been a success.

Lord Nicholls upheld the traditional duty/interest test outlined in *Adam* v *Ward*, stating that the question of whether the public were entitled to know political or other information was a question to be determined by a judge considering all the circumstances of the publication. He put forward ten non-inclusive factors which might be considered when determining whether the duty/interest test would be satisfied, including the seriousness of the allegation, the nature and source of the information, the steps taken to verify it, whether comment was sought from the claimant and whether the article contained the gist of the claimant's version of events. An approach to determining the existence of qualified privilege which involves balancing the competing interests of the parties on a case-by-case basis according to the individual facts would accord with the approach and jurisprudence of the European Court of Human Rights.

On the facts, *The Times* were unable to establish the defence of qualified privilege, as their failure to seek or to publish Mr Reynolds' explanation of events meant that the public had no right to know the information concerned.

Consequences for the protection of freedom of expression
We have seen that the defences available to an action in defamation go some way towards protecting the rights of those who engage in honest political reporting and discussion, at least where the subject matter can be said to relate to the public interest. The decision in *Reynolds* relating to qualified privilege seems to uphold the interests of individual reputations at the expense of freedom of expression. However, this is far from being the true effect of their Lordships' decision. Freedom of expression is now the starting point for the consideration of any claim for qualified privilege by the media, and the courts are instructed to pay particular regard to the vital functions discharged by the press in acting as both 'bloodhound' and 'watchdog'. Lord Nicholls stated that courts should be reluctant to conclude that an article involving political discussion is not in the public interest: any doubts should be resolved in favour of publication. Lord Steyn even suggested at one point that the press have a general duty to inform the public on political matters and that the public has a right to be informed. However, their Lordships ultimately favoured a case-by-case approach to this question. Lord Nicholls affirmed that any unwillingness on the part of newspapers to disclose their sources should not weigh against them when determining the duty/interest test.

The approach of the House is consistent with s12 Human Rights Act 1998 which requires the courts to pay particular regard to the importance of freedom of expression. The law regarding political discussion (and indeed other matters of public concern) has now moved closer to the Australian approach in *Lange*, without the establishment of any new generic category of qualified privilege or precisely defined public interest criteria. It is likely that the courts will, in future, find that qualified privilege exists in cases where reasonable and responsible standards of journalism have been adhered to.

SUGGESTED ANSWER TO QUESTION FOUR

General Comment

This ought to have been a relatively straightforward question for candidates who had a sufficient understanding of the principles of defamation and were aware of the changes brought about by the Defamation Act 1996. It was necessary for candidates to clearly organise their answers, by dealing with the separate potential actions disclosed by the facts under different headings.

Key Points

- Action by Chill and Douche against Flame in slander
- Was this slander actionable per se?
- Were the words defamatory?
- Could Chill and Douche claim as individuals in respect of a 'group' slander?
- Were there any defences available to Flame, eg qualified privilege and fair comment?
- Action by Chill and Douche against the newspaper and others in libel
- Were the words defamatory?
- Could Chill and Douche claim as individuals in respect of a 'group' libel?
- Defences available, eg offer to make amends?
- Action by Flame against the newspaper and others in libel
- Defences available, eg fair comment and offer to make amends

Suggested Answer

The question involves a number of potential claims in the tort of defamation, arising from untrue statements which have injured the reputation of those concerned.

Action by Chill and Douche against Flame in slander

Spoken statements are not in a permanent form and are therefore classified as slanders. Generally, slanders are only actionable if the claimants can show that they have suffered special damage, ie have suffered a loss which is capable of being estimated in money. However, there are a number of exceptional cases where slanders become actionable per se, such as where the statement imputes unfitness to one's trade or calling.

Flame's description of the 'Hitlerite tendency' of the local fire brigade was clearly calculated to disparage Chill and Douche in their profession or calling, and therefore no proof of special damage will be required on their part: s2 Defamation Act 1952.

There is no single definition of a defamatory statement; however, they have been held to include 'words which tend to lower the plaintiff in the estimation of right-thinking members of society generally' (*Sim* v *Stretch* (1936)), possibly exposing him to 'hatred, contempt or ridicule' (*Parmiter* v *Coupland and Another* (1840)), or causing people to shun him or lose confidence in him: *Youssoupoff* v *Metro-Goldwyn-Mayer* (1934). Words may be defamatory 'even though they neither impute disgraceful conduct to the plaintiff nor any lack of skill or efficiency in the conduct of his trade or business or professional activity, if they hold him up to contempt, scorn or ridicule, or tend to exclude him from society': *Berkoff* v *Burchill* (1996). It is submitted that the suggestion that the local fire brigade display 'Hitlerite tendencies' is likely to induce hatred, ridicule and contempt to those at the meeting and even impute disgraceful conduct on the part of the inspectors. On the other hand, Flame might argue that, if the words were uttered in a fit of temper, they should have been understood as amounting to nothing more than vulgar abuse, and therefore not defamatory: *Fields* v *Davis* (1955).

However, a more fundamental issue here is whether Chill and Douche can claim that they have been defamed as individuals when the comments made related to the local fire brigade as a whole. Generally, where the defamatory statement has been directed at a group or class of persons, no individual belonging to that class may sue, unless there is something in the words or the circumstances in which they were uttered which might identify the claimant in particular: *Knupffer* v *London Express Newspapers Limited* (1944). Alternatively, if the group which is alleged to have been defamed is very limited in size, then the statement might be understood as referring to the claimant: *Browne* v *D C Thompson* (1912).

It is submitted that Chill and Douche are likely to experience problems establishing that they, as individuals, have been slandered. Flame's comments were directed at the local fire brigade and made to a group of student representatives several days after the inspection took place. If anyone present at the meeting was to have observed Chill and Douche at work in the building, then Flame's comments might have been taken as being directed at them individually. Otherwise, it is likely that the local fire brigade consists of too many individuals for the comments to be taken as referring to any one of them. However, it should be noted that the subsequent repetition of Flame's words indicate that they were understood as referring specifically to fire inspectors.

Defences: qualified privilege

The effect of this defence is to protect the maker of the statement from liability in defamation provided he acted honestly and without malice. It will be for the claimants, Chill and Douche, to prove that Flame was actuated by malice, ie that he had no honest belief in the truth of his statement, or that he used the occasion for a purpose extending beyond that for which the qualified privilege existed: *Horrocks* v *Lowe* (1975).

However, only statements made in certain circumstance enjoy a qualified privilege. One set of circumstances is 'where the person who makes a communication has an interest, or a duty, legal, social or moral, to make it to the person to whom it is made, and the person to whom it is made has a corresponding interest or duty to receive it. This reciprocity is essential': *Adam* v *Ward* (1917) per Lord Atkinson.

It is clear that Flame has a legal duty (under Health and Safety legislation) or at the very least a social/moral duty to instruct the students not to display notices given the apparent hazards involved and the possible closure of the building. To this extent the students have an interest in receiving the information. However, Flame's comments regarding 'Hitlerite tendencies' indicate that he has used the occasion for a purpose extending beyond that for which the qualified privilege exists, ie to disparage the inspectors. It is submitted that the claimants could rebut a provisional finding of qualified privilege and prove that Flame was actuated by malice.

Fair comment
This defence is relevant where comment is honestly made on a matter of public interest. The defendant must prove four elements.

1. The comments related to a matter of public interest 'such as to effect people at large, so that they may be legitimately interested in, or concerned at, what is going on; or what may happen to them or others': *London Artists Ltd* v *Littler* (1969) per Lord Denning. The prohibition of the display of notices affects the students of the faculty and their ability to continue to use the building, and so Flame's comments are clearly in the public interest.
2. The statement was one of opinion, not fact. It is submitted that Flame's comments regarding the inspectors' 'Hitlerite tendencies' were clearly opinion, based upon his experience of their previous conduct.
3. The comments were fair in all the circumstances of the case. This is an objective test based upon whether any fair-minded person could honestly express the opinion in question, even if it was exaggerated, obstinate or prejudiced. It is difficult to apply this test conclusively to the facts. It might be thought that the inspectors had been overzealous in discharging their duties and that Flame had a reasonable basis for his comments, even if he over-exaggerated. On the other hand, it might be thought that Flame's words were so overstated that his motives must have been improper, and consequently his comments would be regarded as unfair.
4. The comments were not inspired by malice, ie spite, ill-will or any other improper motive.

Is Flame liable for the republication of his defamatory words?
A maker of a defamatory statement may also find himself liable for the damage caused by the repetition of the defamatory statement by a third party, at least where that repetition was reasonably foreseeable. An unauthorised repetition of such a statement by an independent third party (here the Student Union Newspaper and the various distributors) may well be regarded as a novus actus interveniens breaking the chain of causation, provided Flame could not reasonably have anticipated the repetition of his slander as a natural and probable consequence of his original comments: *Slipper* v *British Broadcasting Corporation* (1991).

Claim by Chill and Douche against the Student Union Newspaper and others for libel
Every time a defamatory statement is repeated, the tort is committed again and a fresh cause of action arises. Anyone who participated in the publication of the Student Union Newspaper or its mechanical distribution is potentially liable, subject to a range of defences. Such persons would include the author of the headline, the editor, the printer, the proprietor of the newspaper, the distributors (on campus) and the newsagents.

The headline is potentially a libel as it exists in a permanent form. The words used in the headline are stronger than those originally uttered by Flame and possibly more defamatory. The newspaper might argue that the headline merely reported vulgar abuse spoken by the Dean, and should not be understood to be defamatory of the inspectors themselves. They would argue that an ordinary hypothetical reader, who was not 'avid for scandal', would not necessary believe in the truth of the statement, simply in the fact that it was said. On the other hand it could be argued that an ordinary reader who is neither 'naïve' nor 'unduly suspicious' might read into it an implication of disgraceful conduct on the part of the inspectors 'more readily than a lawyer' having 'indulged in a certain amount of loose thinking': *Hartt* v *Newspaper Publishing plc* (1989). Ultimately, whether the words uttered are reasonably capable of being defamatory is a question of law for the judge before the matter can be put to the jury.

The same problems arise here as to whether Chill and Douche could be said to have been defamed as individuals, given that the statement was aimed at a group of persons. The headline is more specific in that it refers to fire inspectors rather than members of the local fire brigade. Assuming the article goes on to explain the background to the Dean's comments, it is possible that the headline could be taken as inferentially referring to Chill and Douche by those with special local knowledge of the inspectorate: *Morgan* v *Odhams Press Limited* (1971).

Defences: offer to make amends

Under s2(4) Defamation Act 1996 it is open to the newspaper to make an offer to make amends by publishing a suitable correction and apology and to pay compensation. If Chill and Douche were to accept such an offer, any proceedings against the paper would be brought to an end, and if the parties were not able to agree on compensation, this amount would be decided by the court. Under s4, if an offer is not accepted, the fact that the offer has been made is a defence to defamation proceedings unless the claimants can prove that the statement referred to them and was both false and defamatory.

A defence of fair comment would be bound to fail in this case, because the introduction of the word 'scum' seems to indicate an improper motive or malice on the part of the author, thus rendering the comment unfair.

Action by Flame against the Student Union Newspaper and others in libel

The essence of such a claim would be that the newspaper exaggerated Flame's comments in a way that affects his professional standing and raises a question as to whether he is discharging his duties in an appropriate manner. The imputation of 'disgraceful conduct' on Flame's part may hold him up to contempt, scorn or ridicule and lower him in the estimation of right-thinking people. The headline refers to Flame personally and so the only question remaining is whether the newspaper can avail itself of a defence.

Defence: fair comment

If this article is simply about the Dean's outburst, then it might be said to be of public interest in that it calls into question Flame's professional conduct and whether he is discharging his duties in an appropriate manner. A bare statement of fact (for example a verbatim report of Flame's comments) cannot found the defence. However, the words 'fascist scum' seem to represent an opinion of the true meaning of Flame's original words.

It would have to be decided whether a fair-minded person could honestly express the opinion that the Dean, in his original comments, had really been suggesting that the inspectors were 'fascist scum'. The addition of the word 'scum' and the fact that the statement is portrayed as a direct quote (which is clearly inaccurate) might indicate some improper motive to portray the Dean in a bad light, and as such the defence would fail. An offer to make amends to the Dean could also apply here.

SUGGESTED ANSWER TO QUESTION FIVE

General Comment

This question requires the student to highlight the perceived improvements upon the former position, rather than an arid description of the provisions of the 1996 Act. Some emphasis is needed on the summary procedures provided and, if possible, some comment on the 1991 Neill Report. There is scope in this question to deal with the perceived problems that the Act does not really address in detail, such as jury damages awards, 'internet' defamations, exemplary damages etc.

Key Points

- Section 1: innocent dissemination
- Sections 2–4: unintentional defamation and offers of amends
- Section 5: limitation periods
- Sections 8–10: summary disposals
- Section 13: parliamentary waivers
- Damages awards by juries
- New techniques of publication
- Exemplary damages

Suggested Answer

The Defamation Act 1996 has introduced a wide-ranging series of reforms to the existing law, both by way of clarification and substantive reform. Only time and use will show how effective the legislation is, but any assistance at all in this complex area is welcome. The 1996 Act came about as a result of widespread dissatisfaction with the existing law which led to a Lord Chancellor's Consultation Paper in 1990 and the recommendations of Neal LJ in his 1991 Report, many of which are reflected in the Act.

Section 1 has codified the former common law defence of innocent dissemination and, very helpfully, has defined the scope of the defence by exclusion of 'authors', 'editors' and 'publishers', going on in s1(2) to further define the excluded class, and in s1(3) the included class. As at common law, it will be for the defendant to show that he took 'reasonable care' in respect of a publication and that he did not know, and had no reason to believe, that he was publishing a defamation. This is unlikely to prove too onerous a burden for anyone other than a defendant who habitually operates close to the limit.

Sections 2–4 bring in a greatly improved regime for an unintentional defamation defence of apology and offer of amends. This is quite different from the former regime under s4 Defamaton Act 1952 in that it contemplates that, in the event of failure to agree on either the steps to be taken by way of correction, apology and publication or the amount of compensation in amends, both matters will be determined by the court. This will only be appropriate in the circumstance where the sum offered, or likely to be decided upon, is less than £10,000 because that is the current upper limit for summary disposal by the judge alone (s9(1)).

There are other important changes in ss2–4 in that a defendant who intends to rely upon apology and amends as a defence must do so before he puts forward any other defence – it cannot be put forward after service of any other defence (s2(5)) – and once committed to, apology and amends cannot, thereafter, rely upon other defences (s4(4)). The defendant can, however, use an offer to try to mitigate damages whether he has relied on it for a defence or not (s4(5)). An extremely important change is brought in by s4(3) which raises a statutory presumption that the defendant was innocent of the knowledge of reference to the plaintiff and of the defamatory effect upon the plaintiff. This completely reverses the burden of proof on this vital matter and is likely, by itself, to lead to a great increase in using this provision as against its predecessor, s4 Defamation Act 1952.

Section 5 adds new ss4A and 32A to the Limitation Act 1980 so as to reduce limitation periods for defamation and malicious falsehood to one year as against the former three years and six years, subject to a judicial discretion to extend the period on equitable grounds which are wider than the former rules on accrual of knowledge of a right to an action.

Sections 8 to 10 make very sweeping changes in that they allow a judge to take full control of actions where the plaintiff has no realistic prospects of success and there is no other reason to try the claim or an application by the plaintiff for summary disposal, or where matters under ss2–4 are in dispute. In all cases, the disposal is by the single judge and the overall range of matters suitable for summary trial is capped at £10,000 damages. Otherwise than on a plaintiff's insistence the judge will not act summarily unless he is satisfied that summary relief will adequately compensate the plaintiff (s8(3)). This begins to bring defamation proceedings at the lower end of the scale more in line with other types of action, and the intention seems to be that, ultimately, all claims of whatever scale will come before the judge at an interlocutory stage for consideration of the possibility that a summary disposal is possible.

Section 13 brings in, for the first time, a possibility for waiver of the absolute privilege attaching to parliamentary proceedings by persons covered by the privilege so that they may conduct defamation proceedings. This came about as a result of the 'cash for parliamentary questions' issues and is likely to be but sparingly relied upon, although its potential value can be seen.

The Act might have gone further in attempting to deal with the vagaries of awards of damages by juries, perhaps by giving the judge a discretion to remit questionable awards directly to the Court of Appeal for consideration under s8 Courts and Legal Services Act 1990. Time will tell how much such a change is still required or, indeed, whether jury awards should be replaced by the decision of the judges. It may be that the bubble of such awards has been burst by the guidelines in *John* v *MGN Ltd* (1996).

The Act might, similarly, have gone further in response to information technology developments, although s1(3) has arguably touched on the problem of computerised defamations. In this context, *Western Provident* v *Norwich Union* (1997) concerned defamation by e-mail and *Godfrey* v *Demon Internet Ltd* (1999) raised the issue of publication of defamatory material received via internet posting. Also, the immense sums of money to be gained from deliberate defamations with profit in view might well have provided a reason to expand upon the circumstances in which exemplary damage awards might be made. Perhaps the legislators have retained their confidence in the common law and its ability to cope with such matters. The Act has, at least, moved forward on some fronts.

SUGGESTED ANSWER TO QUESTION SIX

General Comment

This is quite a difficult and wide-ranging question on the law of defamation. Students are advised not to embark on such a question if they are unfamiliar with the relevant principles and cases as the scope is quite wide and there is room for confusion.

Key Points

- Definition of defamation
- The principles of defamation
- Is the statement defamatory? – does it refer to the claimants? – has there been publication?
- Availability of defences
- Distinction between libel and slander

Suggested Answer

Defamation has been defined as the publication of a statement which tends to bring a person into hatred, contempt or ridicule. In *Yousoupoff* v *Metro-Goldwyn-Mayer* (1934) it was defined as 'tending to make the plaintiff be shunned or avoided'. It is this aspect of defamation which will give the plaintiffs or complainants in this scenario a cause of action, since their colleagues will no longer wish to work alongside them.

Before looking at Bob's, Jake's and William's causes of action, one must first ask whether the statement in the question was defamatory. Given their natural and ordinary meaning, the words certainly suggest that some drivers have clearly carried councillors and prefer making money to making friends. That is not defamatory. While a statement which disparages a person's reputation in relation to his occupation may well be defamatory, as illustrated in *Turner* v *Metro-Goldwyn-Mayer* (1950), saying that a taxi driver prefers to make a profit does not lower his reputation.

However, in the light of the boycott, the words assume an extra dimension. This is termed a 'true' innuendo, as explained in *Tolley* v *JS Fry & Sons Ltd* (1931). In other words, other taxi drivers reading the statement, knowing of the boycott, will think that some of their colleagues have lacked integrity. Their reputations are damaged and they will be 'shunned and avoided'. Therefore, it is submitted that by innuendo the words are defamatory.

It will be the function of the judge to decide whether the words are capable of being defamatory, as per *Capital and Counties Bank v Henty* (1882), and the jury will have to decide whether they are in fact defamatory.

In this case, there are three potential claimants, so the next question is whether the statement refers to Bob, Jake and William. Although none is mentioned by name, the pictures could be libellous if the claimants could produce evidence from persons who looked at the pictures and understood that, or thought that, they referred to the plaintiffs, as was the case in *Du Bost v Beresford* (1811). There is also, possibly, the defamation of a class – namely those who broke the boycott. In *Knupfer v London Express Newspapers Ltd* (1944) Lord Porter stated that 'a class cannot be defamed as a class, nor can an individual be defamed by a general reference to the class to which he belongs'. The test is how limited is the class that in the circumstances it points to the plaintiffs. Given the size of the class and the circumstances, it is suggested that they could be seen as referring to Bob, Jake and William.

Have the words been published? Publication is the communication of the words to at least one person other than the person defamed: *Bata v Bata* (1948). In this case they are contained in a newsletter and displayed in the window of Safety Taxis' offices. The inclusion in the newsletter is certainly publication. The display of the article is also defamation. In *Byrne v Deane* (1937) a verse put up on a clubhouse wall was held to be a publication. Further, this display may amount to a fresh publication, creating a cause of action against Safety Taxis, as per the case of *Sun Life Assurance Company of Canada v W H Smith* (1934). On the other hand, Safety Taxis would have to argue that the further defamation was unintentional pursuant to s4 of the Defamation Act 1952, so as to raise a defence.

If, therefore, the statement was defamatory, it referred to the claimants and was published. Bob, Jake and William each have a cause of action against the Taxi and Minicab Drivers' Association (TMDA) and Safety Taxis. It is worth noting that if the TMDA is unincorporated, then it cannot be sued in its own name, and the claimants would then have to sue those individuals responsible personally.

In relation to defences, there is one of justification. The plaintiff does not have to prove the statement is false, but the defendant can plead as a defence that it is true. The words contain two charges: namely, carrying councillors and preferring profits. If the defendant can prove that Bob and Jake carried councillors, then (under s5 Defamation Act 1952) if the other charge cannot be proven and it does not materially injure the plaintiffs' reputations, it will amount to a defence.

However, the defendant must make clear and explicit the meaning in his words. In *Jones v Skelton* (1963) the court held that this means the words must convey a direct and unambiguous message. Hence, in this case, it would have to be carrying councillors as fare-paying passengers. Therefore, the defence would only work against Bob as Jake did not accept any fare.

Is the statement fair comment? It is submitted that while it may be a matter of public interest, at least the first charge is an assertion of fact and therefore the defence is unhelpful. The defence of qualified privilege will only work if this statement can be shown to be a fair and accurate report of the findings of the TMDA, as per s15 Defamation Act 1996.

Finally, the defamation in this scenario, being in writing, is libel rather than slander, therefore there is no need for the claimants to prove damage. In conclusion, it is submitted that Jake and William may succeed in their libel action against the TMDA as well as Safety Taxis. The measure of damages they will receive is a matter for the court.

8

Nuisance

Introduction

The tort of nuisance developed to protect persons having an interest in land from unreasonable interference with their use or enjoyment of it. There are broadly two types of nuisance: private and public. Private nuisance is defined as an unlawful interference with a person's use or enjoyment of land, or some right over, or in connection with it. The courts must weigh the interest of the landowner as against the interest of the neighbour in the quiet enjoyment of his land. Only those with an interest in the land affected may sue in nuisance: *Malone* v *Laskey* (1907) and *Metropolitan Properties* v *Jones* (1939). See also the recent case of *Marcic* v *Thames Water Utilities* (2001).

Types of harm covered by private nuisance include: encroachment (*Davey* v *Harrow Corporation* (1980)), landslides (*Leakey* v *National Trust* (1980)), overflow of water (*Sedleigh-Denfield* v *O'Callaghan* (1940)), building collapsing (*Wringe* v *Cohen* (1940)), vibrations (*Hoare* v *McAlpine* (1923)), noise (*Halsey* v *Esso Petroleum* (1961)), smell (*Adams* v *Ursell* (1913)), sex shops (*Laws* v *Florinplace* (1981)) and fumes, heat and dust (*Matania* v *National Provincial Bank* (1936)). For there to be liability in private nuisance, the following elements must be established:

1. The duration of the interference must be unreasonable: *Bolton* v *Stone* (1951) and *Midwood* v *Manchester Corporation* (1905).
2. Sensitivity of the plaintiff: *Robinson* v *Kilvert* (1884) and *Heath* v *Mayor of Brighton* (1908).
3. Locality: *St Helens Smelting* v *Tipping* (1948).
4. The defendant's conduct: *Bellew* v *Cement Co* (1948) and *Andreae* v *Selfridge* (1938).
5. The element of malice: *Christie* v *Davey* (1893) and *Hollywood Silver Fox Farm* v *Emmett* (1936).
6. The House of Lords in *Hunter* v *Canary Wharf* (1997) stated that only a person in exclusive possession could sue and not a mere licensee or occupier. A change in ownership does not necessarily break the chain of continuity: *Delaware Mansions* v *Westminster City Council* (2001).

The potential defendants include: the creator of the nuisance (*Southport Corporation* v *Esso Petroleum* (1954)), the occupier (*Goldman* v *Hargrave* (1967)) and trespassers: *Sedlegh-Denfield* v *O'Callaghan* (1940). Defence of reasonable care was raised in *Goodes* v *East Sussex County Council* (2000), *Holbeck Hall Hotel* v *Scarborough Borough Council* (2000) and *Rees* v *Skerritt* (2001). See also the recent case of *Abbahall Ltd* v *Smee* (2003) on contribution of parties in nuisance. The following are available as defences: Prescription Act 1832, statutory authority, operation of nature, Act of God/stranger and volenti non fit injuria. Remedies include injunctions, abatements and damages. Recent cases in private nuisance include: *Southwark London Borough*

Council v *Mills*; *Baxter* v *Camden London Borough Council* (1999) (HL) and *Hussain* v *Lancaster City Council* (1999) (CA). See also *Lippiatt* v *South Gloucestershire County Council* (1999) (CA).

Public nuisance, on the other hand, is an unlawful act or omission which endangers the life, health, safety or comfort of some section of the public or obstructs the public in the exercise of some common right, for example: unreasonable obstruction of the highway (*Dymond* v *Pearce* (1972)), creating a danger on the highway (*Clark* v *Chambers* (1878)), keeping dangerous premises near a highway (*Tarry* v *Ashton* (1876)). To succeed, the plaintiff must prove three things. First, that he/she belongs to a class or section of people; second, some special damage must have been suffered; and, third, all the elements of private nuisance must also be established. See also the relevance of ss41 and 58 of the Highways Act 1980, in relation to the liability of local councils. The recent Court of Appeal case of *Cross* v *Kirklees Metropolitan Borough Council* (1998) offers a useful illustration of public nuisance and statutory duty. Conversely, see also *Goodes* v *East Sussex County Council* (2000). In *Wandsworth London Borough Council* v *Railtrack plc* (2001) the court held that an owner of property could not sue in public nuisance.

Questions

INTERROGRAMS

1. How may private nuisance be defined?
2. How may public nuisance be defined?
3. What are their similarities and distinctions?
4. To what extent is the tort of nuisance considered as strict liability?

QUESTION ONE

'Originally in private nuisance only the person who by himself or his servant or agent created the nuisance on his land which interfered with the use and enjoyment of his neighbour's land was liable. The position was different in public nuisance where once the existence of a nuisance on his land comes to the knowledge of the occupier it is his duty to abate it or endeavour to do so.' (*Holbeck Hall Hotel Ltd* v *Scarborough Borough Council*, per Stuart-Smith LJ.)

Discuss the scope and purpose of the tort of nuisance in the light of this quotation.

University of London LLB Examination
(for external students) Law of Tort June 2001 Q4

QUESTION TWO

Benison District Council own an inner city site which has been cleared for future development. On the site there is a small gymnasium which has not been demolished. The Council has allowed St Christopher's Church to use the gymnasium each weekday afternoon as a 'drop-in centre' for young homeless people. The church provides a games room, tea and cakes and advice about health and welfare problems. The centre proves very popular, is well attended and often attracts some very rowdy youngsters who are not homeless but hang around the hall all afternoon.

Fenella runs a woman's health club in an adjoining street. She complains that a number of youngsters from the centre are constantly peering through the windows of the club and some of them come in and try to chat to the members of the club. Some of the members have told her that, because they feel uncomfortable and are sometimes frightened to leave the club in the early evening, they have decided not to renew their membership. Every Friday Geoffrey, who occupies the premises next to Fenella, holds meditation sessions for business people afflicted by stress, and complains that the noise from the gymnasium interferes with these sessions.

Discuss whether Fenella or Geoffrey would have a cause of action in nuisance.

University of London LLB Examination
(for external students) Law of Tort June 2000 Q5

QUESTION THREE

'The word "nuisance" is difficult to define precisely. It has been said to be protean when questions are raised as to the conduct which may give rise to liability. But the underlying principles, which distinguish the tort of nuisance from the tort of negligence for example, are, I think, capable of reasonably precise definition in the light of the authorities.' (*Hunter* v *Canary Wharf Ltd* (1997), per Lord Hope of Craighead.)

Discuss.

University of London LLB Examination
(for external students) Law of Tort June 1998 Q1

QUESTION FOUR

The Mudborough Council have maintained a children's playground on one particular site for some 50 years. It is used by children from all over Mudborough, mainly by children under five during school terms, but also by older children during the holidays. Three years ago a private developer built a number of houses on land adjoining the playground. The purchasers of two of these houses, whose gardens back on to the playground are now complaining of interference from the playground.

One, James, complains that the noise the children make prevents him sleeping in the afternoon. He has to do so as he works on night shifts. The other, Keith, complains that the older children climb on his garden fence so that he and his family have no privacy in their back garden. He also complains that children often come into his garden to retrieve balls which have come over the fence.

Both James and Keith want to get the playground closed. Advise them of their legal rights.

Written by the Author

Answers

ANSWERS TO INTERROGRAMS

1. Private nuisance is primarily concerned with conflicts relating to competing uses of land. It can be defined as an unjustified interference by the defendant in the plaintiff's enjoyment of the land.
2. Where a nuisance affects a substantial number of people, it is said to be a 'public nuisance'. This type of nuisance is more concerned with any form of interference with any aspect of the public's rights as opposed to unjustified interference with one's use or enjoyment of land. Public nuisance may be a crime if not a tort.
3. The basic elements which are needed to succeed in a nuisance action (whether private or public) are similar, ie the duration of the interference must be unreasonable, the sensitivity of the plaintiff, the locality, the defendant's conduct and the element of malice. Public nuisance slightly differs because, in addition to these basic elements, the plaintiff has to prove that he or she belongs to a class or section of people and must prove some special damage.
4. Nuisance is considered as strict liability in two instances where liability was on any definition strict. First, liability for damage caused by animals and, second, liability for fire. The third is *Rylands* v *Fletcher* type of instance, which will be considered in the next chapter.

SUGGESTED ANSWER TO QUESTION ONE

General Comment

An essay question should not be used as an excuse to write a general appraisal of the relevant area of law raised by the question, which in this case is private nuisance. The question refers to a specific observation by a judge in a case, and thus calls for critical appreciation within the context of that observation.

Key Points

- Determining liability in private nuisance
- The essential elements
- A brief analysis of the *Holbeck Hall Hotel* case
- The scope and purpose of the tort of nuisance
- Trespassers and acts of nature: are they valid defences?
- Distinction from public nuisance

Suggested Answer

Private nuisance has been defined by Winfield and Jolowicz as 'an unlawful interference with a person's use or enjoyment of land, or some right over, or in connection with it': *Law of Tort*, 15th edn, 1998 at Chapter 14. The House of Lords confirmed in *Hunter* v *Canary Wharf Ltd* (1997) that private nuisance is a tort which attaches to land, and so only those with a proprietorial interest in the land affected may bring an action.

There are many categories of nuisance, but in determining whether the nuisance is actionable the courts must balance the reasonableness of the defendant's activity (which created the nuisance) against the reasonable needs of the claimant to use and enjoy his property. In *St Helens Smelting Co* v *Tipping* (1865), the House of Lords held that there was a distinction between nuisances which cause damage to property and those which cause personal discomfort in the use or enjoyment of land. However, the point raised by the question at hand is not the basis of liability, but rather who the appropriate defendant should be.

Nuisance is essentially a tort of strict liability in the sense that it will be no defence to show that the nuisance was not created intentionally, or even that the defendant used all reasonable care. The leading case that illustrates this point is *Cambridge Water Company* v *Eastern Counties Leather plc* (1994). This case is also significant as it contains a comprehensive restatement of the scope of liability in nuisance and of the relationship between orthodox private nuisance and public nuisance.

In *Holbeck Hall Hotel Ltd* v *Scarborough Borough Council* (2000), a cliff belonging to the defendant council gave way, and as a consequence a hotel on neighbouring land belonging to the plaintiff was destroyed. The case was particularly difficult because while the defendant ought to have foreseen some minor slips causing damage to the plaintiff's rose garden and lawn, there was no reason why it ought to have foreseen the massive slip which destroyed the hotel. In these circumstances, the Court of Appeal held that an occupier that failed to meet the measured duty to take reasonable steps to prevent a nuisance occurring on its land should only be liable to the extent of the damage that ought to have been foreseen. This, it is submitted, is thought to run counter with the usual rule of remoteness of damage: that a defendant is liable for all damage of the same type as ought to have been foreseen, regardless of the extent: *Overseas Tankship (UK) Ltd* v *Miller Steamship Co Pty Ltd, The Wagon Mound (No 2)* (1967).

However, in *Holbeck* the Court of Appeal further suggested that in the circumstances, where the hazard was a result of the forces of nature and the defendant would have gained little benefit from preserving its own land against the hazard, the defendant might well have fulfilled the duty to act reasonably by informing the claimants of the risk and sharing any information relating to it.

Given that the question of whether an occupier will be liable for consequences resulting from a state of affairs he did not create is answered by considering whether the occupier has fulfilled a measured duty of care, it is sometimes suggested that this group of cases should be considered as falling within the tort of negligence. This then raises the question of whether damages can be obtained when a state of affairs only reduces the amenity value of neighbouring land, for example, where an occupier fails to deal with a regular, noisy trespasser, or with smelly rotting rubbish tipped onto his land by trespassers.

In *Southport Corporation* v *Esso Petroleum Co* (1954), it was held that the creator of the nuisance by misfeasance rather than non-feasance may be sued even if he no longer occupies the land from which the nuisance emanates. In *Sedleigh-Denfield* v *O'Callaghan* (1940), it was held that an occupier would be liable for a nuisance created by a trespasser where he continued, or adopted, or in any way authorised or continued to authorise the nuisance. Likewise in *Leakey* v *National Trust* (1980), the court held that the occupier would also be liable for a nuisance arising out of a condition of his land if he knows of the risk and fails to take appropriate action. This arguably also attracts liability under the Defective Premises Act 1972, which imposes a positive duty on the owner/occupier of a property to ensure that his/her property is in good keep and order. Recently, in *Marcic* v *Thames Water Utilities Ltd* (2001), it was held that a nuisance resulting from the breach of the defendant's duty to take such care as is reasonable under the circumstances was actionable. This must, of course, be contrasted with the decision of the Court of Appeal in *Hussain* v *Lancaster City Council* (1999), where it was held that a landlord is not liable in nuisance if an independent third party or a trespasser, over whom the landlord has no control whatsoever, causes a nuisance. This seems to be the view within the ambit of public nuisance.

With public nuisance, there is the availability of the defence of all such care as is reasonable under the circumstances having been discharged, as illustrated in *Goodes* v *East Sussex County Council* (2000). This decision was given support by the case of *Southwark London Borough Council* v *Mills* (1999), where the court held that not all types of interferences would give rise to liability automatically. This contention received further approval in *Wandsworth London Borough Council* v *Railtrack plc* (2001), where the court held that an owner of property could not sue the council in public nuisance because pigeon droppings were falling onto his property.

Perhaps the distinction between private and public nuisance (as observed by Stuart-Smith LJ) is that in public nuisance the owner or occupier has a positive duty to abate or take steps to negative the nuisance. This positive duty, however, is subject to the defence of secret and unobservable operations of nature, as illustrated by *British Road Services* v *Slater* (1964).

Public nuisance, unlike private nuisance, is also a crime as well as a tort. Hence it is deserving of more consideration prior to the imposition of liability in any case.

SUGGESTED ANSWER TO QUESTION TWO

General Comment

Though this appears to be a standard question on private nuisance, attention is drawn to the fact that there are potentially two defendants, the Council and the church. Thus the issue of liability in nuisance should be properly addressed.

Key Points

* Introduction
* Categories of nuisance
* Fenella's claim of nuisance (annoyance): factors or principles of nuisance relevant to establishing liability – who is liable (Council or church)?
* Geoffrey's claim of nuisance (noise): factors or principles of nuisance relevant to establishing liability – who is liable (Council or church)?
* Remedies
* Possible defences

Suggested Answer

Nuisance, particularly private nuisance, can be a complex and confusing area of tort. This confusion arises because there are few hard and fast rules as to what amounts to a nuisance: rather, there are a number of guidelines or factors which the court may, or may not, consider as being relevant in determining whether an activity amounts to a nuisance. In a word, private nuisance regulates unreasonable interference with an occupier's use or enjoyment of his rights over land. The law seeks to find a balance between the legitimate, but conflicting, interests of landowners – the right of an occupier to use his land as he chooses – and the right of his neighbour not to have his use of land interfered with. The litigants in these actions are usually neighbours in the popular sense of the word. It is no wonder that Dean Prosser ((1989) CLJ 55) remarked: 'There is perhaps no more impenetrable jungle in the law than that which surrounds the word "nuisance" '.

As the question concerns the rights of two individuals, Fenella and Geoffrey, each will be dealt with in turn.

Fenella

Fenella's complaint is that there are a number of rowdy youngsters, from the centre run by the church on the premises owned by the Council, who peer through the windows of her health club and have tried to 'chat up' the members of the club, causing fear as well as annoyance. As a result of this, some of the members have informed her that they will not be renewing their membership with the health club.

Clearly, the interference here relates to the enjoyment of the property free from any annoyance. Whilst it is not possible to classify each and every possible activity that may be actionable in nuisance, the three main groups may be identified as the following: cases involving encroachment, as in *Davey* v *Harrow Corporation* (1958); cases involving physical damage to land or property, as in *Sedleigh-Denfield* v *O'Callaghan* (1940); and finally cases involving interference with enjoyment of property, as in *Tetley* v *Chitty* (1986). Fenella's case would clearly fall within the third category.

It must be pointed out that not all interferences give rise to liability: there must be give and take between neighbours and the interference must be substantial and not fanciful, as stated in *Walter* v *Selfe* (1851). This fact was recently reaffirmed in *Baxter* v *Camden London Borough Council* (1999), by the House of Lords. Fenella is not complaining about noise but rather annoyance in the form of harassment from rowdy youngsters, which seems to be scaring away her members. Two cases deserve consideration on this point. In *Hussain* v *Lancaster City Council* (1999), the plaintiffs were subjected to a campaign of harrassment by people who lived as tenants on a council estate owned by the defendant council. This disrupted the plaintiff's business. An action for nuisance against the council failed (apart from on grounds concerning policy issues) on the basis that the claim was in essence related to the plaintiffs' right to be free from racial harassment, as opposed to the right in relation to the use of their land or property. Conversely, in *Lippiatt* v *South Gloucestershire County Council* (1999), a group of travellers allegedly set up camp on land belonging to the council and used the camp as a 'launching pad' for a series of damaging invasions on a neighbouring farmer's property. In this case, the Court of Appeal held that the council was arguably liable for the nuisance resulting from the state of affairs on its land.

In Fenella's case, the annoyance created by the rowdy youngsters does in fact interfere with her rights to use her land and property free from interference. Presumably the church is aware of this and has not done anything to address the issue. Thus Fenella could arguably succeed in an action for nuisance against the church. The church would prove to be a better defendant because they can be said to have created, authorised, adopted or allowed to continue the nuisance. It is likely that the council has knowledge of these matters and hence cannot be implicated for not taking reasonable steps to eliminate the problem. The church is the basis of the cause of the nuisance, and it is them who must be held liable. Fenella must also establish the following conditions in order to be successful. First, that the duration of the interference is continuous and unreasonable: *Harrison v Southwark & Vauxhall Water Co* (1891). Second, that there is no abnormal sensitivity on her part: *Heath v Mayor of Brighton* (1908). Third, that the character of the neighbourhood is such that the annoyance or interference is unjustified: *Bamford v Turnley* (1860). Fourth, the utility of the defendant's conduct in relation to the nuisance concerned: *Bellew v Cement Co* (1948). Finally, the issue of malice or fault on the part of the defendant must also be considered: *Andreae v Selfridge* (1938).

The church has clearly been careless in allowing the annoyance to become excessive and this exposes them to liability in private nuisance. Fenella might apply for an injunction plus damages for the loss that she has suffered. On the facts, the church has no valid defence on which it can rely.

Geoffrey

Geoffrey's complaint is essentially concerned with noise, which is clearly recognised as a category of nuisance, as in *Tetley v Chitty*. However, Geoffrey only holds meditation sessions on Friday's and is thus affected only when he holds these sessions. Geoffrey must also prove all the above elements (as discussed under Fenella) in relation to the duration of the interference, abnormal sensitivity, character of the neighbourhood, utility of the defendant's conduct and malice or fault. Geoffrey may have a problem with proving that he (as well as his clients) are not abnormally sensitive (to noise, in this instance). This would be problematic on the basis that they are all involved in meditation sessions. Are the premises appropriate or useful for such an activity to be conducted in? It is submitted not, on the basis of the decision in *Robinson v Kilvert* (1884). Also, given the fact that the whole area might be subject to future development by the Council, this might arguably change the character of the neighbourhood, which would then prove unsuitable for Geoffrey's activity. If Geoffrey is successful in overcoming the 'abnormal sensitivity' hurdle, then his action would be against the church, which is the sole cause of the nuisance (they have created, adopted or authorised it). As in Fenella's case, the church appear to have no valid defence.

SUGGESTED ANSWER TO QUESTION THREE

General Comment

Recent developments in tort are always likely to form the basis of examination questions, especially important decisions of the House of Lords. Those candidates who had carefully studied the judgment in *Hunter* and its wider implications would have been well placed to answer this question. As ever, a more detailed analysis and comment on the case was expected of candidates, as a compromise to predictability.

Key Points

- Introduce the tort of private nuisance in relation to the *Hunter* case
- Describe why the tort may be said to be 'protean' in nature, given its application to a wide range of scenarios
- What are the distinguishing features of nuisance and negligence (as identified by their Lordships)?
- Why were these important in the *Hunter* case?
- Describe the court's decision regarding standing, damages and the applicability of the tort to interference with TV reception (including Lord Cooke's dissent)
- Conclude by saying something about the importance of the decision in *Hunter* and possible future activity in this area

Suggested Answer

The case of *Hunter* v *Canary Wharf Ltd* (1997) raised important questions as to the scope of the tort of private nuisance. The tort itself is concerned with unreasonable interference with a person's use or enjoyment of his land, or some right over or in connection with his land. The House of Lords in *Hunter* explained the tort as falling within three main categories: nuisance by encroachment on a neighbour's land; nuisance by direct physical injury to a neighbour's land; and nuisance by interference with a neighbour's quiet enjoyment of his land.

These categories are extremely wide in that they cover a large variety of potential claims and factual scenarios. For example, under the third category, interference might be caused by dirt, dust, noise, smoke, smell and vibrations arising from a huge range of activites. In *Thompson-Schwab* v *Costaki* (1956) the sight of prostitutes and their clients entering and leaving neighbouring premises amounted to a private nuisance. In *Khorasandjian* v *Bush* (1993) the Court of Appeal even went so far as to grant an injunction in favour of a young girl against the defendant, who had embarked on a course of harassment against her at the parental home. In *Hunter*, one of the questions before the Lords was whether interference with TV reception suffered by local residents following the construction of the Canary Wharf tower (a building which is almost 250 metres high, over 50 metres square, and clad in stainless steel) could amount to a private nuisance. A second, more fundamental, question related to who had the right to bring an action in nuisance for the interference caused to TV reception, and, in a separate action, for dust caused by the construction of a link road to the Docklands area.

It was this question which prompted the majority of the Lords to comment upon the distinguishing features of actions in nuisance and negligence, and it is this aspect of the *Hunter* case which will be dealt with first.

The distinguishing factors of negligence and nuisance

Lord Hoffmann, quoting from Lord Simonds in *Read v J Lyons & Co Ltd* (1947), noted that nuisance only protects interests in land, and that it is a tort of strict liability ie it is no defence for a defendant to say that he took all reasonable steps to prevent it. Negligence, on the other hand, is fault-based (breach of a duty to take reasonable care) and protects interests of many kinds, not just those in land. Lord Cooke noted that in nuisance, damages may be recovered for interference with the use and enjoyment of land, whereas there is no remedy for discomfort or distress (not resulting in bodily or psychiatric injury) in negligence. Lord Hope, in examining the scope of each tort, noted that the function of nuisance is to control the activities of an owner/occupier of property within the boundaries of his own land which may harm the owner/occupier of neighbouring land. In other words, the duty is owed to owners and occupiers. In negligence, however, the duty extends to those who are foreseeably closely and directly affected by the defendant's act or omission: *Donoghue v Stevenson* (1932). In appropriate circumstances, this might include persons on neighbouring land who are neither owners nor occupiers. It should be noted that in some situations, the two torts overlap and may provide concurrent remedies.

The right to sue in private nuisance

The decision of the majority flowed from the proposition that nuisance is a tort which attaches to land ie is directed against the claimant's enjoyment of the land affected. On this basis, an action in nuisance can only be brought by a person who has an interest in such land. These persons might include one who has actual possession, such as a freeholder, tenant in possession or a licensee with exclusive possession, or a reversioner, where the nuisance is sufficiently permanent in character to damage the reversion itself.

The Lords impliedly accepted the decision of the Court of Appeal in *Foster v Warblington Urban District Council* (1906) which upheld the right, in exceptional cases, of someone who has exclusive possession of land (even though he cannot prove title) to sue in private nuisance. Lord Lloyd stated that the first two categories of private nuisance involve damage to land and therefore only a person who has a proprietary interest in that land can sue. By implication, therefore this must also be true of the third category. Lord Hoffmann agreed that the third category did not constitute a separate tort.

In a powerful dissent, Lord Cooke argued that whilst the decision of the majority achieves symmetry and uniformity in the law of nuisance (the rules being the same for each of the three categories), their approach does not give adequate weight to current perceptions of the rights and status of spouses, de facto partners and children living at home. In relation to children in particular, he noted the recognition given to the interests of children by international convention. Article 16 of the UN Convention on the Rights of the Child protects children from unlawful interference with their home. Article 8 of the European Convention for the Protection of Human Rights and Fundamental Freedoms recognises the right to respect for private and family life, aimed in part at protecting the home. Jurisprudence of the European Court of Human Rights shows that the protection of the home extends to protection from nuisance, even though children clearly have no proprietary rights over the family home.

Lord Cooke therefore considered the Court of Appeal decision of *Khorasandjian* to have been correctly decided and regarded the fact of 'occupation of property as a home' to be an acceptable basis from which to bring an action in nuisance. He felt that other resident members of the family, de facto partners and lodgers, could as a matter of policy be allowed to claim in private nuisance if they had suffered a 'truly serious interference with domestic amenities'.

However, the majority of their Lordships overruled *Khorasandjian*, Lords Goff and Lloyd stating that the Court of Appeal had simply exploited the tort of nuisance in order to introduce, by the back door, a tort of harassment out of sympathy with the claimant. They noted that a tort of harassment had since received statutory protection under the Protection from Harassment Act 1997, and a remedy was no longer needed at common law. The approach taken in *Khorasandjian* was to transform the tort of nuisance to one which attaches to the person rather than to land. The effect would be to allow a claimant to recover for loss less severe than personal injury upon criteria relating only to the balancing of the interests of neighbours, rather than negligence.

Damages

The proposition that the tort of nuisance attaches to land only also formed the basis of the decision of the majority as to the correct measure of damages recoverable in nuisance. Under the first two categories of nuisance involving damage to land, compensation will be assessed according to the diminution in value of the property. This will normally be the cost of remedial work and repair. However, where a nuisance simply affects the enjoyment of land, then damages will be assessed according to the loss of the amenity value of the land, assuming the nuisance does not affect the overall market value. This would be a relatively low single payment to the proprietor(s) of the land, and will not depend upon the overall number of people who were affected.

Although not necessary for the actual decision in *Hunter*, considerable doubt was cast upon the question of whether damages for personal injury are recoverable in private nuisance. Lord Goff stated that the correct action for the recovery of such loss is negligence. Lord Hoffmann drew attention to the anomalous outcome of compensation for personal injury being easier to recover if suffered at home rather than at work.

TV reception

It was agreed unanimously that interference to TV reception in the circumstances did not amount to a private nuisance. The Lords held that a building, which by its mere presence prevents something from reaching the claimant's land, is not a nuisance. The tort must take the form of something emanating from the defendant's land, or, occasionally, from some offensive conduct of neighbours. The blocking of TV reception was comparable by analogy with the loss of a view, which is not actionable in private nuisance. Lords Goff and Hoffmann agreed that at common law, people are entitled to build freely on their land unless restricted by a covenant or an easement. It was further doubted whether an easement could exist against the interruption of TV/radio signals.

A common theme of the majority of their Lordships' judgments related to the unpredictability of building developments causing interference with TV reception, and the large number of potential claimants involved in such a situation. Lords Goff and Hoffmann pointed out that the most appropriate time to raise an objection to possible

TV interference would have been at the stage of application for planning permission to the local planning authority, although it was noted that this course of action would not have been open to the residents in this case. Lord Cooke preferred to approach the question according to the reasonable user test, holding that Canary Wharf Tower had been a reasonable development in all the circumstances.

Conclusion

The decision in *Hunter* is an important one, because it preserves the distinction between nuisance and negligence as two separate torts subject to different rules. It settled the question of who can sue in private nuisance and the basis for awarding damages for loss of the use and enjoyment of land. It might be argued that Lord Cooke's approach to the question of standing should achieve favour in the future, as the courts are now under an obligation to decide a case's compatibility with Convention rights (unless prevented from doing so by primary legislation), and to take into account the jurisprudence of the European Court of Human Rights in doing so: Human Rights Act 1998. The protection of the home, as an aspect of the right to respect for private and family life, contained in art 8 of the Convention, seems to require protection to be given to all members of the household against nuisances.

Important questions have yet to be answered following *Hunter*; for example, whether damages for personal injury are available in nuisance and whether interference with TV reception caused by something emanating from the defendant's land can form the basis of an action. Further judicial activity in this area can be anticipated. For the time being, the House of Lords appear to have applied the brakes to the development of the tort of nuisance to cover novel situations.

SUGGESTED ANSWER TO QUESTION FOUR

General Comment

Another common question examining the liability of a local authority in private nuisance and, possibly, negligence. The availability of the equitable remedy of injunction and possible defences must also be discussed.

Key Points

- Private nuisance
- Definition
- Interference
- Unreasonableness
- Character of neighbourhood
- Loss of enjoyment/damages
- Defence of prescription
- Availability of damages/injunction as a remedy

Suggested Answer

James and Keith would be advised to bring an action in private nuisance and will seek the remedy of a mandatory injunction against the Council so that the playground may be closed.

The essence of the tort of nuisance is unreasonable interference with another's enjoyment of his land. Private nuisance has been defined as being committed when a person is held responsible for an act indirectly causing physical injury to land or substantially interfering with the use or enjoyment of land or of an interest in land, where in the light of all the surrounding circumstances, this injury or interference is held to be unreasonable. The plaintiff's case will be based on the fact that there has been a substantial and unreasonable interference with their enjoyment of their property: see *Walter* v *Selfe* (1851).

'Substantial interference' will exclude any interference which is trivial, and although the loss of one night's sleep has been held not to be trivial (*Andreae* v *Selfridge* (1938)), the interference suffered by James and Keith must generally not be an isolated incident and it may, however, be a 'state of affairs, however temporary': per Oliver J in *Bolton* v *Stone* (1950). The Court of Appeal's decision in *Southwark London Borough Council* v *Mills*; *Baxter* v *Camden London Borough Council* (1999) lends support to this contention.

James claims that he is unable to sleep not at night but in the afternoons and therefore it may be argued that he is an abnormally sensitive plaintiff. However, those cases concerning abnormal sensitivity suggest that the sensitivity lies in the use to which the house is put, rather than personal sensitivity on the part of the plaintiff himself: *Robinson* v *Kilvert* (1884).

Unreasonable interference concerns several factors which will apply to both James's and Keith's cases. As the House of Lords in *Sedleigh-Denfield* v *O'Callaghan* (1940) pointed out: 'A balance has to be maintained between the right of the occupier to do what he likes with his own land and the right of the neighbour not to be interfered with. It is impossible to give any precise or universal formula but it may broadly be said that a useful test is perhaps what is reasonable according to the ordinary usages of mankind living in society'.

The character of the neighbourhood is taken into account in assessing what is reasonable (*Bamford* v *Turnley* (1860)), save in cases involving physical damage: *St Helen's Smelting Co* v *Tipping* (1865). At this point, it must be said that in this case, both plaintiffs have come to the nuisance; the nuisance has not come into existence after they have moved in. The playground has been run for 50 years; the houses were built only three years ago. The court would therefore expect greater tolerance by the plaintiffs since they have chosen to live near the playground and may have had some idea of the problems they might have to face. If, however, the nuisance is sufficiently great, the case may be actionable regardless of the locality: *Halsey* v *Esso Petroleum* (1961). Applying the test used in Halsey by Veale J the standard is that of the ordinary and reasonable man who lives in the vicinity of the playground. It is submitted that noise will be expected during the daytime and in school holidays, so that James's claim may fail under this head, although Keith's claim in relation to children climbing over the fence should not be affected by this consideration.

The Council may attempt to set up the defence of prescription (as in *Miller* v *Jackson*

(1977) by claiming that they have a right to commit the alleged private nuisance over a period of at least 20 years with continual use and that the plaintiffs (or their predecessors in title) knew of the nuisance. The defence was raised in *Sturges* v *Bridgman* (1879) but the court held that the defence must fail since the time ran from when the nuisance became apparent. Applying that decision to the facts of the case, the nuisance has only existed for a maximum of three years, so that this defence must fail.

James's claim is arguably doubtful but Keith should have an arguable case. In deciding whether to grant the injunction, the court will have regard to the public interest as opposed to the infringement of the individual's rights. In *Miller* v *Jackson* (above), the public interest suggested that an injunction should be refused where to hold otherwise would have meant that the playing of cricket would be prevented although this approach was not followed in *Kennaway* v *Thompson* (1981).

Keith may have an alternative action in trespass which involves the 'intentional or negligent entering on or remaining on, or directly causing any physical matter to come into contact with land in the possession of another' (Street). The children have entered Keith's garden clearly without his permission or consent, but the problem here is whom to sue. It would be extremely difficult to bring in the Council as defendants and it may not be worthwhile to bring such an action. Although trespass is actionable per se, many trivial trespassers where no damage is caused to the land are ignored, and this may well be one of those cases.

9

The Rule in *Rylands* v *Fletcher*

Introduction

Strict liability is a general term used to describe forms of liability that do not depend upon proof of fault. These are instances where the plaintiff may succeed without proving fault on the part of the defendant, provided he proves actual damage has been suffered. The philosophy behind strict liability is that the defendant has chosen to engage in an activity which increases the dangers to others. The classic example of strict liability in English law was illustrated in *Rylands* v *Fletcher* (1868) in the House of Lords. Their Lordships had to develop a new principle as none of the available tortious concepts was appropriate – for example, trespass, nuisance or negligence. Hence, the rule in *Rylands* v *Fletcher*. Four elements must be established in order to succeed in an action under the *Rylands* heading. Note also that liability may arise under the *Rylands* principle where there is evidence of negligence: *Ribbee* v *Norrie* (2000).

1. There must be dangerous substances or things likely to do mischief if they escape: *Read* v *Lyons* (1947) and *Crowhurst* v *Amersham Burial Board* (1878).
2. The 'thing' must have been accumulated by the defendant: *Giles* v *Walker* (1890) and *Rigby* v *Chief Constable of Northamptonshire* (1985).
3. The 'thing' must escape from the defendant's place or control and do damage elsewhere: *Miles* v *Forest Rock Granite* (1918) and *Powell* v *Fall* (1880).
4. The use of the defendant's land must be a non-natural one: *Rickards* v *Lothian* (1913), *Musgrove* v *Pandelis* (1919), *British Celanese* v *Hunt* (1969) and *Cambridge Water* v *Eastern Counties Leather* (1994). The House of Lords in *Hunter* v *Canary Wharf* (1997) has finally settled the issue of the status of the plaintiff. To be able to sue in nuisance, the plaintiff must be in exclusive possession and not a mere licensee or occupier. Defences include: consent (*Attorney-General* v *Cory Bros* (1921)), plaintiff's default (*Eastern and Southern African Telegraph* v *Cape Town Tramways* (1902)), act of God (*Greenock Corporation* v *Calendonian Railway* (1917)), act of stranger (*Rickards* v *Lothian* (1913) and *North Western Utilities* v *London Guarantee and Accident* (1926)) and statutory authority and necessity. See also *British Gas plc* v *Stockport Metropolitan Borough Council* (2001).

Questions

INTERROGRAMS

1. What are the facts of *Rylands* v *Fletcher*?
2. How is *Rylands* v *Fletcher* distinct from ordinary nuisance?
3. What is meant by non-natural user?
4. Are damages for personal injuries and economic loss recoverable?

QUESTION ONE

Ronald leased a small country house from Percival. With Percival's consent, he assigned the unexpired two years of the lease to Stewart in 1998. A shed in the garden contained a considerable amount of rubbish including some paint tins. Stewart did not want to use the shed, did not ask Ronald to remove the rubbish and did not investigate what was there. The paint tins had in fact been used to store a highly corrosive chemical. It has now destroyed the containers and seeped into the adjoining property of Terence. It has made it impossible to grow flowers in a large part of Terence's garden and has destroyed his prize sunflowers. Stewart has disposed of the paint tins but says that he cannot do anything about the chemical which has seeped into the soil. Terence knows that Stewart always likes to watch the 'Newsnight' programme at 10.30 each evening on television and Terence always uses electrical equipment at the time in order to interfere with reception. Ronald's present whereabouts are unknown.

   Advise the parties.

University of London LLB Examination
(for external students) Law of Tort June 1999 Q8

QUESTION TWO

Cruella Enterprises Ltd manufacture leather garments. They receive a threat from an 'animal rights' organisation that their factory will be occupied by protesters. This is reported to the managing director who decides that it is a hoax and takes no special security measures. Two weeks later a bomb explodes beside a drum of acid which the company uses in its manufacturing processes. The acid pours into the adjoining premises of DeVile Ltd where a large number of used car tyres are stored. Thousands of pounds worth of damage is done to the tyres and the reaction with the acid unexpectedly produces toxic vapours. Neighbouring factories have to close down for several days until the vapours have dispersed.

   Advise Cruella Enterprises and DeVile.

University of London LLB Examination
(for external students) Law of Tort June 1997 Q4

QUESTION THREE

'I incline to the opinion that, as a general rule, it is more appropriate for strict liability in respect of operations of high risk to be imposed by Parliament, than by the courts. If such liability is imposed by statute, the relevant activities can be identified, and those concerned can know where they stand.' (*Cambridge Water Co Ltd* v *Eastern Counties Leather plc* (1994), per Lord Goff of Chieveley)

a) What is the significance of this case?
b) Do you agree with Lord Goff's view about the respective roles of the courts and Parliament?

University of London LLB Examination
(for external students) Law of Tort June 1994 Q1

QUESTION FOUR

Andrew, Basil and Clive each leases premises on an industrial estate. Andrew has recently greatly increased the use of his premises and often overloads the drains and sewage system. There is frequently an unpleasant smell hanging over the other workshops and both Basil and Clive find that there is sometimes a flow back of sewage into their systems.

Basil uses his premises for his photography business. He has chemicals stored in his basement. These are kept in accordance with the manufacturers' instructions. However water has seeped into the basement from Andrew's overflowing sewage system and this results one evening in a violent explosion. Bricks and glass shower down on Clive's premises damaging some goods stored there and Daphne, who was walking past in the street, was showered with broken glass.

Discuss the issues of liability in tort raised by these facts.

University of London LLB Examination
(for external students) Law of Tort June 1993 Q8

Answers

ANSWERS TO INTERROGRAMS

1. The defendants were millowners. Wanting to improve their water supply, they employed independent contractors who were apparently competent to construct a reservoir on their land which would supply them with water. During the course of their work, the contractors discovered some underground passages and mines on the land where the reservoir was to be built. They did not seal these mines and shafts properly with the result that, when the reservoir was filled with water, the water burst through into the mines and shafts and flooded the plaintiff's coal mine, causing damage agreed at £937. The House of Lords held that the defendants were liable.

2. The requirements of *Rylands* v *Fletcher* type of nuisance is distinct in a sense that there has to be a dangerous substance which must have been accumulated by the defendant, and which said dangerous thing must escape and cause damage elsewhere. Another important feature is the requirement that the use of the defendant's land must be a non-natural one.

3. It simply means any use which is not ordinary, normal, usual or natural, ie, an extra-ordinary use. As Lord Moulton stated in *Rickards* v *Lothian* (1913), 'it must be some special use bringing with it increased dangers to others, and must not merely be the ordinary use of the land or such use as is proper for the general benefit of the community.'

4. Authorities on this point swing in both directions. As regards personal injury, *Hale* v *Jennings* (1938) states that the plaintiff would be able to claim for personal injuries but the decision in *Read* v *Lyons* (1947) doubted that. It is thus arguable whether *Rylands* v *Fletcher* could be extended to encompass personal injuries. With respect to economic loss, the position is the same. Whilst *Weller* v *Foot & Mouth Disease Research Institute* (1966) states that there is no liability for economic loss, the

decision in *Ryeford Homes* v *Sevenoaks District Council* (1989) argues otherwise. In principle, therefore, it is submitted as recoverable on a 'direct result' basis.

SUGGESTED ANSWER TO QUESTION ONE

General Comment

Students who were well aware of the House of Lords' decisions in *Hunter* v *Canary Wharf* and to a lesser extent *Cambridge Water* would have been well placed to answer this question. A thorough knowledge of the rules would have been necessary to have made some observations on the question of whether Percival might be liable to Terence in respect of the escaped chemicals.

Key Points

- Terence
- Action in private nuisance for the escaped chemicals
- Does Terence have sufficient standing to bring a claim?
- Can a single event give rise to liability in private nuisance?
- Who can Terence sue?
- Measure of damages
- Alternative action in *Rylands* v *Fletcher*
- Whether the storage of the chemicals was a non-natural use of the land
- Who can Terence sue?
- Stewart
- Whether interference with TV reception can form the basis of an action in private nuisance
- Whether nuisance is actionable (noting the relevance of malice)
- Brief mention of remedies

Suggested Answer

Damages for the clean up costs of Terence's land and the destroyed flowers are potentially recoverable in both the tort of private nuisance and under the rule in *Rylands* v *Fletcher* (1868).

Private nuisance
Private nuisance has been defined by Winfield and Jolowicz as 'an unlawful interference with a person's use or enjoyment of land, or some right over, or in connection with it.' The House of Lords in *Hunter* v *Canary Wharf Ltd* (1997) confirmed that private nuisance is a tort which attaches to land, and so only those with a proprietorial interest in the land affected may bring an action. Terence must therefore be a freeholder, a tenant in possession or a licensee with exclusive possession of the neighbouring premises in order to have sufficient standing to bring a claim.

Generally, nuisances may take three different forms: encroachment on a neighbour's land, direct physical injury to a neighbour's land or interference with a neighbour's quiet enjoyment of the land. Whilst Terence's land has suffered direct physical damage, there is some uncertainty as to whether an isolated or a single escape can constitute a nuisance. The position appears to be that if damage resulted from a pre-existing state of affairs, it will constitute a nuisance: see *Midwood* v *Manchester Corportation* (1905) in which a gas explosion was held to be an actionable nuisance as it followed a build-up of gas in the main. It is clearly arguable that the migrating chemical which caused damage to Terence's land resulted from their storage and gradual escape from the shed next door over a period of time, and it is therefore submitted that this amounted to a pre-existing state of affairs giving rise to a nuisance.

Who can Terence sue?

Ronald's whereabouts are unknown and so Terence's potential claims are against Percival (the reversioner) and Stewart (the tenant). It is not clear whether it was Ronald or Percival who accumulated the paint tins. Stewart was not responsible for their presence. If Percival was responsible for the storage of the chemical, he may be held liable as a previous occupier of the premises, because he knew, or ought to have known, of the hazardous state of affairs: *St Anne's Well Brewery Co* v *Roberts* (1928).

As for Stewart, there is authority to suggest that he will be liable as an occupying tenant of the premises: *Montana Hotels* v *Fasson Pty* (1986). Stewart's liability, notwithstanding his ignorance of the hazard, would seem to be consistent with the notion of strict liability in the tort of private nuisance.

Was this an actionable nuisance?

In determining whether the nuisance is actionable, the courts balance the reasonableness of the defendant's activity (which created the nuisance) against the reasonable needs of the claimant to use and enjoy his property. However, in *St Helens Smelting Co* v *Tipping* (1865), the House of Lords held that there was a distinction between nuisances which cause damage to property and those which cause personal discomfort in the use or enjoyment of land. It is easier to establish nuisance in the former case, as the courts do not take into account the character of the area as a relevant factor. We have already seen that single escapes of the type which occurred in this case can amount to actionable nuisances, and it is submitted that the fact of physical damage to Terence's land in the circumstances will allow him to claim. There appear to be no problems as to whether damage of the kind that took place in this case was foreseeable, given the highly corrosive nature of the chemical being stored: *Cambridge Water Company* v *Eastern Counties Leather plc* (1994).

Damages

Terence will be able to claim compensation according to the diminution in value of his land. This is likely to be equal to the cost of re-instatement, ie the clean up costs. Terence ought to be able to claim, in addition, compensation for the cost of the plants and flowers destroyed. There seems to be no English authority on the question of whether Terence could claim for any economic losses flowing from prizes he might have won in respect of the sunflowers.

Rylands *v* Fletcher

Since the *Cambridge Water* case, it is clear that this tort is nothing more than a specific application of the law of private nuisance in relation to isolated escapes. For liability to attach under this rule, it must be proved that:

1. the defendant brought something onto his land in the course of some non-natural use of it;
2. there has been an escape of that thing from the defendant's land to the claimant's land;
3. damage has resulted to the claimant's property; and
4. it must have been foreseeable that damage of the kind that took place would occur.

The only issue here is whether the corrosive chemical amounted to a non-natural use of the land. This concept receives no precise definition in the authorities, although Lord Goff in the *Cambridge Water* case stated: 'The storage of substantial quantities of chemicals on industrial premises should be regarded as an almost classic case of non-natural use.' Whether the storage of some paint tins containing a highly corrosive chemical on residential premises would be regarded as a non-natural use is uncertain. It might be argued that if the storage of chemicals is a non-natural use of industrial premises, it certainly ought to be so regarded on residential premises, even if the quantities involved are less. In general, the more dangerous a thing is, the more likely it is to constitute a non-natural use.

Who can Terence sue?
In *Rylands* v *Fletcher* Blackburn J spoke of a person who 'for his own purposes' brings things onto his land. This would appear to rule out Stewart as a potential defendant, liability thus depending upon whether it was Percival or Ronald who was responsible for the storage of the paint tins. However, in *Cambridge Water*, the rule in *Rylands* v *Fletcher* was held to be an offshoot of the tort of private nuisance. In view of this, it is might be argued that the same rules should apply in relation to potential defendants as were discussed for private nuisance.

Is Terence liable to Stewart for the interference with TV reception?
Stewart, as a tenant, has a proprietorial interest in the land affected by Terence's activities and therefore has sufficient standing to mount an action in private nuisance. The first issue is whether interference with TV reception can amount to a private nuisance. Comments made by Buckley J in the case of *Bridlington Relay Ltd* v *Yorkshire Electricity Board* (1965) suggested that, at the time of that case, TV reception could not be regarded as such an important part of an ordinary householder's enjoyment of his property so as to amount to a legal nuisance. However, more recent cases in other common law jurisdictions have held that TV viewing is an important incident of the ordinary enjoyment of property and should be protected. In *Hunter*, the House of Lords held that interference with TV reception caused by the blocking of such transmissions by the erection of a building did not constitute a nuisance. However, obiter comments of Lords Hoffman and Cooke suggest that interference with TV reception could, in some circumstances, amount to a nuisance. In the light of the decision in *Hunter*, it is submitted that where such interference is caused by something emanating from the defendant's land, such as Terence's use of electrical equipment, then an action will lie.

The point remains to be firmly decided.

Assuming that such interference can form the basis of a claim in nuisance, it must be decided according to the balancing test whether or not there is an actionable nuisance. All the factors in this case point to the resolution of that balancing exercise in favour of Stewart. In the normal course of events, relevant factors would be as follows.

1. The character of the neighbourhood in which the nuisance took place. The facts of the question indicate a residential countryside area, where interference with TV reception is likely to be uncommon and therefore subjectively more disturbing.
2. The fact that the interference took place at night time, when residents are most likely to be viewing TV.
3. The fact that this was a repeated and continuing interference.

Moreover, the fact that Terence was motivated by malice tips the balance very firmly in Stewart's favour (*Christie* v *Davey* (1893)) and it is submitted that the court is likely to be persuaded to grant an injunction restraining or restricting Terence's use of the electrical equipment. Stewart may also be entitled to damages for the loss of amenity value to his property covering the period of intentional interference up to the time of any injunction. Any such award would consist of a relatively low one-off payment.

SUGGESTED ANSWER TO QUESTION TWO

General Comment

Students should be prepared to deal with the general question of whether a duty exists to prevent the acts of third parties and how far such a duty might extend. The question also requires a consideration of the law of nuisance and *Ryland* v *Fletcher*. The nature of the damage will also require some discussion of unlikely or remote consequences, and pure and consequential economic loss. The vicarious liability of the company for the torts of its managing director should be discussed.

Key Points

- Whether there is a duty to prevent the acts of third parties: *Smith* v *Littlewoods*
- The claim by DeVile Ltd: negligence, nuisance and *Rylands* v *Fletcher*
- The claims brought by the neighbouring factories against Cruella Enterprises Ltd and DeVile Ltd
- The unexpected consequences – *Cambridge Water* v *Eastern Counties Leather* – remoteness of damage
- The range of recovery – consequential economic loss – pure economic loss
- Vicarious liability

Suggested Answer

The original source of the damage in this situation is the unlawful bombing of Cruella's factory and, if it were possible to find the miscreants, they could be held to account. But, as this result is unlikely, Cruella will be probably forced back upon their insurers for their own property damage. The real question is to what extent, if at all, will Cruella be liable for damage to others. The complaint that will be levelled against the company and its managing director is that they failed to prevent the act of the 'animal rights' third party. This directly raises the question whether, and in what circumstances, such a duty arises. The leading case is now *Smith* v *Littlewoods Organisation Ltd* (1987), from which it is clear that no such operational duty exists but that within certain exceptional situations, Lord Goff illustrating four, a duty may arise.

In Cruella's situation, some of the exceptional features may be present. Lord Goff pointed to the case where a landowner allows or knows that a source of danger on his land is being created by a third party as a situation where a duty might arise; similarly, a duty may arise where a person has created or tolerated a potential danger which only needs the agency of a third party to 'trigger off' a risk to others as in *Haynes* v *Harwood* (1935). It is assumed for present purposes that such a duty is owed by Cruella and, in the absence of evidence of how secure the site and acid storage is under normal circumstances, that the duty is breached. This duty will be owed, at least, to adjoining owners such as DeVile Ltd under conventional 'neighbour' principles: per Lord Atkin in *Donoghue* v *Stevenson* (1932).

The claim by DeVile Ltd may, as outlined above, be brought on ordinary negligence principles. If, however, it were found that Cruella's security was such that no special measures were needed or, perhaps, practicable, this cause of action would disappear. It would then be necessary to consider alternatives, and the ones that suggest themselves are nuisance and/or *Rylands* v *Fletcher* (1868) liability. A claim might be brought in private nuisance, even for an isolated escape, if there is evidence of a generally insecure site with an underlying, unsatisfactory state of affairs as in *British Celanese* v *A H Hunt Ltd* (1969), but this sort of claim would fail in the circumstance of a reasonably secure site and storage as with the claim in negligence. It might, however, succeed if the overall site security was good (preventing a negligence claim) but the storage of acid left something to be desired. A more promising probability would be under *Rylands* v *Fletcher* on the basis that Cruella had brought a substance onto their premises which was likely to do harm if it escaped. This use of their land would, undoubtedly, be a 'non-natural' use and this is the very type of situation for which the remedy is intended. The acid has simply escaped under gravity, but there is a defence to *Rylands*, that of the act of a stranger as in *Perry* v *Kendrick Transport Ltd* (1956). However, as Cruella knew that there was a possibility of sabotage, this might not be a defence here. Liability under *Rylands* v *Fletcher* depends very much upon reasonable foreseeability, both of the escape and of the consequences of the escape: *Cambridge Water* v *Eastern Counties Leather plc* (1994).

The neighbouring factories, if they claim against Cruella, may have some difficulties whatever cause of action they rely upon. The problem is that the rules of remoteness of damage laid down in *The Wagon Mound (No 1)* (1961) show that property damage of a type that is not reasonably foreseeable is unrecoverable. This would seem to bar a negligence action based on toxic vapours, and a very similar result obtains in nuisance and *Rylands* v *Fletcher* since the *Cambridge Water* case. This would not, of course, prevent a claim by DeVile Ltd against Cruella for direct acid damage to the tyres.

An even more formidable obstacle for the neighbouring factories is that most of their loss appears to be in the form of lost production. There are two possibilities here. First, that there may be stock or material which has been damaged or rendered useless by the closures and, second, that the loss is pure economic loss in the form of lost productivity and continuing overhead costs. If the factories can get a claim going against Cruella (perhaps on the basis that the vapours are of the general acidic nature of the escape), they may be able to recover for the first head of the loss as that can be seen to be consequential economic loss. They will be unable to recover for the pure economic loss in negligence or *Rylands*: *Spartan Steels and Alloys Ltd* v *Martin & Co (Contractors) Ltd* (1973). The question whether such a loss is recoverable in nuisance is unclear but, as the interference is with the enjoyment of land as manufactures, there seems no reason in principle why such loss should not be recoverable.

There would be little doubt that any negligence by the managing director would be 'within the course of his employment' so as to bring down vicarious liability on Cruella.

There is the possibility that the neighbouring factories may wish to claim against DeVile for the escape of fumes from their premises under *Rylands* v *Fletcher*. This could probably be met by a defence of lack of reasonable foreseeability under *Cambridge Water* v *Eastern Counties Leather plc* or possibly act of a stranger as in *Perry* v *Kendrick Transport Ltd*.

SUGGESTED ANSWER TO QUESTION THREE

General Comment

This involves discussing a quotation from a judgment in relation to both its context in that judgment, and on a wider, more practical basis. The scope for moving outside the confines of the question is great, but should obviously be avoided.

Key Points

a) • Nuisance
   • *Rylands* v *Fletcher*
   • Damage/harm
   • Foreseeability
   • Natural v non-natural use
b) • Strict liability
   • Statute v common law
   • Parliamentary supremacy/separation of powers
   • Rule of law

Suggested Answer

a) The most significant aspect of the *Cambridge Water* (1994) decision appears to relate both to nuisance and to the rule under *Rylands* v *Fletcher* (1866), and to a consideration of whether foreseeability of a particular type of harm was necessary in determining an award of damages. The case also involved an attempt to clarify the issue regarding the assessment of the use of land as either natural or non-natural. The latter, subsidiary point was only considered briefly as the main decision of the court rendered fuller discussion irrelevant. The House of Lords appears to have concluded that foreseeability of harm of the *relevant type* by the defendant was a prerequisite for the recovery of damages, in both nuisance and under *Rylands* v *Fletcher*.

The *Cambridge Water* case revolved around an almost typical nuisance/*Rylands* v *Fletcher* scenario. The defendant was using and storing a chlorinated solvent, a mile from a borehole belonging to and used by the plaintiff for the abstraction of water for domestic use. The solvent, over a period of time, seeped into the water supply and, as a result of a European Commission ruling, the water was classed as being unfit for human consumption. As a result, the plaintiff claimed damages in, alternatively, negligence, nuisance and under the rule in *Rylands* v *Fletcher*. The case made a steady progression through the court hierarchy, until it fell for the House of Lords to decide upon the issues raised. The Court of Appeal had declined to determine the case on the basis of the rule in *Rylands* v *Fletcher*, but instead held that there was a parallel rule of strict liability in nuisance. The House of Lords felt unable to agree with the stand taken by the inferior court and considered that this was not a case in which extending the bounds of nuisance was proper and appropriate. In reviewing this whole area, their Lordships turned firstly to the question of foreseeability of damage in nuisance. Although the appearance of the liability is strict, in that the fact that the defendant has taken all reasonable care will not exonerate him from liability, the principle of 'reasonable user' acts as a form of control mechanism. Within this area of law no suggestion is made, however, that the defendant should be held liable for damage of a type which he could not reasonably foresee. This appears to have been the view of the Privy Council in *Overseas Tankship (UK) Ltd* v *Miller Steamship Co Pty, The Wagon Mound (No 2)* (1967). In that case, Lord Reid felt unable to discriminate 'between different cases of nuisance, so as to make foreseeability a necessary element in determining liability'.

It was against this general background that Lord Goff turned to the rule in *Rylands* v *Fletcher* and, in particular, the judgment of Blackburn J. It was possible to discern a view that foreseeability of the risk was a prerequisite to the recovery of damages. His Lordship considered some of the authorities that had been presented as offering an opposite perception. However, it was felt that the undeniable connection between the rule in *Rylands* v *Fletcher* and nuisance meant that it was merely a logical step to afford the same test for both types of claim. This was not to say that the rule in *Rylands* v *Fletcher* was, as the examination of the point by the House of Lords in *Read* v *J Lyons & Co Ltd* (1947) revealed, to be the development of a test of strict liability. It appeared that the House of Lords was concerned to have the *Rylands* v *Fletcher* rule considered as an extension of the law of nuisance to cases of isolated escapes from land. As the quotation suggests, Lord Goff did not consider that is was for the judiciary to take the law down that particular path.

The second point, that was mentioned only for the sake of completeness, related to the discussion of whether storing of solvent on land was a natural or non-natural use of land. In the original action, the trial judge had attempted to label it a natural use and thereby allow the exception to come into play. However, the House of Lords felt bound to decide that the storing of such chemicals was a non-natural use.

b) Looking at the respective roles of the courts and Parliament involves considering their places within the constitution of this country. At its most basic, Parliament makes the law, and it is left to the courts to interpret that law, in accordance with general presumptions and both internal and external aids to construction. There is a whole wealth of issues pertaining to the separation of powers within constitutional law, to which this question could relate. However, it is the extent to which the courts should take their role of interpreters of the law which appears to have been behind Lord Goff's consideration, and correct assessment, of these issues.

In general, it seems that those producing legislation are doing so in a way that is both carefully structured and well-informed. This being so, it means that the need for the courts to try and achieve the same ends via the use of the common law is reduced. This can only be of benefit as the common law is, and can only be, of general application. The 'system' is called upon to operate in so many differing environments that it cannot be too specific. Therefore, it would be unfair to expect the common law to accommodate areas of law that are overly technical. It must be left to the agency that can afford to meet those technical challenges head on and, as Lord Goff goes on to say, 'statute can where appropriate lay down precise criteria establishing the incidence and scope of such [strict] liability'.

The inherent dangers in allowing the courts to take a more active role in the defining of such controversial issues are a price too high to pay just to answer the courts' fears of a reluctant legislature. There may well come a time, and probably a judiciary, when the failure of Parliament to meet the challenges set by areas such as environmental pollution will lead to the redefining of roles. This would be a great shame and could lead to the judiciary's 'floodgate' fears acting in their favour, but against the general rule of law.

The imposition of liability in a haphazard and general way on the basis of 'no fault' may have quite a dramatic effect on the commercial ability of some businesses to survive. If, in relation to 'strict liability', Parliament is reluctant to create such a duty, it cannot really be for the courts to do it on Parliament's behalf. It seems that until the legislature can develop a fair and sophisticated system of compensation, then the courts' hands will be, and must remain, tied.

SUGGESTED ANSWER TO QUESTION FOUR

General Comment

This question is essentially concerned with interference to land and the torts of nuisance – both private and public – and the rule in *Rylands* v *Fletcher*, as well as negligence. It is a wide-ranging question and most students will probably have found a lot to say.

Key Points

* Private nuisance – factors to consider
* Public nuisance

- The elements of *Rylands* v *Fletcher*
- Negligence and the question of remoteness

Suggested Answer

This question is concerned with property being used in such a way that it annoys or damages other people. It is therefore concerned with the torts of private and public nuisance and the rule in *Rylands* v *Fletcher* (1866) as well as with negligence.

The first problem to deal with is the smell hanging over other workshops owing to A overloading the drains and sewage system. Any action would be in private nuisance, which can be defined as unlawful interference with a person's use and enjoyment of land. An unpleasant smell is sufficient to constitute a nuisance: eg *Rapier* v *London Tramways Co* (1893).

B and C are both leaseholders and therefore have sufficient interest in the land to sue in nuisance: *Inchbald* v *Robinson* (1869). They can sue A because presumably he or his servants or agents created the nuisance. The damage is not tangible and has not caused material damage, therefore one has to consider a number of factors to decide whether or not A acted unreasonably and created a smell which constitutes a nuisance.

One of these factors is the nature of the locality. As was memorably stated by Thesiger LJ in *Sturges* v *Bridgman* (1879), 'What would be a nuisance in Belgrave Square would not necessarily be so in Bermondsey'. A, B and C all lease properties on an industrial estate, therefore it might be felt that unpleasant smells are a hazard of such places. However, it is submitted that the fact the smell emanates from overloading the drains and sewage systems, rather than from the proper use of the premises, makes the nature of the location less relevant. Smells from drains are equally unpleasant everywhere.

It may be that A is involved in some activity of general benefit, which would be a factor in his favour, although in the Irish case of *Bellew* v *Cement Co* (1948) the court forbade a nuisance even though it meant closing the only cement factory in Ireland. In A's case, whatever the activity, he has overloaded the system which would surely negate the mitigating effect of social utility.

The court would not take account of any abnormal sensitivity on the part of A or B: eg *Heath* v *Mayor of Brighton* (1908). On the other hand, the fact that the smell is frequent is important for the success of the action, since a temporary or occasional smell would probably be insufficient: eg *Bolton* v *Stone* (1951).

These are the issues of liability with regard to the smell and, on the facts, it seems likely that B & C's action in private nuisance would succeed. The remedy they would be seeking would be an injunction to bring the nuisance to an end.

What has been said about the smell will also apply to the flow back of sewage into B and C's systems with regard to an action in private nuisance, although if the flowback has caused material damage, the additional factors become less relevant, since the nuisance is tangible. The remedy would be in damages.

Is there an action in public nuisance? The smell is a nuisance which materially affect the reasonable comfort and convenience of a class of Her Majesty's subjects, namely the occupants of the industrial estate. It arises from A overloading the drains and sewage system. B and C have also suffered additional, particular damage – the flow back of sewage – beyond the general inconvenience caused by A's behaviour. Therefore they could sue in public nuisance also.

Turning to B, he has brought chemicals onto his premises. Since these have been kept in accordance with manufacturers' instructions, it does not appear that he has acted negligently, unless it could be argued that it was negligent to keep them there in the first place. Nevertheless, they have come into contact with water and exploded, causing damage to C's premises and personal injury to D. The action that one is looking at here is under the rule in *Rylands* v *Fletcher*.

The rule as stated by Blackburn J is this: a person who for his own purposes brings on his lands and collects and keeps there anything likely to do mischief if it escapes, must keep it at his peril, and, if he does not do so, is prima facie answerable for all the damage which is the natural consequence of its escape. This rule was somewhat tempered by Lord Cairns LC in the House of Lords when he relied upon the 'non-natural use' of the land to uphold the decision. Subsequent case law has similarly relied upon this additional element, which has weakened the strict liability that would otherwise apply. (Indeed, were this not the case, then B and C might have been helped by one of Blackburn J's examples, that of the person whose cellar is invaded by the filth of his neighbour's privy!)

Applying the rule to the facts of this case: the rule in *Rylands* v *Fletcher* has been applied to explosions: *Miles* v *Forest Rock Co* (1918). The chemicals have been accumulated on B's land for his own purposes, in other words for his own benefit. There has been an escape, in that the explosion has extended beyond B's land: see the House of Lords' decision in *Read* v *J Lyons & Co Ltd* (1947). Keeping combustible chemicals carries with it inherent risks and it is submitted that this is non-natural use of the land. The most commonly used definition is from *Rickards* v *Lothian* (1913):

> 'It must be some special use bringing with it increased danger to others and must not merely be the ordinary use of the land or such a use as is proper for the general benefit of the community.'

The risk is B's and, subject to any defences, he is therefore liable under the rule. While C could certainly recover damages for property damage, there has been some uncertainty over recovery for personal injury. Although the House of Lords in *Read* v *Lyons* doubted whether there could be recovery for personal injury, given the context of the original decision in *Rylands* v *Fletcher*, there have been decisions in which damages for personal injuries were allowed: eg *Perry* v *Kendricks Transport Ltd* (1956). Therefore D would be able to recover.

B will argue, in his defence, that the explosion was caused not by him, but by A and that A's act was an unforeseeable one. He will say that he has followed the manufacturers' instructions and has not been negligent and, if he can prove this and that the seeping water was unforeseeable, he has a defence to the claim. From the facts, this may seem to be the case.

Finally, there is the issue of A's negligence. He owes a duty of care to B and C as well as to D, the passer-by, not to injure them by his negligent acts. He has breached this duty by unreasonably unloading the drains and sewage system. This breach may have caused damage to B and C's sewage systems, in which case they can sue him for damages. It has also caused the damage to C's premises and to D, since 'but for' A's negligence, the explosion would not have occurred: *Barnett* v *Chelsea and Kensington Hospital Management Committee* (1969).

However, it is arguable whether it is foreseeable that overloading one's drains will lead to an explosion and therefore A will argue that the damage to C and D is too remote. The test of foreseeability is contained in *The Wagon Mound (No 1)* (1961), namely that the damage is too remote if a reasonable man would not have foreseen the consequences.

10

Trespass to Persons

Introduction

This tort seeks to provide a remedy for directly inflicted intentional interference with the person. It includes battery, assault and false imprisonment. A point that needs noting here is that where force is applied negligently, the action lies in negligence; whereas the action would lie in trespass if the force was intentional. Interestingly, the Court of Appeal recently struck out a case on harassment: see *Thomas* v *News Group Newspapers Ltd* (2001). See also *R* v *Colohan* (2001).

BATTERY (ACTIONABLE PER SE)

Battery is the intentional and direct application of force on another. It must be direct (*Scott* v *Shepherd* (1733)); it must be intentional (*Letang* v *Cooper* (1965), *Miller* v *Jackson* (1977) and *Wilson* v *Pringle* (1987)); it must be hostile (*Wilson* v *Pringle* (1987) and *F* v *West Berkshire Health Authority* (1989)); and, finally, it must involve contact with the complainant (*Cole* v *Turner* (1704)). Defences include: consent (*Chatterton* v *Gerson* (1981) and *R* v *Billinghust* (1978)), self-defence (*R* v *Duffy* (1967) and *Lane* v *Holloway* (1968)), contributory negligence (Law Reform (Contributory Negligence) Act 1945 and *Murphy* v *Culhane* (1977)) and inevitable accident.

ASSAULT

Assault involves putting the plaintiff in reasonable apprehension of immediate physical violence to his person. There is no need for words as mere action suffices: *Martin* v *Shoppee* (1828). Words without any action will also do: *R* v *Wilson* (1955). Words may also negate assault: *Tuberville* v *Savage* (1669) and *Read* v *Coker* (1853).

FALSE IMPRISONMENT

This is committed when the defendant intentionally and without lawful justification restrains a person's liberty within an area delimitated by the defendant. The plaintiff's liberty must be totally restrained: *Bird* v *Jones* (1845). It is not necessary for the imprisoned person to be aware of his imprisonment: *Herring* v *Boyle* (1834). In *Murray* v *Ministry of Defence* (1988) the court held that knowledge is not relevant to the cause of action but rather to the recoverability of damages.

Where a person intentionally, but indirectly, inflicts physical harm on another, then that person may be found liable on the basis of the principle in *Wilkinson* v *Downton* (1897). Note the relevance of the harassment legislation – the Protection from Harassment Act 1997 – in this context. See also the relevance of the recent Court of

Appeal case of *Roberts* v *Chief Constable of the Cheshire Constabulary* (1999). The case of *Gregory* v *Portsmouth City Council* (2000) discusses malicious prosecution.

Questions

INTERROGRAMS

1. Is it an assault to point an unloaded gun at another person?
2. Would kissing without the consent of the other amount to a battery?
3. What are the remedies for false imprisonment?
4. What is the rule in *Wilkinson* v *Downton*?

QUESTION ONE

Arthur has agreed with Bertram to use his front room on the day following the Cup Final in order to watch the local team return triumphant or otherwise, with the Cup. He agrees to pay five pounds for this. On the morning of the day in question Arthur arrives with several friends, some of whom appear to be still intoxicated after the celebrations of the previous night, Bertram says: 'The deal's off. Take this mob away.'

Arthur says: 'You can't do this. We agreed. Let me through.'

He pushes Bertram aside and sits down in the room. Bertram fetches his friend Bruce who throws Arthur out onto the road and injures his back. Arthur's friends who have retreated out of the house in some disarray throw bottles through the windows of Bertram's house.

Advise Bertram.

Written by the Author

QUESTION TWO

Alan is an old age pensioner living with Brian, his nephew, in Stoketon. Brian treats Alan badly, threatening to punch him if he leaves his room without permission. Alan is too frightened to disobey. Their neighbour, Clive, suspects that Alan is badly treated and tells Diane, the Stoketon social services supervisor. Diane tells Clive that social services will arrange a visit but they fail to do so and simply pass on the information to a local pensioner support group. Edward, a volunteer from the group, calls but fails to recognise the signs of age abuse which would be obvious to a professional. Alan becomes so depressed that he tries to commit suicide by jumping out of his window. He breaks his leg and is taken to Stoketon Hospital where Fiona, an experienced medical student working in casualty, fails to recognise the problems that can be caused by bone fractures in the elderly. As a result, Alan does not receive proper treatment and will always have towalk with the aid of a stick. If Alan had received proper treatment, he would have had a reasonable chance of making a full recovery.

Advise Alan.

University of London LLB Examination
(for external students) Law of Tort June 1991 Q5

QUESTION THREE

Keith is a lecturer in law at the University of Slumsville. One of his duties is to organise moots and mock trials. He arranged with Lucy, a mathematics student, and Mark, a law student, that they would stage an incident which would be the basis of a mock trial. In accordance with the arrangement, as Lucy walked into a mathematics lecture, Mark seized her from behind, tore her shoulder bag from her and rushed from the room. Lucy collapsed and another student, Noel, sprang from his seat and tackled Mark. In the ensuing scuffle, Mark suffered a dislocated shoulder and Noel lost several teeth.

Lucy suffered from a rare medical condition and the incident caused a spasm which constricted her throat and she died of asphyxiation. Neither Lucy nor anyone else had known that she suffered from this condition, but the evidence now is that she could have died at any time if she suffered severe shock. Mark's shoulder injury did not respond to treatment and he is likely to have a permanent disability. He was so distressed by learning of Lucy's death that he suffered a complete nervous breakdown and is unlikely to be able to resume his studies.

Advise Mark, Noel and Lucy's father as to any possible claims in tort.

University of London LLB Examination
(for external students) Law of Tort June 1990 Q3

Answers

ANSWERS TO INTERROGRAMS

1. Since assault is concerned with the apprehension of fear of immediate physical violence, it is how the complainant reacts which is important. The person pointing the gun maybe aware that the gun is unloaded but the victim does not know this and therefore he fears the worst. That is sufficient for assault to subsist.
2. Although the Court of Appeal in *Wilson* v *Pringle* (1987) stated that it was not 'practicable' to define the tort of battery in terms of 'physical contact which is not generally acceptable in the ordinary conduct of daily life', the act must be hostile, intentional and consent must be lacking. In that sense, kissing someone without their consent may amount to battery.
3. More often than not damages are awarded as compensation. A declaration may also be sought at times.
4. This is where the defendant has done a wilful act calculated to cause some physical damage to the plaintiff, though he may not have willed the ultimate consequences of his actions. So long as it is reasonably foreseeable that someone might sustain injury, that is enough. It applies to practical jokers and the like.

SUGGESTED ANSWER TO QUESTION ONE

General Comment

A general question on trespass requiring an analysis of the distinction between contractual licences and bare licences. The question also tests the student on aspects of assault, battery, trespass to land, defences and criminal damage.

Key Points

- Distinguish as between the type of licence possessed
- Elements of assault
- Elements of battery
- Trespass to land
- Criminal damage

Suggested Answer

When Arthur agrees with Bertram to use his front room in return for £5, he is given a contractual licence to enter the premises. Arthur's friends, however, are not part of the agreement, and when they walk up Bertram's path to his house, they have merely an implied gratuitous licence.

Both contractual and gratuitous licences are 'bare licences' and should be distinguished from a licence coupled with a grant where the licensee is granted a proprietary interest in the land to which the licence is ancillary to enable the licensee to enjoy the grant. A bare licence can be revoked at will, subject to the payment of compensation in the case of a contractual licence, whereas a licence coupled with a grant cannot be revoked arbitrarily. Therefore, when Bertram says, 'The deal is off. Take this mob away', he is withdrawing Arthur's contractual licence in respect of which Arthur may be able to claim compensation (although it could be an implied term of the agreement that he would be in a condition suitable to entering the premises) and Arthur's friends' gratuitous licence.

When Arthur pushes Bertram aside and enters the house, there is an assault if Bertram apprehended fear of battery, and a battery since Arthur has intentionally applied force to Bertram. The lightest touch of a person is actionable: *Cole* v *Turner* (1704). Both torts are actionable per se, ie without proof of damage although, if no damage is established, Bertram's entitlement is to nominal damages only, ie a few pounds in recognition that the plaintiff's rights have been infringed.

When Arthur sits down in the front room, he also commits a trespass to land because he has entered without lawful authority or the permission of Bertram, the person in possession. Again, this tort is actionable per se.

When Bertram's friend, Bruce, throws Arthur out of the house and injures his back, he is ejecting a trespasser. If a trespasser enters forcibly the occupier may use reasonable force to eject him without a prior request to leave. Third parties may intervene only as agents of the occupier, and the force used may only be such as is necessary to remove the trespasser; it may not be used as chastisement.

Here Bruce is acting as Bertram's agent, but the force used, if excessive, may be both an assault and a battery and, since injuries were sustained, if Arthur is successful he will recover substantial, as opposed to nominal, damages. The question of whether the force employed was reasonable is a question of fact to be decided by the court in all the circumstances.

Throwing bottles through Bertram's window is an act of criminal damage by Arthur's friends. If Bertram was in the room at the time, it is an assault and battery. The acts also amount to a trespass to land, for this tort can be committed by putting things on to the land: *Turner* v *Thorne and Thorne* (1959); *Gregory* v *Piper* (1829). This is actionable at the suit of Bertram, the person in possession.

SUGGESTED ANSWER TO QUESTION TWO

General Comment

A number of complex issues arise on the facts given. In particular, detailed knowledge of the rule on omissions in the tort of negligence, including the duties of public authorities to protect vulnerable citizens and even to prevent suicide attempts! Recent caselaw is available concerning the policy on these matters, and the general issue of the 'duty to rescue' has been the subject of academic research; probably the best is Bowman and Bailey's analysis in the 1984 Public Law Journal, which can be cited here. The problem also involves the law on medical negligence; students need to be familiar with the standard of care and its applicability to inexperienced staff. Probably most difficulty will be caused by the causation issue and the question of whether loss of a chance of recovery can be the subject of a claim in tort. A helpful analysis of the leading authority is provided by Hill in the 1991 Modern Law Review.

Key Points

- *Alan* v *Brian*: ingredients of torts of assault and false imprisonment
- *Alan* v *Stoketon Council*: vicarious liability for Diane – the law on omissions – is there a duty to rescue? – the special rules for public authorities – causation – prevention of suicide attempts – 'novus actus interveniens'
- *Alan* v *Edward*: standard of care from a volunteer
- *Alan* v *Stoketon Hospital*: direct and vicarious liability for hospital staff – standard of care – inexperienced staff – causation – balance of probabilities test – is loss of a chance recoverable in tort?

Suggested Answer

A number of possible claims arise out of the facts given and it will be convenient to consider them separately, although in some claims there will be similar or overlapping issues (such as causation).

Alan *v* Brian

Alan may sue Brian for assault. Assault is any act (including words) which causes another person to apprehend the infliction of immediate unlawful force: *Wilson* v *Pringle* (1987). Brian's threat to punch Alan falls within this definition.

Alan may also sue Brian for false imprisonment, which involves the unlawful imposition of constraint on one's freedom of movement from a particular place: *Wilson* v *Pringle*. Brian's confinement of Alan to his room under duress falls within this definition. In *Roberts* v *Chief Constable of the Cheshire Constabulary* (1999) the Court of Appeal held that the plaintiff was falsely imprisoned when his detention did not take place on time.

Both torts are actionable per se.

Alan *v* Stoketon Council

If Diane was negligent the Council will be vicariously liable as her employer for acts or omissions occurring during the course of her employment.

The first difficulty is in establishing that the Council owed Alan a duty of care. The failure to arrange the promised visit by the social services department is an example of a pure omission and the law of tort does not impose a positive duty to act (here, effectively, a duty to rescue) unless there is a special relationship between the parties in which one exercises control and the other is dependent on the controlling party.

Mere status does not imply control or duty to rescue; there must be also practical ability to control the particular situation, such as in the case of a lifeguard on the lookout for swimmers in distress: example given by Bowman and Bailey (1984) PL 277.

The courts are especially reluctant to impose positive duties on public authorities which may be faced with limited resources and difficult operational decisions, eg it has been held that the police are not under a duty to answer a burglar alarm or 999 emergency call in the absence of a contract or other special relationship with the plaintiff: *Alexandrou v Oxford* (1993); see also *Hill v Chief Constable of West Yorkshire* (1988) and *Knight v Home Office* (1990).

However, in the present problem Diane had promised to investigate Alan's circumstances and such assumption of responsibility might be enough to give rise to the duty of care. If so, it is advised that the Council were in breach of that duty by 'passing the buck' to an unprofessional organisation.

The next issue is one of causation. If Alan had suffered further abuse from Brian as a result of the failure to investigate, there would be little doubt as to the Council's liability. However, Alan's actual damage is the broken leg caused by a suicide attempt at a time when he was depressed. Although the Council were under a duty to exercise supervision, it would be going too far to suggest that they were under a duty to prevent a suicide attempt, because they did not have sufficient degree of control over Alan's hour-by-hour movements. Even if they had had such control (eg, if Alan had been transferred into their custody) a suicide attempt would be unforeseeable in the absence of direct knowledge of A's clinical depression and suicidal tendencies.

For those reasons the present facts are distinguishable from *Kirkham* v *Chief Constable of Greater Manchester Police* (1990) where the police had known of such tendencies in a remand prisoner but had failed to alert the hospital wing which would otherwise have taken protective action. The prisoner's widow was successful in suing the police for negligence (defences of 'ex turpi causa', and 'volenti' were rejected, and the plea of contributory negligence was also regarded as unavailable).

Hence, although the Council were in breach of their duty of general supervision, Alan cannot sue them for the damage to his leg, which was not caused by such breach of duty. The suicide attempt could be described as a 'novus actus interveniens' breaking the chain of causation leading from the breach of duty to the actual damage sustained.

Alan *v* Edward

On the existence of a duty of care it has been said that if a person undertakes to perform a voluntary act he is liable if he performs it improperly: per Willes J in *Skelton* v *L & NW Ry* (1867). Hence the issue here is whether Edward was in breach of the duty he undertook to investigate Alan's circumstances. The standard of care expected from him was that which would be expected from a member of a 'pensioner support group'. Since the objectives of such a group are wide-ranging and involve activities of a political nature rather than medical or quasi-medical the law would not impose on its members the standards expected from a professional social services worker. Since the facts indicate that the signs of Alan's age abuse were not obvious to a non-professional such as Edward, he was not in breach of his duty to Alan. Even if there were a breach of the duty of care, Edward would not be liable because of the causation issue, which would apply in the same way as in Alan's claim against the Council (above).

Alan *v* Stoketon Hospital

If Fiona was negligent Stoketon Hospital would be liable, either directly for failure to provide competent medical staff or vicariously for the individual act of negligence committed by an employee in the course of employment: *Cassidy* v *Ministry of Health* (1951).

On the issue of medical negligence the test will be whether Fiona failed to diagnose a problem which would have been diagnosed by a responsible body of medical practitioners: *Bolam* v *Friern Hospital Management Committee* (1957). On that test Fiona is in breach of her duty of care to Alan and her inexperience will not affect her liability because a uniform standard of care is required from all those who undertook the practice of medicine in the casualty unit of the hospital, be they doctors of 30 years' experience or, like Fiona, a student 'learning on the job': *Wilsher* v *Essex Area Health Authority* (1988). In the law of tort the duty is tailored to the act being performed and not to the actor performing it: *Nettleship* v *Weston* (1971) (driving a car: learner-driver under same standard of care as qualified driver).

However, even though Fiona was in breach of her duty of care, the issue of causation remains: did her breach cause Alan's permanent disability? If it can be shown that it was more probable than not that Alan would have been permanently disabled in any event as a result of the suicide attempt, that will conclude the issue in the hospital's favour, because evidence that D's conduct may have caused or contributed to P's injury will only result in a finding that it did cause that injury if there is no or inadequate evidence of any other causal factor which on the balance of probabilities resulted in the injury: see *Hotson* v *East Berkshire Area Health Authority* (1987) where it was found that there was a 25 per cent chance that the delay in diagnosis contributed to the development of D's condition but a 75 per cent chance that it would have happened anyway as a result of established other causes. It was held that the delay in diagnosis was not a cause of the injury on the civil standard of probabilities and so the hospital escaped liability. It was left open whether a lost chance of recovery which could be proved to result from a breach of duty could be compensated in tort, as it clearly is in contract law (*Chaplin* v *Hicks* (1911)): see, further, article by Hill (1991) MLR 511.

In the present case the facts would seem to suggest that it was Fiona's negligence which prevented Alan's complete recovery and therefore Alan may have at least an arguable case for compensation on the basis of his lost chance of complete recovery.

SUGGESTED ANSWER TO QUESTION THREE

General Comment

This problem concerns trespass to the person and the relevant defences. The possibility of vicarious liability should also be briefly considered.

Key Points

* Definition of trespass
* Elements of the tort of battery
* Defence of consent
* Powers of arrest – s24(4) PACE 1984
* Remoteness and remedies
* Vicarious liability (Keith)

Suggested Answer

As regards the incident between Lucy and Mark and its consequences, as Mark's act is intentional we must consider trespass to the person and in particular the tort of battery which consists of the intentional and direct application of force to another person. In *Letang* v *Cooper* (1965) it was held that where the act which caused the damage was intentional the cause of action lies in trespass to the person, and this was accepted by the Court of Appeal in *Wilson* v *Pringle* (1987). Thus it would appear that there is no overlap between the torts of trespass to the person and negligence.

Clearly Mark's actions constitute an intentional and direct application of force to Lucy. However, Lucy has a problem in establishing liability in that in *Wilson* v *Pringle* it was held that the act of touching the plaintiff had to be a 'hostile touching'. In view of Lucy's agreement with Mark to stage the incident the touching would appear to be non-hostile. A further problem for Lucy is that she has consented to the physical contact by Mark and volenti would provide a complete defence to Mark. Even if Lucy was unaware of the exact incident, providing she was aware in general terms of what was to happen this would be enough to support the defence of volenti: *Chatterton* v *Gerson* (1981).

Noel has committed a battery on Mark as Noel's actions were direct and intentional. Noel would seek to raise the defence of acting in support of the law as he thought that Mark had stolen Lucy's property. By s24(4) Police and Criminal Evidence Act 1984 a person may arrest without warrant any person who is, or who he suspects with reasonable cause to be, in the act of committing an arrestable offence. Section 24(5) also allows any person who has reasonable cause to believe that a person is guilty of an arrestable offence to arrest that person without warrant if that arrestable offence has in fact been committed. Thus Noel has fallen foul of the trap in *Walters* v *W H Smith* (1914) in that he must prove that an offence has actually been committed, and it is no defence to show there were reasonable grounds for believing the person arrested to be guilty. Hence Noel cannot rely on the defence that he was acting in support of the law and is liable to Mark in battery. Noel will be prima facie liable for the damage to Mark's shoulder and as regards Noel's lost teeth, he will be regarded as the author of his own misfortune.

Noel could also attempt to justify his attack on Mark on the grounds that Mark was a trespasser in so far as Mark is a law student and the lecture was a mathematics lecture. However, as Noel is not the occupier of the lecture theatre he will have to show that he has the authority of the occupier to eject a trespasser, which seems unlikely. Noel would also have to show that Mark was requested to leave the premises, had a reasonable opportunity to do so, and failed to leave. As no request was made for Mark to leave Noel cannot raise this defence.

As regards the injury to Mark's shoulder, as Noel intended to inflict harm on Mark no question of remoteness of damage will arise: *Quinn* v *Leatham* (1901); *Doyle* v *Olby (Ironmongers) Ltd* (1969) and Noel will be liable for the damage to Mark's shoulder. As regards Mark's nervous breakdown the question of causation arises, ie what event caused the breakdown. We are told that it was caused by Mark's distress at Lucy's death. Turning to Lucy's death we are told Lucy collapsed after Mark removed her shoulder bag and that Noel attacked Mark after this occurrence. I assume that the 'incident' referred to in the problem which caused the spasm was therefore the removal of the bag by Mark. As Mark intended to harm Lucy then again no question of remoteness of damage would arise and Mark would be liable to Lucy's death, but as we have seen Lucy's consent will provide a total defence to Mark's actions.

Thus we should advise Mark that he can sue Noel in respect of his dislocated shoulder, but that he has no remedy for the nervous breakdown he has suffered. We should advise Noel that he is liable to Mark for Mark's shoulder injury, but has no remedy as regards his lost teeth. We should advise Lucy's father that he has no claim.

We could also consider whether Keith is vicariously liable for the actions of Lucy or Mark. Keith is not the employer of Lucy or Mark but we should consider whether an ad hoc agency has arisen as in *Ormrod* v *Crossville Motor Services* (1953) where Keith is the principal and Lucy and Mark are his agents acting on his behalf. If so, then the University of Slumsville would be liable for Keith's acts as they are his employer, Keith is their employee and Keith was organising the incident in connection with a mock trial and so was acting in the course of his employment. However, this would not affect the liabilities of the parties as described above.

11

Employers' Liability and Breach of Statutory Duty

Introduction

EMPLOYERS' LIABILITY

Employers owe certain duties to employees. These duties may arise at common law or as a result of statutory provisions. The common law duties are classified as four separate duties. They are:

1. To select competent staff: *Hudson* v *Ridge Manufacturing* (1957).
2. To provide proper plant and equipment: *Smith* v *Baker* (1891) and *Coltman* v *Bibby Tankers* (1988). See also the effect of the Employers' Liability (Defective Equipment) Act 1969.
3. To provide a safe place of work: *Latimer* v *AEC Ltd* (1953) and *Gitsham* v *Pearce* (1992). See also *Fairchild* v *Glenhaven Funeral Services Ltd* (2002).
4. To manage a safe system of work: *General Cleaning Contractors* v *Christmas* (1953) and *Walker* v *Northumberland County Council* (1995).

Certain duties are personal (*Paris* v *Stepney London Borough Council* (1951)) and non-delegable: *McDermid* v *Nash Dredging* (1987) and *Morris* v *Breaveglen* (1993). Employers are not liable for employees' economic welfare: *Reid* v *Rush & Tompkins Group plc* (1990). See also *Alderson and Another* v *Beetham Organisation Ltd* (2003).

BREACH OF STATUTORY DUTY

Breach of statutory duty by the defendant gives rise to a cause of action in tort. Since, in every case, there are statutes involved, in determining whether a statute gives rise to civil action for breach of statutory duty the courts seek to determine whether Parliament intended there to be an action: *Cutler* v *Wandsworth Stadium* (1949), *X* v *Bedfordshire County Council* (1995) and *Lonrho* v *Shell* (1982).

Another frequent question asked is: Whether the Act says anything as regards remedies? If the Act is silent then the presumption is that the breach does give rise to a cause of action: *Wentworth* v *Wiltshire County Council* (1993) and *Thornton* v *Kirklees Metropolitan Borough Council* (1979). There are some statutes which confer benefit to certain class: *Groves* v *Lord Wimborne* (1898), *West Wiltshire District Council* v *Garland* (1995) and *Richardson* v *Pitt-Stanley* (1995). The distinction between statutes which create public rights and statutes which merely prohibit what was previously lawful activity must be noted. The plaintiff must prove that the injury or damage suffered was of a kind which the statute intended to prevent: *Gorris* v *Scott* (1874) and

McWilliams v *Sir William Arrol* (1962). Defences include volenti non fit injuria (*ICI* v *Shatwell* (1968)) and contributory negligence: *Westwood* v *Post Office* (1974) and the Law Reform (Contributory Negligence) Act 1945. For a recent illustration of negligence in the exercise of statutory power: see the House of Lords' case of *Barrett* v *Enfield London Borough Council* (1999). Also relevant are *Cross* v *Kirklees Metropolitan Borough Council* (1998) and *Goodes* v *East Sussex County Council* (1999). The case of *Todd* v *Adams* (2001) raises the issue of civil law rights within the context of breach of statutory duty. Other important recent cases include *Barrett* v *Enfield London Borough Council* (1999), *Gower* v *Bromley London Borough Council* (1999), *Jarvis* v *Hampshire County Council* (2000), *Kane* v *New Forest District Council* (2001), *Phelps* v *Hillingdon London Borough Council* (2000), *Bradford-Smart* v *West Sussex County Council* (2000) and *S* v *Gloucestershire County Council* (2000).

Questions

INTERROGRAMS

1. What is the old doctrine of common employment?
2. What is the present position as regard employers' liability?
3. What is the difficulty with breaches of statutory duty?
4. What sort of considerations do the courts follow?

QUESTION ONE

The Food Standards Act 1999 has established the Food Standards Agency. Under s6 it has the functions of '(a) developing policies ... relating to matters connected with food safety or other interests of consumers in relation to food; and (b) providing advice, information or assistance in respect of such matters to any public authority'.

The chief executive of the Agency has asked you to prepare a report for its first meeting explaining the circumstances in which the Agency might be held liable in tort in the discharge of these functions. Write the report.

University of London LLB Examination
(for external students) Law of Tort June 2000 Q1

QUESTION TWO

The (fictitious) Industrial Premises (Alcohol Restriction) Regulations 1999 provide: 'No alcoholic substance shall be taken into or consumed within any premises to which these regulations apply.' The regulations apply to the premises of Goat & Sheep Ltd. Alf, who works at Goat & Sheep, buys four bottles of wine at lunchtime, brings them back to work and places them in a bag on top of the cabinet in the recreation room. During the lunch break, Bill and Clive, who also work at Goat & Sheep, and Des, a lorry driver who has been delivering supplies there, are sitting in the recreation room throwing a frisbee to each other. When Bill throws the frisbee, it strikes the bag containing the wine bottles. They are shattered; broken glass falls on Clive and Des, who are cut, and each of them loses an eye.

Advise Clive and Des.

University of London LLB Examination
(for external students) Law of Tort June 1999 Q6

QUESTION THREE

Richard worked as a gardener with the Peony District Council. He was planting out a bed of rose bushes which the council had purchased from the Floribunda Nurseries. The bushes had been treated with a spray to repel greenfly. It is known that a number of people react to the spray for some days after it has been applied. Richard began to feel breathless, but, before anyone could come to his assistance, he had collapsed. It appears that he is abnormally allergic to the spray. He has suffered permanent brain damage. He is happy and in no physical pain but is unable to look after himself, to work or to pursue his hobby of darts. His mother Stella has given up her job in a supermarket to look after him, but she is quite elderly and it is expected that Richard will eventually have to go into a home.

Advise Richard (a) as to any claims he may have in tort and (b) as to the assessment of damages.

University of London LLB Examination
(for external students) Law of Tort June 1998 Q6

QUESTION FOUR

Statutory regulations impose upon employers and employees in the chemical manufacturing industry an obligation to ensure that prescribed protective equipment (including special gloves) are worn when workers are handling chemicals. The regulations apply to the premises of Stinks Ltd. George, Hamish and John, who are all employed there, were engaged in loading chemicals on to a lorry and were all wearing the prescribed clothing. George and Hamish were passing casks containing chemicals up to John who was standing on the back of the lorry. A fly went into John's eye suddenly and he removed his glove to wipe it away. George did not notice and passed a cask up to him. John was unable to hold it. Some of the chemical spilled over his hand. He screamed in agony and clung on to Hamish in desperation.

John suffered serious burns to his hand. He will be permanently disfigured and will not be able to obtain manual employment. Hamish has suffered from severe depression since the incident and has not been able to return to work.

University of London LLB Examination
(for external students) Law of Tort June 1994 Q7

Answers

ANSWERS TO INTERROGRAMS

1. The old doctrine of common employment had the effect of reducing the liability of an employer towards his employees. The doctrine dictated that an employer was not liable where injury was negligently inflicted by one employee on another on the ground that the employee had consented to the risks involved in his employment. The doctrine was abolished by s1 of the Law Reform (Personal Injuries) Act 1948.
2. Currently, employers are liable both at common law and statute. They owe a common duty of care to employees under the negligence doctrine. They may also be vicariously liable.
3. The difficulty lies where statutes overlap. If this happens, it can give rise to difficulties in discerning which statute actually imposes liability. Even if that is not a problem, sometimes a statute may not prescribe any remedy whatsoever. Sometimes statutes are clearly worded, so as to impose liability, but in the majority of cases the statutes are either ambiguous or completely silent as to whether the breach gives rise to a cause of action in tort.
4. In deciding whether the breach of statutory duty confers upon the plaintiff a cause of action in tort, the general approach which the courts adopt is one of construction. That is, does the Act, on its true construction, confer upon the plaintiff a right to an action in respect of the breach of the statute? The normal rules as regards statutory interpretation would be applicable in this context.

SUGGESTED ANSWER TO QUESTION ONE

General Comment

This looks like a straightforward question on negligent or faulty advice on food safety, but as there is a statute involved, namely the Food Standards Act 1999, it requires consideration of the tort of breach of statutory duty.

Key Points

- Nature of a breach of statutory duty
- Does it impose liability in tort?
- Relevant principles in establishing liability
- Examples of cases where liability has been imposed
- Remedies

Suggested Answer

It would appear from the facts of the question that the Food Standards Agency is a creature of statute and hence is to be treated as a public body for all intents and purposes. Under common law, a public body owes a duty of care in respect of all its functions and obligations that affect others. Therefore, to establish negligence at common law on the basis of *Donoghue v Stevenson* (1932) would be an easy task. But one is not dealing with the ordinary principles of common law. Rather, there is a statute, namely the Food Standards Act (FSA) 1999, which is the subject matter of the question. The FSA 1999 sets out the duties, functions and obligations of the Food Standards Agency. Thus, any liability on its part (the Agency's) must be determined on the basis of its breach of statutory duty.

The Food Standards Agency, it would seem, has essentially two basic statutory functions. One is to develop policies related to matters connected with food safety and other interests of consumers in relation to food, and the other involves the provision of advice, information and assistance in respect of such matters to any public authority.

The Agency therefore not only deals with consumers who are members of the public, but it also deals with public authorities and other corporations, such as manufacturers and producers. In discharging its statutory functions, the Agency has to balance both these interests so as to avoid any possible conflict. On the one hand, if it is not sufficiently interventionist, public health might be comprised, resulting in the outbreak of serious diseases. On the other, if it is too interventionist, it may damage the commercial interest of food producers, or even add to production costs unnecessarily. For example, in *Welton* v *North Cornwall District Council* (1997) the local authority was held liable where an environmental health officer negligently required the owner of food premises to undertake unnecessary works to secure compliance with the Food Standards Act 1990. It is also arguable that where a public body takes on the role of providing a quasi-professional service, which corresponds to a service that might well be provided by the private sector (such as the provision of information, advice and assistance, for example), the authority can be liable for negligence in the provision of that service. In *E (A Minor)* v *Dorset County Council* (1995), the House of Lords held that a local authority could be both directly liable in negligence and vicariously liable for the negligence of an educational psychologist in assessing a child's special educational needs.

The crucial point is not the breach of the statutory duty itself, but whether the breach gives rise to a cause of action in tort. The statute may expressly exclude a civil right, for example, as in the Post Office Act 1969 and the Guard Dogs Act 1975, or the statute may provide a cause of action where none previously existed, for instance as in the Race Relations Act 1976. However, it is quite common for the statute to be silent as to whether or not it gives rise to an action in tort. Therefore, it is for the courts to determine the intentions of Parliament by construing the words or provisions of the statute in question. There are two presumptions in this context. First, if the Act in question imposes a duty but provides no remedy for the breach, then the presumption is that the breach would give rise to an action in tort, as confirmed by the court in *Thornton* v *Kirklees Metropolitan Borough Council* (1979). The second presumption is that if the Act provides a remedy (civil or criminal), then it is harder or more onerous to show that the breach gives rise to a cause of action in tort. Recently, in *Todd* v *Adams* (2001), the Queen's Bench Division held that an action could not succeed in tort as the Act in question had already provided a remedy itself.

However, every case has to be decided on its own facts and merits, and the court has on previous occasions held that, notwithstanding a remedy within the statute, a civil action in tort was nonetheless possible: *Groves* v *Lord Wimborne* (1898).

As such, the Food Standards Agency, in exercising its statutory functions, ought to be vigilant and diligent so as not to fall below the standards of legitimate expectation. If a breach of duty of care at common law is actionable, then the breach of a statutory duty would impose a higher duty, perhaps even strict liability. For example, if the Agency develops a policy (negligently) which results in an outbreak of a serious disease amongst some consumers, then an action in tort for compensation would undoubtedly result. The plaintiff(s) would have to establish three things. First, the act which caused the damage is regulated by statute; second, the plaintiff(s) belong to the class of people which the Act intended to protect; and, third, the damage suffered is of the kind that the Act intended to prevent. These principles were highlighted and confirmed in the case of *Gorris v Scott* (1874). As mentioned earlier, there is not a consistent or uniform principle which has been enunciated to determine the remedy in tort for a breach of statutory duty. The courts have said 'yes' in some cases and 'no' in others. Two principles, however, lie at the heart of this area. One is parliamentary intention, and the second is judicial construction, or the interpretation of that intention.

The other related and relevant issue is whether there is any breach under the European Convention on Human Rights committed by these public bodies if they are found to be in breach of their statutory duty. The Human Rights Act 1998 now provides a remedy in respect of breaches of duty by a public body. In *Osman v United Kingdom* (1998), the European Court of Human Rights strongly suggested that to impose 'no duty of care in tort' might be equivalent to the grant of an immunity to public bodies and local authorities. *Osman* was, of course, a controversial decision which attracted both judicial and academic criticism. The question in the end is for the courts to decide on the basis of what is just, fair and reasonable under the circumstances.

SUGGESTED ANSWER TO QUESTION TWO

General Comment

This is a question which required candidates to sift through a number of possible claims in tort arising from the facts, and to concentrate on those which showed the most promise. Note that the balance of the discussion should have related to breach of statutory duty rather than common law negligence.

Key Points

- Breach of statutory duty
- Discuss whether the regulations might allow for the bringing of private civil actions in tort, either expressly or by presumption
- Examine the elements of a breach of statutory duty
- Identity of the defendant?
- Was a duty owed to the claimants?
- Were the injuries suffered of a type contemplated by the regulations?
- Did any breach of duty cause the damage complained of?
- Were Goat & Sheep Ltd vicariously liability for breach of statutory duty (if duty imposed only upon employees)?

- Liability in negligence
- Did Bill owe Clive and Des a duty of care, and if so, was it broken?
- Were Clive and Des contributory negligent?
- Was Alf negligent in leaving the bottles on top of the cabinet?
- Were Goat & Sheep Ltd vicariously liable for any negligence on the part of Alf or Bill?
- Employer's liability of Goat & Sheep Ltd?

Suggested Answer

Breach of statutory duty

The first issue to be decided in this question is whether a possible breach of the duty contained in the Industrial Premises (Alcohol Restriction) Regulations 1999 can give rise to private civil actions for breach of statutory duty in respect of the injuries suffered by Clive and Des. Such an action might lie against Goat & Sheep Ltd or Alf, depending upon whether the duty is imposed upon employers or employees. If a duty falls upon employees, there is the further question of whether Goat & Sheep Ltd can be vicariously liable for the breach of statutory duty of one of its employees.

Does an action for breach of statutory duty lie at all?

One possibility is that the regulations may expressly state whether or not civil liability will arise from their breach. If civil claims are possible, then it will be necessary to apply the elements of the tort. If not, then no action for breach of statutory duty will be possible.

If the regulations make no mention of the possibility of civil actions, then the court will have to determine whether, on their true construction, they were intended to confer a right of action in tort upon the claimant for their breach. The general rule was laid down by the House of Lords in *Lonrho Ltd* v *Shell Petroleum Co Ltd (No 2)* (1982). Where the legislation creates an obligation and a specified means for enforcing performance of that obligation, for example by criminal penalty, there is an initial presumption that performance cannot be enforced in any other way. However, as an exception to this general rule, the courts will presume a right of action for breach of statutory duty where an obligation has been imposed for the benefit of a class of people, such as employees. Such a right may be held to exist even if the legislation does provide for criminal penalties in the event of breach: *Groves* v *Lord Wimborne* (1898).

The Industrial Premises (Alcohol Restriction) Regulations 1999 are clearly designed to provide safety in employment and thus intended to benefit employees as a class of people. Even if the regulations do not expressly confer a right to bring a civil claim for their breach, there will certainly be a presumption to this effect.

Elements of breach of statutory duty: identity of the defendant

It is unclear from the brief quote from the regulations as to whether the duty is imposed upon employers (to prevent employees from bringing alcohol on to industrial premises and consuming it there) or upon employees, or both. This of course is a matter of interpretation. If the duty falls wholly upon employees, then an action for breach of statutory duty lies against Alf only. If, on the other hand, the duty falls wholly or partly upon employers, then Goat & Sheep Ltd are potentially liable.

Duty must be owed to the claimant

Assuming that the duty does fall upon employers, it seems likely that the regulations may only have been passed to benefit employees. Des is not an employee of Goat & Sheep Ltd. As such, only Clive would be able to claim in respect of a breach of the regulations. A similar result was arrived at by the court in *Hartley* v *Mayoh & Co* (1954) in which a fireman's widow was unable to claim for breach of statutory duty against the defendant, in whose factory her husband had been killed, because the regulations concerned only conferred a duty upon 'persons employed'.

Injury must be of a kind which the legislation is intended to preven: Gorris v Scott (1874)

A further problem arises in respect of the manner in which Clive and Des' injuries occurred. It seems likely that the regulations were intended to prevent injuries sustained in the workplace caused by employees under the influence of alcohol, and not by accidents caused by the smashing of unattended bottles in incidents such as the one described. Clearly, the injuries suffered by Clive and Des would have been identical whether or not the bottles left on top of the cabinet contained alcohol. It is submitted that Clive and Des' injuries may therefore be of a type which these regulations were not intended to prevent. Such was the case in *Nicholls* v *Austin (F) (Leyton) Ltd* (1946) in which a workman was unable to claim for breach of statutory duty under the Factories Act 1961 for injuries sustained when a component flew out of a machine whilst in use. The requirement that the machinery should be securely fenced was intended to prevent the workers from making contact with the machine and not vice versa.

However, Winfield and Jolowicz (*Tort* (15th edn, 1998) at p261) point out that the modern approach is not to apply this requirement too strictly, and that if the damage suffered by the claimant was of the kind that the regulations were designed to prevent, then it does not matter that the precise method by which the injuries occurred was not contemplated by the legislation. Such an approach would be consistent with the decision of the House of Lords in *Hughes* v *Lord Advocate* (1963).

A breach of the legislation has caused the damage complained of

The duty is framed in absolute terms: 'no alcoholic substance shall be taken into' and therefore Alf's action in leaving the bag containing the wine in the recreation room appears to give rise to a breach of duty. The breach has certainly caused Clive and Des' injuries in fact, and it has already been pointed out above that according to Hughes, the injuries are unlikely to be regarded as too remote to recover for. However, it might be argued that the conduct of the claimants, Clive and Des, in playing frisbee in the recreation room was so unreasonable as to amount to a novus actus interveniens, breaking the chain of causation: *McKew* v *Holland & Hannen & Cubitts (Scotland) Ltd* (1969). It is more likely, however, that Clive and Des will be regarded as partly at fault for their loss, and that any damages awarded will be reduced according to an apportionment of blame under the Law Reform (Contributory Negligence) Act 1945.

Vicarious liability

If the regulations are construed as imposing duties upon employees, then the question arises as to whether Goat & Sheep Ltd could be held vicariously liable for Alf's breach of statutory duty. It has never been positively decided whether vicarious liability could exist in these circumstances, and the better approach may be for the courts to decide that a duty is imposed upon both employer and employee by the regulations. A major problem in the establishment of vicarious liability in this case is whether Alf can really be said to have been acting in the course of his employment when he brought alcohol onto Goat & Sheep Ltd's premises for his own purposes.

Negligence

Liability of Bill

It must first be considered whether Bill owes a duty of care to Clive and Des. The three part test to determine whether such a duty exists was most recently stated in *Caparo Industries Ltd plc v Dickman* (1990). The first requirement is that the injuries suffered by the claimant must have been reasonably foreseeable, secondly that a close relationship of proximity existed between Bill and the claimants, and finally that it should be fair, just and reasonable in all the circumstances for the courts to impose a duty. It is arguable that a reasonable person would have foreseen some form of injury resulting from the throwing of a frisbee in an enclosed space, especially with glass or loose objects in the vicinity (although the wine bottles were concealed in a bag). The courts will readily hold that a relationship of proximity is present where physical injury has been sustained by the claimant, and it is relevant that a pre-existing relationship exists between the parties here. The most difficult element to satisfy in these circumstances is likely to be the fair, just and reasonable element of the duty test, although it is submitted that there are no specific policy considerations why Clive and Des should be denied a claim.

As to whether Bill's conduct fell below the standards to be expected of the reasonable person, it is submitted that the decision to participate indoors in an outdoor activity is in itself likely to give rise to a breach of duty to take reasonable care. It cannot be said that the risk of harm being inflicted is so unlikely that that no breach has taken place: *Bolton v Stone* (1951).

No issues of causation appear to arise here. However, it is almost certainly the case that Clive and Des' voluntary involvement in the game will be regarded as a partial cause of the injuries they have suffered, and that any damages awarded will be reduced 'to such extent as the court thinks just and equitable having regard to the claimant's share in the responsibility for the damage': s1(1) Law Reform (Contributory Negligence) Act 1945. It will be for Bill to prove that Clive and Des' injuries resulted from a risk which their own fault or negligence exposed them to, and that this negligence contributed towards their injuries. It is submitted that the observations above relating to the existence of Bill's own breach of duty apply equally to Clive and Des, and that a court would probably regard them as being equally responsible for the injuries they suffered.

Once again, it is highly unlikely that Bill could be regarded as acting in the course of his employment at the time of this accident, and so Goat & Sheep Ltd are unlikely to be held vicariously liable for his negligence.

Liability of Alf

It is just possible that Alf might have been negligent in leaving the bottles on top of the cabinet, especially with seating in the vicinity. However, liability is much less likely to arise in Alf's case for the following reasons.

1. A duty of care is less likely to exist in that injuries to those in the recreation room are less foreseeable in the circumstances – unless Alf is aware that people play frisbee there, or the bottles are left in such a position that they might easily be knocked off the cabinet causing injury. It is also less likely that a court would think it fair, just and reasonable to impose a duty.
2. Novus actus interveniens arising from the independent and unreasonable actions of the claimants in playing frisbee indoors is more likely to be relevant here, breaking the chain of causation and relieving Alf of liability for Clive and Des' injuries.
3. Once again, Goat & Sheep Ltd are unlikely to be held vicariously liable for any negligence on the part of Alf. The leaving of the bottles of wine in the recreation room could hardly be described as taking place in the course of Alf's employment.

Employers' liability of Goat & Sheep Ltd

Whilst employers owe certain non-delegable duties to their staff, such as the duty to provide competent fellow employees and a safe system of working, it is submitted that it is highly unlikely that Goat & Sheep Ltd could be in breach of any of these requirements as they are, no doubt, unaware of their employees activities in the recreation room.

SUGGESTED ANSWER TO QUESTION THREE

General Comment

It was important that candidates noted the ambiguity in the facts of this question. It was not made clear whether it was the council or the nursery who were responsible for the spraying of the rosebushes, and the precise nature of liability would have varied accordingly. Candidates could have chosen to deal with employers' liability first, although it might have been more logical initially to consider Floribunda's liability for the possible supply of a defective product. This is because an employer's vicarious liability for the provision of defective equipment depends upon the fault of the third party who supplied it.

Key Points

a) • Product liability
   • Examine Floribunda's potential liability under the Consumer Protection Act 1987
   • Is a rosebush a 'product' within the meaning of the Act?
   • Discuss the possibility of liability at common law under the narrow rule in *Donoghue* v *Stevenson*
   • Employers' liability
   • Is Peony vicariously liable for providing Richard with defective equipment under the Employers' Liability (Defective Equipment) Act 1969?
   • Is a rosebush 'equipment' within the meaning of the Act?
   • If Peony was responsible for the spraying of the rosebush, are they in breach of their non-delegable duty to provide a safe system of working?

b) • The assessment of damages
  • Identify the aim of damages in tort and explain the heads of loss relevant to Richard's circumstances, under which damages will be awarded
  • Make particular reference to future loss of earnings, the provision of care by a relative and loss of amenity

Suggested Answer

a) *Claims in tort: liability for defective products – Floribunda Nurseries*

If, as seems likely, Florinbunda were themselves responsible for growing the rose bushes and for spraying them with the greenfly repellent, the question arises as to Floribunda's liability as producers of a defective product. Section 2(1) Consumer Protection Act 1987 provides that 'where any damage is caused wholly or partly by a defect in a product, every person to whom subsection (2) … applies shall be liable for the damage.' Section 2(2) lists a number of potential defendants, including the producer of the product, further defined in s1(2)(c) as including a person who carried out (for example in relation to agricultural products) an industrial or other process.

An immediate problem for Richard here is that agricultural products, defined in s1(2) as including 'any produce of the soil' are excluded from the provisions of the Act unless they have undergone an 'industrial process' before supply. The definition is aimed at the processing of raw foodstuffs so that, for example, the processing of meet into beef burgers would be caught by the provisions of the Act. It is submitted that the mere spraying of agricultural produce would not be regarded as an industrial process, and so the rosebushes are not 'products' for the purposes of the Act. If the spraying of crops were to be regarded as an industrial process, the exemption of agricultural produce from the provisions of the Act would be meaningless and ineffective.

Common law

The so-called narrow rule laid down by Lord Atkin in *Donoghue v Stevenson* (1932) imposes a duty on manufacturers of products to the ultimate consumer in certain circumstances:

> '… a manufacturer of products, which he sells in such a form as to show that he intends them to reach the ultimate consumer in the form in which they left him, with no reasonable possibility of intermediate examination, and with the knowledge that the absence of reasonable care in the preparation or putting up of the products will result in an injury to the consumer's life or property, owes a duty to the consumer to take that reasonable care.'

The duty as originally defined has been extended in many respects, and could apply to Richard's circumstances for the following reasons.

1. Whilst the grower of plants might not be regarded as a 'manufacturer' in the traditional sense, the duty has been extended to cover a range of persons who create dangers in relation to products, such as repairers, erectors and builders. It is submitted that growers would also fall within the scope of the duty.

2. The duty, whilst originally relating to food and drink, has been held to apply to a range of products, eg tombstones and cars, so rosebushes are presumably covered.

3. The duty extends to the ultimate user of the product as well as those within close proximity of it. It is submitted that Richard, as a gardener who plants the product, is within sufficiently close proximity to come within the scope of the duty.

4. The possibility of an 'intermediate examination' of the rosebushes by Richard is unlikely to exonerate the nursery. The presence of a chemical residue on a plant could not be discovered by a reasonable examination, unless a specific warning had been provided: *Andrews v Hopkinson* (1957).

5. It will be for Richard to prove that the nursery failed to take reasonable care by spraying the rosebushes with a dangerous insect repellent. This should not cause any great difficulty. If it can be shown that the Council were not responsible for the spraying, then on the balance of probabilities, it must have been Floribunda who did so. In view of the known risks associated with this particular insect repellent, a finding of breach of duty appears likely.

6. Richard's abnormal sensitivity to the spray does not render the serious physical injuries he sustained too remote from any negligence on the part of Floribunda. A tortfeasor takes his victim as he finds him. So long as physical injury was foreseeable (there were known risks of adverse reactions to this chemical spray lasting some days after application) the claimant can recover damages, even if the extent of those injuries could not have been foreseen: *Smith v Leech, Brain & Co* (1962).

It would appear that Richard's claim in respect of a defective product would therefore lie in common law negligence, rather than under the Consumer Protection Act 1987, due to the exclusion of agricultural products from the scope of the latter.

Liability of Peony District Council as employers

Peony District Council's liability to Richard as his employer will depend upon who was responsible for the application of the insect repellent. If the nursery were responsible for the spraying, then Peony may be vicariously liable for the supply of defective 'equipment' attributable to the fault of a third party under s1(1) Employers' Liability (Defective Equipment) Act 1969. If the spray was applied by the Council, then it would be more appropriate to consider whether Peony were in breach of their non-delegable common law duty to provide a safe system of work.

Employers' Liability (Defective Equipment) Act 1969

Section 1(1) states that:

> 'Where ...
> (a) an employee suffers personal injury in the course of his employment in consequence of a defect in equipment provided by his employer for the purposes of his employer's business; and
> (b) the defect is attributable wholly or partly to the fault of a third party (whether identified or not),
> the injury shall be deemed to be also attributable to negligence on the part of the employer ...'

In other words, the Council will be vicariously liable for defective equipment supplied to Richard for the purposes of his job, if the defect arose through the fault of Floribunda Nurseries.

The main issue here is whether a rosebush could be said to be 'equipment' within the meaning of the Act. Section 1(3) defines 'equipment' as 'any plant and machinery, vehicle, aircraft and clothing.' In fact, the courts have adopted a wide, purposive approach to the interpretation of this section. For example, in *Knowles* v *Liverpool City Council* (1993) the House of Lords held that a flagstone, which broke whilst being handled by an employee, causing personal injury, should be regarded as equipment even though it was, in fact, 'material upon which the employee used the equipment.' Thus it is clearly arguable that a rosebush, which will have been planted with the use of gardening tools, should be regarded as 'equipment' within the meaning of the Act. If Richard can show that the spray residue caused his injury and that there must, on the balance of probabilities, have been negligence on the part of Floribunda Nurseries (see above), then the Council as well as Floribunda will be liable to him, even though the Council were not to blame.

Safe system of work
If Peony District Council was responsible for the application of the greenfly repellent, then there is likely to have been a breach of their duty as employers to take reasonable care in devising and operating a safe system of work. Such a breach of duty would arise from the use of a known allergen to spray the bushes rather than some safer alternative, and the failure to provide adequate warnings, instructions and personal protective equipment to those employees handling the plants which have been sprayed with the substance. As explained above, Richard's abnormal sensitivity to the spray residue will not render the serious physical injuries he sustained too remote from any negligence on the part of his employer.

b) *The assessment of damages*
Any award of damages will be payable as a lump sum, unless the parties were to agree to a structured settlement. The aim of such an award will be to restore Richard, in so far as money will allow, to the position he was in before the tort(s) took place. An award of damages is usually considered in two parts: 'special damages' covering precisely calculable losses, normally arising pre-trial, and 'general damages', which are not capable of precise mathematical calculation and normally arise post-trial. It is also customary to classify losses sustained as being either pecuniary or non-pecuniary in nature.

Pecuniary losses: loss of earnings
This will include any loss of Richard's earnings both before and after trial. The large part of the award will be for loss of salary post-trial, as Richard is now unemployable on a long-term basis. Any award will include prospective earnings during any 'lost years' due to a reduced life expectancy and loss of pension rights associated with a future loss of salary.

The court will award Richard a lump sum which, when invested, will be sufficient to produce an income equal to the loss of his future salary. The calculation is approached in two stages. The court will first assess Richard's net annual loss, by taking his gross earnings at the date of the accident, but also making an allowance for the possibility of an increase in pay or for promotion. Once this sum has been calculated, a deduction will be made for the income tax and social security contributions he would have paid on his earnings.

The court will then select a multiplier based upon the likely duration of the disability. However, this will not be the same as the number of years Richard would have worked before retirement, because the courts apply a reduction to take account of the possibility that future events might have cut his working life short, eg early death or unemployment. A reduction is also applied to take account of the fact that a lump sum payment will produce an investment income of its own.

Medical expenses reasonably incurred

This includes the cost of nursing care and travel expenses to and from hospital. The cost of nursing care provided by Stella can be recovered by Richard himself: *Hunt* v *Severs* (1994). In *Housecroft* v *Burnett* (1986) it was decided that where a relative gives up work to look after the claimant, the court will award reasonable recompense to the carer, but the ceiling on such an award is the commercial rate for providing such care. It is unlikely that Stella would be paid more than her existing salary whilst she is still able to look after Richard, if her current salary is less than the commercial rate of remuneration for professional nursing care. However, a full commercial rate ought to be recoverable for the years during which Richard will have to spend in a home. The damages awarded in respect of the carer will be held on trust for Stella by Richard: *Cunningham* v *Harrison* (1973). Further deductions will be made to reflect any social security benefits that Richard has received as a result of his injuries since the accident.

Non-pecuniary losses

Richard's non-pecuniary losses include his loss of amenity, ie the loss of capacity to engage in activities which he enjoyed before trial (playing darts) and compensation for his actual injuries. The amounts awarded under these heads are usually assessed by reference to past cases. An award would usually be made for any pain and suffering endured by the claimant; however, Richard appears to be perfectly happy and in no pain, and so damages are unlikely to be awarded under this head.

Finally, Richard will receive interest on the lump sum payment reflecting the lapse in time between the accident and the trial.

SUGGESTED ANSWER TO QUESTION FOUR

General Comment

This question is specifically addressed as a possible breach of statutory duty, although it could be argued that the employer owed a like duty in the tort of negligence. The importance of the dual heads of liability is that the statutory duty could be pitched at a higher level than the duty of care in negligence. The question does not indicate the level of duty imposed by the regulations, but suggests that the duty is one of 'strict liability'.

Similarly, the question does not actually specify what is required of the student, and this answer is based on the presumption that John and Hamish require advice on liability and assessment of damages.

Key Points

- The concept of employers' liability
- Statutory duty and strict liability
- Distinction between strict liability and liability for negligent acts or omissions
- Method of assessment of damages in personal injuries cases

Suggested Answer

If John and Hamish are to rely on the tort of negligence as the basis of their claim against their employer, they face an onerous task.

An employer owes certain duties to his employees. Those duties are derived from both common law and statutory sources. For many years an employer was not liable for injury negligently inflicted by another employee on the ground that the employee had consented to the risks involved in his employment: *Bartonshill Coal Co* v *Reid* (1858). This doctrine was finally abolished by s1 of the Law Reform (Personal Injuries) Act 1948.

The employer may now be vicariously liable for the negligence of his employee committed in the course of his employment or for breach of his own non-delegable duty.

In the question set, any negligence appears to be limited to (a) John removing his glove; (b) George failing to notice and passing him a cask; and (c) John clinging on to Hamish in desperation. The question does not specifically ask, but it must be presumed that John wishes to claim damages for his burns injury, and Hamish for his depression and loss of earnings.

I will first address John's potential claim. As against his employer, a claim would lie for the negligence, if any, of George, for which the employer would be vicariously liable, and for the primary negligence of the employer for failing to provide a safe system of work: see *General Cleaning Contractors* v *Christmas* (1953).

John will be in great difficulty if he is to claim negligence in respect of either of these heads of allegedly negligent acts. There is nothing to suggest that George was negligent in passing the cask up in circumstances where he and Hamish were engaged in an ongoing process of 'passing casks' to John. That is a matter open to argument on the facts.

Similarly, the employer appears to have discharged his duty to provide a safe system of work by providing gloves.

However, John may have a claim for breach of statutory duty, namely the regulations cited in the question. The duty imposed was an 'obligation to ensure that prescribed protective clothing (including special gloves) are worn when workers are handling chemicals'. If that duty is strict, it matters not that the act of a fly causing John to suddenly remove his glove to wipe his eye was in no way the fault of the employer.

It will be left to the court to determine whether these regulations afford a remedy to an individual employee who suffers injury as a result of breach: *Cutler* v *Wandsworth*

Stadium Ltd (1949). The court will look to see if the regulations specifically provide for a remedy, and if not, will determine whether the regulations are directed at protecting a class of persons as opposed to society as a whole.

In this case, the effect of the regulation is to provide protection to employees in John's position, and it is highly likely that the court would find that he is entitled to a personal remedy, namely compensation, if the employer breached the duty: *John Summers & Sons Ltd v Frost* (1955).

Volenti is not a defence to breach of an employer's statutory duty. However, the defence that the employer did all that was reasonably practicable is often provided in regulations: see *Larner v British Steel plc* (1993).

There is no information in the question as to whether such a defence is provided in the regulations in issue. If not, it will be assumed that the liability is strict. In view of the unexpected way in which John came to remove his gloves, nothing short of strict liability will assist him. I do not think he has a claim in negligence, nor for breach of statutory duty if the employer's liability is limited to doing what is reasonably practicable.

It should be noted that a person who is the subject of a statutory duty cannot generally discharge that duty by entrusting it to someone else.

Presuming that the duty is strict, it is clear that the breach of duty (ie not ensuring that the gloves were worn for that short period during which John suffered the injury) caused John's injury, and he would therefore be able to claim damages.

The issue of contributory negligence arises, and would go to reduce the employer's liability in a negligence claim, and arguably a breach of statutory duty claim. Although the courts are very reluctant to find contributory negligence in employer/employee cases, as the regulations are designed to protect the employees (see *Caswell v Powell Duffryn Associated Collieries Ltd* (1940)), they will do so if the employee has himself been very foolish or fails himself to comply with the regulations, as in *Bux v Slough Metals Ltd* (1974) where an employee removed protective goggles which were misted up.

John's reason for removing his gloves is apparently more legitimate, and verging as it does on an 'emergency' or instinctive situation (see eg *Jones v Boyce* (1816)), it is unlikely that there would be any finding of contributory negligence.

Hamish's claim is in some respects similar to John's, in that he will only have a claim if the duty is a strict one. He has an added difficulty in that he has to prove that the breach of statutory duty regarding John wearing gloves caused his loss, and that the loss suffered is a recoverable loss.

In terms of causation, the employer will perhaps argue that John's act of grabbing Hamish was a 'novus actus', breaking the chain of causation instituted by the initial breach. The court may well take the view that injury by chemicals, and specifically, by shock brought about by seeing the effects of a chemicals-related injury, was foreseeable, so not too remote. Lord Reid in *Hughes v Lord Advocate* (1963) said:

> '... a defendant is liable, although the damage may be a good deal greater in extent that was foreseeable. He can only escape liability if the damage can be regarded as differing in kind from what was foreseeable.'

Finally, for Hamish to succeed his 'depression' must fall into the recognised category of 'nervous shock', in that it must be more than simply grief and sorrow and must be a pathological nervous injury: see *Brice* v *Brown* (1984).

If the extent of his depression is of a clinical nature, he will be able to recover if he falls into the category of persons whose relationship to the primary injured person is sufficiently close to justify the imposition of liability on the tortfeasor. The test of proximity has been recognised in several cases, and it is submitted that a worker whose co-employee grabs hold of him whilst the two are engaged in a joint task is sufficiently proximate for his nervous shock to be foreseeable.

In conclusion, the cases of John and Hamish hinge on the degree of liability attaching to the regulations. If strict, their claims have a good chance of success. If there is a statutory defence within the particular regulations of 'reasonable practicability', I feel that their respective claims will fail.

12

Product Liability

Introduction

With regard to consumers, remedies at common law in relation to loss, harm or damage caused by defective products are available both in contract and in tort. *Donoghue* v *Stevenson* (1932) laid the foundations in which liability for defective products was subsequently developed. The Consumer Protection Act (CPA) 1987 was enacted as a compliant to the European 'Products Liability' Directive. See also the recent General Product Safety Regulations 1994. Originally, only manufacturers were liable, but now the rule extends to any supplier who is under a duty to inspect the goods. The CPA 1987 applies to all products: *Grant* v *Australian Knitting Mills* (1936). An express warning of the danger will discharge the manufacturer's duty: *Kubach* v *Hollands* (1937). The nature of the loss recoverable must relate to the consumer's life or other property: *Aswan Engineering* v *Lupdine* (1987). Further, it must relate to the nature of the defendant's obligation: *Mason* v *Williams and Williams* (1955) and *Evans* v *Triplex Safety Glass* (1936).

Where the damage is purely economic, no claim lies tort. The claim is one of contract: *Daniels* v *White and Sons* (1938). The main provisions of the CPA 1987 are:

- Section 2 provides the general principle governing liability for defective products.
- Section 3 outlines the safety element in products.
- Section 4 provides the defences. See, in this context, the recent case of *EC Commission* v *United Kingdom* (1997) in the ECJ where the 'development risks' defence was debated as being available under the CPA 1987.
- Section 5 damage covered includes death, personal injury and property damage other than the defective product itself.

The Act does not apply to damage below £275, and liability under s2 cannot be excluded or restricted.

Questions

INTERROGRAMS

1. How did the decision in *Donoghue* v *Stevenson* affect product liability?
2. What were the common law limitations?
3. When does the CPA 1987 describe a product to be defective?
4. What type of losses are recoverable under the Act?

QUESTION ONE

Discuss the following cases:

a) A supermarket chain sells many lines under its own brand name 'Salmonella'. Peggy buys a packet, labelled 'Salmonella sliced apples. Produce of England. Vacuum packed. Suitable for home freezing. Freeze immediately on purchase. Eat within three months.' Peggy puts them in her home freezer as soon as she gets home two hours after she has purchased them. She uses them two months later. She and her daughter Queenie suffer severe food poisoning which is traced to the apple slices.

b) Ruth buys in England some marker pens manufactured by Ecoli GmbH in Germany. Her teenage son Simon uses the red and white pens to paint a St George's Cross on his face before he joins the spectators at an international soccer match. The red pen contains a pigment which causes a severe rash and itching on Simon's face, which persists for several months.

University of London LLB Examination
(for external students) Law of Tort June 1997 Q5

QUESTION TWO

Geoffrey, a student, took a holiday job last summer as a gardener at Barsetshire Hall, a stately home owned by Lord Trollope. He was working one day using a rake which had been manufactured by Dudtools plc and recently purchased by Lord Trollope from a reputable supplier. When he had finished work, he discovered that the door of the toolshed had stuck. As he was in a hurry, he tried to pull it open using the prongs of the rake. After a few moments the shaft of the rake split and a large splinter pierced the palm of his hand. Because of a rare blood condition (of which he had until then been unaware), he suffered very severe poisoning and lost a year before he could return to his university studies.

Advise Geoffrey as to any causes of action in tort (a) against Dudtools plc and (b) against Lord Trollope.

How (if at all) would it affect your answer if Geoffrey had known of the blood condition and had told Lord Trollope at the time he took the job?

University of London LLB Examination
(for external students) Law of Tort June 1996 Q4

QUESTION THREE

Fanny and Gordon were married last year. They received a very expensive record player and stereo system manufactured by Botchit Ltd as a wedding present from Henry, a business associate of Fanny's father. For the first few weeks the equipment caused much trouble. There were unexplained surges of power and the equipment would cut out. The service engineer reported (correctly) that the motor was faulty and could not be repaired. They had to buy a new motor unit at considerable expense.

Two months later smoke started to pour from the turntable. It seems that the original surges of power had damaged the turntable drive, which had now started to overheat when in use. Fanny and Gordon had to buy a new turntable and had to buy new curtains and redecorate the room as the smoke had destroyed the original curtains and decorations.

Fanny and Gordon do not know where Harry bought the equipment and do not want to tell him that his present has caused such trouble. Advise them whether they have a remedy against Botchit Ltd.

University of London LLB Examination
(for external students) Law of Tort June 1993 Q2

QUESTION FOUR

'The provisions of Part I of the Consumer Protection Act 1987 are to be welcomed, but there is scope for the role of fault in the law of tort to be further diminished.'
   Discuss.

University of London LLB Examination
(for external students) Law of Tort June 1988 Q5

Answers

ANSWERS TO INTERROGRAMS

1. Prior to *Donoghue,* consumers had no right of action against manufacturers because of the privity element of the law of contract. Since the House of Lords' decision in *Donoghue v Stevenson* the shackles of privity are now broken so as to impose liability on manufacturers of defective of dangerous goods.
2. The doctrine of privity of contract limited the contractual remedies in two respects. First, liability could only arise in favour of the person who had bargained for the goods and, second, it would be the seller of the goods and not the manufacturer who would be held liable to the consumer. Hence, there was no way in which affected third parties could seek redress.
3. The CPA 1987 does not hold a producer liable for all the harm caused by his products. He may only be liable if his product is defective, for which a test is prescribed by s3 which states that a product is defective if the safety of the product is not such as persons generally are entitled to expect.
4. As a general rule personal injury and/or property damage suffered as a result of a defective product is recoverable. There are some restrictions governing recoverability in property damage. There are three instances where compensation will not be awarded. First, where the damage is to the product itself, or to any product supplied with the product in question, no liability arises. Second, where the damaged item is not either of that which is ordinarily intended for private use or that which is intended by the plaintiff for his own private use. Third, where the total property damage complained of is valued at no more than £275.

SUGGESTED ANSWER TO QUESTION ONE

General Comment

The question is clearly concerned with processed or manufactured products which have caused personal injury to persons who could be described as 'consumers'. Some analysis of the terms of the Consumer Protection Act (CPA) 1987 is called for and, perhaps, some comment on the improved situation under the CPA 1987 as against the common law.

Key Points

- Scope of the Act and incidence of liability – type of product
- Producers, suppliers and liability to person supplied and others
- Nature of the damage and 'defects' – range of recoverable damage
- Defences

Suggested Answer

a) Peggy and Queenie have both suffered personal injury as a result of eating apple slices which, by reason of having been machine sliced and packaged, could be said to be a 'product'. This is very important because it brings the matter within the general sphere of product liability as compared with untreated, unprocessed, agricultural produce which is governed by an altogether looser regime imposed by the law of sale of goods and the common law. The Consumer Protection Act (CPA) 1987 provides a very comprehensive and effective type of strict liability where damage has been caused by a 'defect' in a product in a 'consumer' situation. Section 2(4) implies that agricultural produce which has 'undergone an industrial process' is within the ambit of the Act.

   The incidence of liability is set out in s2(2) and (3) and it clearly attaches to the 'producer' (s2(2)(a)) and others who hold themselves, by brand or mark, out as the producer (s2(2)(b)), thus catching the supermarket chain. The chain will also be caught as a 'supplier' within s2(3) regardless of the fact that they did not supply the goods direct to Queenie. This express inclusion of suppliers goes a long way towards remedying the severe limitations on the liability of suppliers which were imposed by the common law and only partly remedied by the 'manufacturer's role' in *Donoghue* v *Stevenson* (1932).

   Section 2(3) also shows that the basis of liability is damage 'caused wholly or partly by a defect in a product'. Clearly, there is no room for foreseeability here and the damage, once causation has been established, is strict so it is obvious that one great drawback with the foreseeability-based common law approach has been removed; the problem from *Evans* v *Triplex Safety Glass Co Ltd* (1936) has disappeared. A 'defect' is defined by s3(1) as meaning that 'the safety of the product is not such as persons generally are entitled to expect', with s3(2) going on to highlight particular circumstances which need to be taken into account in considering what 'persons generally are entitled to expect'.

   The instructions on the package (s3(2)(a)) may be adequate, but it is a question of fact whether there is enough information about the need to maintain the vacuum or otherwise for the safety of the consumer. Apart from that, there is the possibility that a two-hour delay, particularly if temperatures were high during the two hours, might have affected matters. But a one- to two-hour delay ought, perhaps, to be anticipated by a producer. In all other respects, the food has been used in accordance with the instructions and there are strong indications of a defect. The range of recoverable damages clearly contemplates personal injury (ss3(1) and 5(3)), but not loss in respect of the product itself (s5(2)), and the liability cannot be ousted by disclaimers, notice etc: s7.

The liability is strict, but not absolute, so the statutory defences within s4 must be considered. The vitally important point about s4 is that the legal burden of proof of the defence is placed upon the defendant producer/supplier by s4(1). The only defence that seems able to be run by the defendant in this case is that in s4(1)(d), ie 'that the object did not exist in the product at the relevant time', the relevant time here being the time of supply. This will be a heavy burden for the chain to discharge in the circumstances.

b) The marker pen is clearly a 'product' and the incidence of liability will apply to the 'producer', Ecoli GmbH: s2(2)(a). This provision is likely to apply to the UK supplier if it fails, on request for information about the manufacturer by Simon as the person who suffers damage, to supply details: s2(3)(b). If the supplier were liable, the liability of producer and supplier would be joint and several. As outlined above, the supply to a person other than the damaged person does not matter provided that there was a supply 'to another' (s4(1)(b)) and that it was a normal business supply: s4(1)(c).

There could be some real difficulties in establishing that there is a 'defect' within s3 in that it is highly likely that the marker pens carried some sort of warning against using on skin. If they did not, there is likely to be an argument that there should be a warning unless Simon has a highly sensitive skin. The express requirement under s3(2)(b) to consider 'what might reasonably be expected to be done with or in relation to the product' would seem to indicate against there being a defect.

The type of damage is within the range of the Act, but if the evidence showed that appropriate medical testing had failed to indicate such a reaction, ie Simon was hypersensitive, the 'development risks' defence within s4(1)(e) might well be relied upon. Recently, the ECJ in *EC Commission* v *United Kingdom* (1997) approved this defence. The Act seems to be working very well in that there is almost a complete absence of case law on the 'defects' provisions, so closer analysis of high-sensitivity complainants must necessarily await judicial examination of the Act.

Neither (a) nor (b) above seem to fall outside the Act so it is not necessary to consider the residual common law jurisdiction which will now mainly apply to non-consumer situations.

SUGGESTED ANSWER TO QUESTION TWO

General Comment

The question raises issues of Lord Trollope's liability as an employer and also issues of manufacturer's liability for defective products. The final part of the question requires consideration on issues of contributory negligence and volenti.

Key Points

- Dudtools' liability: under the Consumer Protection Act 1987 and at common law – defences
- Lord Trollope's liability: safe plant and equipment – volenti and contributory negligence

Suggested Answer

Geoffrey will wish to show that Dudtools plc are liable for the defective rake. One should first look to the Consumer Protection Act (CPA) 1987 to see if Geoffrey is afforded any statutory protection by it. The rake is clearly a product or 'goods' for the purposes of s1(2) of the Act, and the loss suffered, personal injury, is also covered under s5(1) of the Act. Geoffrey will then have to establish that the damage was caused wholly or partly by a defect in the rake. The standard laid down in s3 of the Act is that the safety of the product must be such as 'persons generally are entitled to expect'. One of the relevant factors in assessing whether the product has achieved this standard is 'what might reasonably be expected to be done with ... the product'. It is here that Geoffrey may experience some difficulties, for it would seem that the rake was not manufactured for the purpose of opening jammed doors. It is arguable, however, that the rake might be expected to be robust enough to cope with general wear and tear of work in the garden. A lot would depend here on the individual facts of the case, eg whether the rake was a plastic garden rake or a heavier hay rake. In any case Geoffrey will have to establish that his injuries are a result of a particular defect in the rake, and not his application of too much force on the rake.

Assuming Geoffrey would be able to establish this, we will consider the defences available to Dudtools. Section 4 of the Act lays down a number of statutory defences to an action for defective products. None of these defences seems to be applicable here. The development risks defence laid down in s4(1), recently approved by the ECJ in *EC Commission v United Kingdom* (1997), has regard to the state of scientific knowledge at the time of manufacture, but this relates to the defect in the rake, not to Geoffrey's condition, and would be irrelevant unless the defect was caused by something very obscure and untraceable. The defence of volenti would also be inapplicable – as Geoffrey was not aware of the extent of the risk of poisoning, he could not have consented to it. The key issue here is what caused the injury: was it Geoffrey's carelessness, or a defect in the rake? Were it to be the former, Geoffrey would not recover, and were it to be the latter Dudtools would have no defence. The evidence points to a conclusion half way between these positions, ie that the injuries were caused by some defect in the rake, coupled with some fault or carelessness on Geoffrey's part. I would advise, then, that Geoffrey would recover a reduced amount of damages in an action against Dudtools, by virtue of the Law Reform (Contributory Negligence) Act 1945. There is also a possibility of a common law action against Dudtools on *Donoghue v Stevenson* (1932) principles. However, if anything the standard of care required at common law from a manufacturer is lower than that required under the CPA 1987 (hence the raison d'etre of the Act itself) and so Geoffrey's case would be no stronger. Had Geoffrey known of his condition I would submit that this would have the effect of weakening his claim against Dudtools, as he should have taken more care in the circumstances.

Geoffrey's claim against Lord Trollope will be governed by the duty of care owed by an employer to his employee. The extent of this duty was defined most notably in *Wilsons and Clyde Coal* v *English* (1938). One aspect of this is the duty to provide adequate plant and equipment. Geoffrey will argue that there has been a breach here in that both the shed door and the rake constitute defective plant and equipment. The standard of care required of an employer is the same as that in negligence, ie he is required to take reasonable care, effectively therefore Lord Trollope is obliged to inspect and check the equipment thoroughly enough to spot a defect: *Murphy* v *Philips* (1876). It may be the case that the defects would not have been discoverable even on a thorough investigation, in which case Lord Trollope would not be liable – this argument would seem stronger in relation to the rake than to the door. Again much will depend on the circumstances surrounding the injury, but there is an arguable case that the equipment is defective.

Assuming Lord Trollope has been in breach of the duty outlined above, the question arises as to whether the loss sustained is too remote a consequence of the breach, as the blood condition is unknown to Lord Trollope. Although Lord Trollope could not have predicted the extent of the injuries caused, due to his ignorance of Geoffrey's condition, the so-called 'eggshell skull rule' will apply here. The rule dictates that as long as some damage to the person is a foreseeable consequence of negligence it generally does not matter that the precise nature and extent of the damage were unforeseeable: *Dulieu* v *White & Sons* (1901). A narrower approach was taken in *Tremain* v *Pike* (1969) where the plaintiff contracted Weil's disease while employed by the defendants. The disease is very rare and caused when human beings come into contact with rats' urine. There was no evidence that the defendants were aware of the possibility of the disease being contracted and it was held that the defendants were not liable as the damage suffered was 'entirely different in kind' from that which could have been foreseen by the defendants. The Court of Appeal has more recently disapproved this decision in the similar (contract) case of *H Parsons Ltd* v *Uttley Ingham & Co* (1978). Lord Denning stated in *Parsons* that the issue of foreseeability applied equally in contract and tort, so this case would imply that the damage suffered by Geoffrey would not be considered too remote in that some injury would be a foreseeable consequence of the provision of a defective door or rake, if it can be established that Lord Trollope failed to inspect the equipment adequately.

As with Geoffrey's potential claim against Dudtools, the court may choose to reduce damages because of Geoffrey's partial fault under the Law Reform (Contributory

Negligence) Act 1956, and will reduce the amount according to the relative fault of Geoffrey, although the courts apply this provision reluctantly in employment cases: *Caswell* v *Powell Duffryn Associated Collieries Ltd* (1940), which indicates that Geoffrey may fare better in his action against Lord Trollope than against Dudtools in this respect. Finally, had Geoffrey known about his condition this would work against him only as regards the defence of volenti. Had he not known of the disease the defence cannot be established, as he could not consent to a risk he knew nothing about. Where he knew about the condition it is arguable that he knew of the risk and therefore assumed it. This presumes, however, that Geoffrey's knowledge of his blood condition extends to the knowledge that a splinter would cause him such severe poisoning, which would seem unlikely. Furthermore the courts are reluctant to allow the defence of volenti in employment cases (*Smith* v *Baker* (1891)) as employees may be under understandable pressures to accept risks at work which they would not normally accept in other situations. This would make it less likely that Lord Trollope could establish a defence of volenti, although Geoffrey's knowledge could increase the court's assessment of fault on his part, and thereby reduce the damages.

SUGGESTED ANSWER TO QUESTION THREE

General Comment

This question concerns liability for defective products and is a fairly straightforward problem. Much of the question concerns the Consumer Protection Act but it is also necessary to consider the position at common law.

Key Points

* Consumer Protection Act 1987 – who is a producer? – what is a product? – what is a defect? – what damage is covered? – are there any defences?
* Position at common law

Suggested Answer

This problem concerns a defective product manufactured by Botchit Ltd, the potential defendants. The plaintiffs are put to expense in mending the product and then replacing it, as well as in repairing the damage it causes to their property.

One should first look to the Consumer Protection Act 1987 to see if Fanny and Gordon are afforded statutory protection. The stereo system is a product covered by the Act, since s1 defines product as meaning any goods. Under s2(2) of the Act, the producer of the product is liable for the damage caused by a defect in the product. Botchit Ltd, we are told, manufactured the system and are therefore producers covered by this section. F and G do not know the name of the supplier and do not want to ask H where he bought it. While the supplier can also be held liable under s2(3) of the Act, this would be where the supplier fails, upon request being made within a reasonable period after the damage occurs, to identify the producer. Therefore F and G are unaffected by their lack of knowledge of the supplier.

The next question that F and G need to consider is whether there has been a defect within the meaning of the Act. A defect exists, under s3, 'if the safety of the product is not such as persons generally are entitled to expect'. 'Safety' is construed widely and includes safety in the context of risks of damage to property. The problems that occurred in this case arose from the faulty motor, both before and after it was replaced, and meant that the system was not of the safety that one would reasonably expect in a new product. Therefore, the defect falls within the definition of the Act.

Next, the plaintiffs must consider the damage. Unfortunately for them, the Act restricts recovery for property damage in that there is no liability in respect of loss of or damage to the product itself: s5(2). Therefore they cannot recover under the Act for the defective motor unit and turntable. They can only recover for the damage the product causes to their property. Presumably this damage is quite extensive and, in any case, is above the £275 threshold demanded by the Act.

It does not appear that any of the defences provided by s4 of the Act will apply, unless this is a 'state-of-the-art' stereo and Botchit can claim that 'the state of scientific and technical knowledge at the time was not such that a producer of products of the same description as the product in question might be expected to have discovered the defect if it had existed in his products while they were under his control': s4(1)(e). This is the so-called 'development risks' defence, which was recently approved by the ECJ in *EC Commission* v *United Kingdom* (1997).

Therefore Fanny and Gordon can recover under the Act for the damage to their property but not for their outlay on repairing and then replacing the stereo. The next question, then, is whether that expense can be recovered. Obviously there is no contract between plaintiffs and defendants and Fanny and Gordon do not want to involve Henry, who was a party to the contract. So any remedy must lie in tort.

Liability at common law for defective products was most famously stated in *Donoghue* v *Stevenson* (1932). However, it applies where the product causes damage to other property than the product itself. There is no general liability at common law for loss to the product. This is despite the House of Lords' decision in *Junior Books* v *The Veitchi Co Ltd* (1983) which purported to allow such liability but which has since been disapproved. This is properly the sphere of contract law and I would advise the plaintiffs that they will not recover for damage to the property itself in tort.

SUGGESTED ANSWER TO QUESTION FOUR

General Comment

This essay question focuses upon the provisions of Part I of the Consumer Protection Act 1987 but it also requires consideration of the desirability of no-fault liability and whether or not it is desirable that the imposition of such liability should be extended. You should resist the temptation to write everything you know about the CPA 1987 and try to use your information to answer the question.

Key Points

- CPA 1987

- Strict liability
- Who is liable?
- Defective
- Defences
- Damage
- Is Act welcome?
- Other examples of strict liability
- *Rylands* – animals – fire – vicarious liability – nuisance? – res ipsa loquitur?
- Other extensions?
- Causation and *Wilsher*
- Replacement of present system by comprehensive no-fault accident compensation scheme

Suggested Answer

The provisions of Part I of the Consumer Protection Act (CPA) 1987 were introduced to implement the provisions of an EEC Directive relating to product liability. The CPA 1987 purports to introduce a regime of strict liability in the sphere of product liability. Before considering whether or not the Act is to be welcomed it is necessary to outline the principal provisions of the Act.

The main provision of the Act is contained in s2(1) which states that where any damage is caused wholly or partly by a defect in a product then certain persons shall be liable for the damage which is occasioned. The persons who may be liable are the producer of the goods, any person who holds himself out as being a producer of the goods, the importer of the goods into the EEC and, in certain circumstances, the supplier of the product. The liability of the supplier is, however, a secondary liability; that is to say that the supplier may discharge liability by identifying the producer of the goods and it is only where he fails to so this that he will be liable. A product is defined in s1(2) as any 'goods or electricity' and goods is further defined in s45.

The consumer is left with a problem, however, in establishing that the product was defective. A product is defective where the 'safety of the product is not such as persons generally are entitled to expect': s3(2). Thus the product must in some way be unsafe; it will not generally suffice to say that the goods simply did not live up to expectations. A court is to have regard to all the circumstances of the case in considering whether a product is defective but relevant factors include the marketing of the product, any warnings contained on the product and the use to which the product might reasonably be put.

The Act contains a number of defences, the most important of which is the 'state of the art' defence contained in s4(1)(e) which states that it is a defence to show 'that the state of scientific … knowledge at the relevant time was not such that a producer of products of the same description … might be expected to have discovered the defect'. The presence of this defence makes it difficult to say that the role of fault has been completely eliminated under the CPA because the factors to which a court will have regard in considering whether the state of the art defence has been established are similar to the factors which a court will have regard to in a negligence action. This defence, which is also known as the 'development risks' defence, recently received approval from the ECJ in *EC Commission* v *United Kingdom* (1997).

Finally it should be noted that only certain types of losses are recoverable under the Act. Damages are recoverable for personal injury and death and in relation to damage to property (provided that it exceeds £275) but damages are not recoverable for the defect in the product itself: s5.

The provisions of the Act are generally to be welcomed in that they improve the position of the consumer who suffers injury as a result of a defective product. But difficulties will remain due to the presence of the state of the art defence which may be invoked by many manufacturers, particularly in relation to the manufacture of drugs. Difficulties will also remain in showing that the product was defective and where the goods themselves are defective and do not cause any other injury no remedy will lie under the Act and the remedy (if any) will be in contract.

These provisions of the CPA are not, however, the only example of liability without fault in English law. Other examples of strict liability in English law are the rule in *Rylands* v *Fletcher* (1866), vicarious liability (as the employer does not commit a tort), liability under the Animals Act 1971 and liability for the escape of fire. More debatable examples of strict liability are nuisance (although the role of fault within this tort is unclear see Lord Reid in *The Wagon Mound (No 2)* (1967) and res ipsa loquitur. Another source of strict liability is contractual liability, particularly in relation to the merchantable quality provisions of the Sale of Goods Act 1979. Liability depends on proof that the goods are unmerchantable and not on proof that the vendor was in some way at fault.

Despite the fact that there are a number of areas in which English law recognises liability without fault there is no general principle in English law of liability without fault and there is still room for the extension of no fault liability as can be seen from the recent case of *Wilsher* v *Essex Area Health Authority* (1988). The House of Lords held that the plaintiff must in all cases prove on a balance of probabilities that the negligence of the defendant was the cause of the loss to the plaintiff. This is likely to cause problems for plaintiffs in medical negligence cases such as *Wilsher* where it is uncertain which of a number of competing causes was the cause of the damage to the plaintiff. If the plaintiff can surmount the problems of proof he can recover for all his losses; if he cannot surmount this hurdle he will recover nothing. It seems rather arbitrary that enormous sums of money should hinge on such difficult evidential questions.

Wilsher also demonstrates other deficiencies of a fault based system. The plaintiff's parents have now been fighting for a number of years to recover damages for their son but as a result of the decision of the House of Lords they are now no nearer to recovery than they were when the case first started. Large amounts of time and money have so far been spent on seeking to show that the defendant's fault was the cause of the damage to the plaintiff. The Pearson Committee discovered that the cost of operating the tort system accounted for some 85 per cent of the sums paid to accident victims.

Similarly it is questionable whether the presence of fault should make such a difference to the plaintiff in *Wilsher*. His needs are the same whether the negligence of the defendants was the cause of his loss or not. It is difficult to justify a system in which he recovers extremely large sums of money if he can prove the necessary causal link but nothing if he fails. It may be said that the presence of fault is the differentiating factor but in cases such as *Nettleship* v *Weston* (1971) the role of personal fault in a negligence action appears to have almost entirely disappeared.

Dissatisfaction with the tort system in New Zealand was such that the tort action has been abolished in relation to personal injury cases and replaced by a comprehensive no-fault accident compensation scheme which covers all accidental injury, except diseases (other than occupational diseases) and is financed by a levy on motor vehicles, employers and employees and out of general taxation.

Such a scheme is likely to ensure a greater extent of equality as between different victims of misfortune in society. It is true that such a system would be expensive to operate but at least more of the money would get to the claimants and not be tied up in administration as in the present fault based system. It is therefore suggested that there is scope for the extension of no fault liability in English law and that serious consideration should now be given to implementing a comprehensive no-fault accident compensation scheme.

13

General Defences

Introduction

These are defences which are common throughout the law of tort, although each tort may have a number of defences which are specific to that tort. Contributory negligence and volenti non fit injuria which are two of the principal defences are dealt with under negligence.

MISTAKE

Although it is not a general defence in a tort action, it can operate as a defence, for instance an honest but mistaken belief in the truth of a statement will negative liability in deceit.

NECESSITY

It can operate as a complete defence in tort. The defendant can argue that his course of action was the lesser of two evils and that he has intervened to prevent greater damage being occasioned. The acts of the defendant must by synonymous to that of the reasonable man: *Southwark London Borough Council* v *Williams* (1971). For a recent illustration of the applicability of this defence: see *Monsanto plc* v *Tilly* (1999) (CA).

LIMITATION

Statute has intervened to impose time limits within which an action in tort must be brought against a defendant. The rule contained in s2 of the Limitation Act 1980 is that an action in tort cannot be brought more than six years from the date on which the plaintiff's cause of action accrued. See also the recent Court of Appeal cases: *Byrne* v *Hall Pain & Foster* (1999) and *James* v *East Dorset Health Authority* (1999). See also the recent case of *KR and Others* v *Bryn Alyn Community (Holdings) Ltd* (2003), as well as *Cave* v *Robinson Jarvis & Rolf* (2002).

ILLEGALITY

Based on public policy, ie ex turpi causa non oritur actio – no right of action accrues from a bad cause. Therefore, if the plaintiff suffers damage because of the defendant's tort while participating in a crime, then no action will lie: *Ashton* v *Turner* (1981), *Pitts* v *Hunt* (1990) and cf *Tinsley* v *Milligan* (1993). *Clunis* v *Camden and Islington Health Authority* (1998) decided by the Court of Appeal also provides a useful illustration.

STATUTORY AUTHORITY

Some statutes specifically authorise certain acts. In such cases, no action will lie for doing that act or for any necessary consequence of that act: *Allen* v *Gulf Oil Refining* (1981) and *Hampson* v *Department of Education and Science* (1990).

Questions

INTERROGRAMS

1. What is meant by the maxim ex turpi causa non oritur actio?
2. Is necessity a recognised defence in tort today?
3. Why are there limitation periods?

It must be noted that there are rarely examination questions that are asked exclusively on defences. They usually form part of a question. Hence, although the following questions overlap with other areas of tort, focus should be placed with the operation of defences therein.

QUESTION ONE

a) Discuss the concept of necessity as a defence to an action in trespasss.
b) Hilda enters hospital for major abdominal surgery. Ingrid, the surgical registrar, describes the nature of the operation to her and she signs a form consenting to the surgery. During the operation Ingrid notices that Hilda's appendix is diseased and is likely to cause her serious problems in a year or two. She therefore removes it. Hilda is annoyed when she discovers that this has happened.
      Advise her.

University of London LLB Examination
(for external students) Law of Tort June 1988 Q8

QUESTION TWO

Fergus is employed as a driver by the Egmont Engineering Co. It is a company rule that only their employees may be carried in their vehicles. A notice is displayed on the dashboard of Fergus's van, reading:

> 'Egmont employees only in this van. The company can accept no liability towards any other persons riding in this vehicle.'

One day Fergus has to drive to the premises of a supplier to collect some materials. George, an employee of a firm of electrical contractors repairing machinery at the Egmont plant, asks if he can have a lift to collect some supplies urgently needed for their repairs. Fergus agrees, but on the way he is gripped by severe chest pains, George asks him, 'Are you feeling well enough?' Fergus replies, 'Yes, just a touch of indigestion.' George allows him to continue to drive. A few minutes later Fergus loses control of the van and crashes into a lamp-post. George is thrown out of the van and is severely injured.

He had not been wearing a seat belt because he felt trapped if he did so. If he had been wearing a belt, his injuries would have been slight.

It is later discovered that Fergus had had a heart attack and he can now remember nothing of the accident.

Advise George.

Written by the Author

QUESTION THREE

Green is a famous and highly paid violinist. He is travelling with his wife in a taxi to a concert in which he is to perform when the taxi is involved in a collision with a car. The collision is caused solely by the negligence of Brown, the driver of the car. Green is not injured but his Stradivarius violin, worth £50,000, is destroyed. He is also too shaken to be able to perform the concert, for which his fee was to have been £1,000. Green cannot afford to buy a new Stradivarius immediately although he knows of one for sale in London. He hires one for three months at £300 a month until he is able to buy one.

The taxi driver, White, is uninjured but the taxi is damaged so that it cannot be used for four weeks. White does not own the taxi, but hires it from Taxicab Ltd. Taxicab Ltd cannot supply another taxi, so that White cannot work for four weeks.

Violet, a pedestrian, witnesses the accident. As she is trained in first aid, she immediately rushes across the road to see if any of the occupants of the vehicles require assistance and is struck and injured by another car.

Advise Green, White and Violet.

Written by the Author

Answers

ANSWERS TO INTERROGRAMS

1. Essentially, the maxim means that one cannot derive a benefit or expect to gain benefits out of an illegal act. It basically means that no action arises from a disgraceful cause. It is for the defendant to show that the plaintiff's activities were so thoroughly tied up with illegality that the two cannot fairly be separated.
2. Although some authors seem to doubt the utility of necessity as a defence today on the basis that carelessness or recklessness is not excusable, it seems arguable that necessity could surely in some cases justify the defendant running a risk of injury to the plaintiff. The courts are however very reluctant to allow this plea to succeed except in the most exceptional cases: *Cope v Sharpe (No 2)* (1912), *Southwark London Borough Council v Williams* (1971) and cf *Rigby v Chief Constable of Northamptonshire* (1985). See also *Monsanto plc v Tilly* (1999).
3. First, it would be grossly unfair to leave the defendant at risk of a legal action indefinitely or for too long. Hence, the law imposes time frame within which certain types of action must be initiated. The governing legislation is the Limitation Act 1980.

SUGGESTED ANSWER TO QUESTION ONE

General Comment

It is clear that students need to have a very detailed knowledge of the defences to actions in trespass, particularly in respect of trespasses to the person, in order to do justice to this question.

Key Points

a) Discuss the limited nature of the defence of necessity to actions in both trespass to property and to the person, using past cases by way of illustration
b) • Discuss whether the removal of Hilda's appendix might have been covered by the terms of her original written consent
   • If Hilda's consent was not expressly provided, might the courts imply such consent?
   • Discuss whether the defence of necessity might justify additional procedures being carried out where other medical conditions are discovered during an operation

Suggested Answer

a) Necessity is, by definition, an extremely limited defence in trespass as it allows a defendant to lawfully protect his, or another's, person or property, even though the result is that an innocent person suffers a loss in the process. It is likely that the defence will only be available in emergency situations where it is necessary for private citizens to avert immediate and serious dangers to life or property, and where the citizen acts reasonably in all the circumstances. Thus, defendants who take personal action, when a call to the emergency services would have been a reasonable alternative course of action, are unlikely to avail themselves of the defence.

On this basis, campaigners against field trials of genetically modified plants had no defence to an action in trespass after entering land to destroy some of the crops, even though they claimed such action was necessary to raise public awareness and to protect the public: *Monsanto plc* v *Tilly* (1999). In *Southwark London Borough Council* v *Williams* (1971) necessity was also held to be no defence to actions in trespass brought against homeless persons squatting in empty local authority housing, Lord Denning stating that otherwise, necessity '… would be an excuse for all sorts of wrongdoing. So the courts must, for the sake of law and order, take a firm stand.'

However, necessity has been successfully used as a defence to trespass to property in a variety of circumstances such as the following.

i) The prevention, by diversion, of flood water from entering a defendant's land, with the result that a neighbour's land was flooded: *Home Brewery plc* v *William Davis & Co (Loughborough) Ltd* (1987).
ii) The prevention of a plague of locusts from entering the defendant's land

(achieved by entering the land of a third party) with the result that the insects re-entered the plaintiff's land, destroying crops: *Greyvensteyn v Hattingh* (1911).

iii) The firing, by a police officer, of a CS gas cylinder into a building in order to flush out a dangerous psychopath: *Rigby v Chief Constable of Northamptonshire* (1985). However, whilst the defence was held to apply in the circumstances, damages were awarded against the defendant as the officer responsible was found to have been negligent in firing the cylinder without having fire fighting equipment to hand.

iv) The throwing of goods overboard in a storm in order to save the passengers on a ship: *Mouse's* Case (1609).

Necessity is also a limited defence to trespasses against the person. Most cases have arisen where medical treatment has been administered without a patient's consent, but even here the courts have taken an extremely restrictive approach to the availability of the defence, the sanctity of the human body being a fundamental basic principle.

Necessity would be applicable in those circumstances where a doctor is forced to give medical treatment to an unconscious patient in order to preserve life or prevent permanent damage to health. It might also extend to the administration of treatment to a conscious adult who is temporarily or permanently incompetent to give consent by reason of mental illness or because of the undue influence of others. For example, in *F v West Berkshire Area Health Authority* (1989) the House of Lords allowed the defence of necessity to justify the sterilisation of a 36-year-old woman who was a voluntary patient in a mental hospital. It was held that the defence would be available in similar circumstances where a reasonable body of medical opinion was in favour of allowing the treatment in the best interests of the patient. Not only would treatment be justified in order to save life or to prevent permanent injury, but also in cases of routine medical treatment.

However, the defence will not operate where a mentally competent patient refuses life-saving treatment provided there is a full understanding of the consequences of that decision. This principle extends to the refusal of a caesarean section, even if that would mean the death of the mother's unborn child: *Re M B (Caesarean Section)* (1997). Nor could the defence be used to justify the force-feeding of prisoners on hunger strike: *Secretary of State for the Home Department v Robb* (1995).

b) The issues to be decided here are whether Hilda has in fact given her consent (express or implied) to the removal of her appendix and if not, whether its removal by the hospital was justified on the grounds of necessity. The basic position was stated by Lord Brandon in *F v West Berkshire Area Health Authority*:

> 'At common law, a doctor cannot lawfully operate on adult patients of sound mind … without their consent. If a doctor were to operate on such patients, or give them other treatment, without their consent, he would commit the actionable tort of trespass to the person.'

In other words, the hospital may have committed a battery on Hilda in going beyond the scope of the original abdominal surgery. Whether such a battery has taken place here will depend upon the scope of the defences available to the hospital.

Did Hilda provide her express consent to the removal of her appendix?

We are told that Hilda signed a consent form covering, at the very least, major abdominal surgery. Such written consents normally contain a declaration, on the part of the patient, that the nature and effect of the treatment has been explained to them, and provided that the patient has in fact been advised of the broad nature of the operation by a doctor, consent will have been lawfully given. Whether Hilda has expressly consented to the removal of her appendix appears, therefore, to depend upon how closely this further procedure matched the precise nature of the operation previously explained to her. It is possible that the diseased appendix related to the condition originally requiring surgery, in which case Hilda's actual consent is more likely to authorise the removal of the organ. Another possibility is that the original written consent may have authorised such further treatment as the doctor considered necessary or desirable in the circumstances. Such a wording, if present, would appear to cover the removal of the appendix.

Did Hilda impliedly consent to the removal of her appendix in the circumstances?

Consent to a course of medical treatment can sometimes be implied from the claimant's conduct, eg where a patient holds out her arm in order to receive an injection. It is clearly much more difficult to imply such consent if a patient is unconscious when the need for a consent first arises. It might be thought that the courts would approach the issue on the basis of whether a reasonable person would have wanted their appendix removed during an operation for some other matter, given that it's removal would have been inevitable at some stage in the future. This would obviously depend upon whether any additional risks were involved. However, the courts prefer to approach these questions according to the defence of necessity rather than upon issues of implied consent (*F* v *West Berkshire Area Health Authority*), and it is submitted that this is the likely basis on which the hospital would have to justify their actions.

Can the removal of the appendix be justified by the defence of necessity?

It has already been noted that that a doctor would be justified in administering urgent, necessary medical treatment where a patient is unconscious and not known to object to it. However, this exception appears to be confined to cases where immediate action is necessary to preserve life or prevent permanent damage to health. It is clear that Hilda's diseased appendix does not pose any immediate threat to her health, and on this basis, it is submitted that she ought to have been given the opportunity to provide her consent to the procedure, even if that meant a further operation.

There does not appear to be any explicit UK authority on whether consent to one medical procedure justifies another. Whilst the issue was considered by the Canadian courts in *Marshall* v *Curry* (1933) and *Murray* v *McMurchy* (1949) (and resolved as suggested above), the question was expressly left open in *F* v *West Berkshire Area*

Health Authority by Lord Goff. It is submitted that necessity will be no defence in the circumstances described.

SUGGESTED ANSWER TO QUESTION TWO

General Comment

A general problem on negligence, and particularly the tort of vicarious liability. It also raises the defences of contributory negligence and volenti non fit injuria as appropriate.

Key Points

- Elements of the tort of negligence
- Reasonable person test
- Element of vicarious liability
- Defence of contributory negligence
- Defence of volenti non fit injuria
- Relevance of UCTA 1977 as regards exclusion of liability

Suggested Answer

George will base his action on Fergus' negligence, and may be in a position to sue Fergus' employers should they be vicariously liable.

He must first prove that Fergus owed him a duty of care to take reasonable steps for his safety while he is a passenger, and a duty of care has been found to exist between passenger and driver in cases such as *Froom v Butcher* (1976). Since Fergus should have George in his reasonable contemplation as he may be harmed by his carelessness, it is submitted that he is under a duty of care. A breach of that duty will be proved if a reasonable man would not have acted in the same way: *Blyth v Birmingham Waterworks* (1856). On the facts, it is not per se a breach that Fergus lost control of the vehicle, but a reasonable and prudent driver may, on feeling unwell, pull into the side of the road and stop his vehicle, especially if he had a passenger, and so Fergus is in breach by continuing to drive when he feels unwell. Res ipsa loquitur has no application here since the reason for Fergus' loss of control is ascertainable: *Barkway v South Wales Transport* [1950]. Fergus' breach has caused George's injuries, so that negligence has prima facie been made out.

The second issue is whether Egmont Engineering Co is vicariously liable for Fergus' negligence. Fergus must be their employee, which is apparent from the facts, but it must also be determined whether he is 'in the course of employment'. This phrase has in recent times been construed by the courts very liberally. The question to be asked is whether Fergus was performing an act which he was authorised to do or which was reasonably incidental to his employment, even though he may have been doing it in an unauthorised manner; if he was his employers will be liable.

The fact that Fergus undoubtedly knew of his employers' prohibition on the carrying of non-employees is, it is submitted, by no means decisive. In *Limpus v London General Omnibus Co* (1862), contrary to his employers' express instructions, a bus driver obstructed buses from a rival company and caused an accident; it was held that the employers were still vicariously liable because the driver's act was merely a wrongful act of carrying out an authorised act, ie the driving of buses, and was not an act which he was not employed to do at all. The prohibition related to the mode of performing his job and not to the scope of his employment: cf *Beard* v *London General Omnibus Co* (1900).

A contrary view was taken as to a prohibition in *Twine* v *Bean's Express* (1946), a case with facts similar to those in George's case, except that in *Twine* a hitch-hiker was given a lift. It was held that an employee giving a lift to an unauthorised person is acting outside the course of his employment. Since the plaintiff was a trespasser, the employers owed him no duty of care. The latter reason now seems erroneous in the light of *British Railways Board* v *Herrington* (1972) and the Occupiers' Liability Act 1984, where a modified duty of care was held to apply to trespassers, but the main distinction is that the court in *Twine* based vicarious liability on a duty of care owed by the employer to the plaintiff, a view which today has lost favour, so that modern courts examine instead the employer/employee relationship.

The decision in *Twine* was disapproved of by a majority of the Court of Appeal in *Rose* v *Plenty* (1976) where the trespassory status of the plaintiff in the milk-float was regarded as irrelevant, and in any event the presence of the boy was in effect furthering the employer's interests in helping to deliver milk.

It is submitted that *Rose* is the preferable decision to apply in this case so that the prohibition relates only to the way in which Fergus is to carry out his job as a driver and it is immaterial that George is a trespasser. It may further be argued that George's presence is indirectly furthering Egmont's interests, since he is an employee of contractors repairing machinery at the Egmont plant. As long as Fergus has not deviated from his route, he is not on a frolic of his own.

Egmont's notice should also be read in the light of s2 of the Unfair Contract Terms Act 1977, so that the employers could not rely on the notice to the extent that it purports to exclude liability for death or personal injury caused by negligence.

Fergus and Egmont would be able to claim contributory negligence against George on two possible grounds. The clearest is his failure to wear a seat-belt and he must face a reduction in his damages of 20 per cent – 15 per cent since his injuries would have been slight had he worn one (*Froom* v *Butcher* (above)). His aversion to seat-belts is unlikely to affect this, per Denning MR in *Froom*, unless his aversion amounted to a 'phobia': *Condon* v *Condon* (1978). He may also have acted without regard for his own safety by allowing Fergus to continue driving when he felt unwell; this case is different from decisions such as *Owens* v *Brimmell* (1977) where the plaintiff knew of the defendant's disability (drunkenness) before he accepted a lift, so that this ground is less certain to succeed.

Volenti may also be raised against George for accepting a lift in view of the notice displayed in the van. For this defence to succeed, George must have voluntarily submitted to the risk of injury, and must have had knowledge of the danger. It is therefore unlikely to succeed on these facts, since George, by ignoring the notice, has not consented to the risk of injury by Fergus' negligence: s2(3) Unfair Contract Terms Act 1977.

SUGGESTED ANSWER TO QUESTION THREE

General Comment

A general question on recoverability of damages under the different heads. The question also raises the defences of contributory negligence and volenti non fit injuria.

Key Points

- Negligence, causation and remoteness
- Claim in respect of violin – foreseeability and remoteness
- Claim in respect of hiring – mitigation and remoteness
- Recoverability for economic loss
- Defence of contributory negligence
- Defence of volenti non fit injuria

Suggested Answer

All parties concerned will base their respective claims for damages on negligence, but the main issue here is whether Green and White will be able to recover their total loss in full since part of that loss is economic, as opposed to physical damage.

We are told that Brown, the defendant, has been negligent in causing the collision, but the damage caused must be a reasonably foreseeable consequence of his negligence (*The Wagon Mound (No 1)* (1961)) and must be a type of loss which is recoverable.

Considering, first of all, the claim of Green, it seems that he will wish to recover for the loss of the violin, the loss of the concert fee and the cost of hiring a replacement violin. Until the decision in *Junior Books v Veitchi* (1983), a plaintiff could only recover for economic loss if it was consequential upon personal injury or damage to property; that rule was relied upon in *SCM (UK) v W J Whittall* (1970) and in *Spartan Steel v Martin* (1973). Applying that principle to the facts of this case, it is quite clear that the most immediate loss flowing from the destruction of the violin is the value of the instrument itself, ie £50,000. The loss of the concert fee is not so immediately consequential. However, in considering remoteness principles, it is clear that the defendant must take his victim as he finds him, either in relation to physical weaknesses (eg *Smith v Leech, Brain and Co* (1962) or to the value of the property damaged. Since damage to Green's property is reasonably foreseeable, Green will be able to recover the value of the destroyed instrument regardless of its rarity. It is submitted that it is also reasonably foreseeable that Green will be unable to attend the concert, either through the physical effects suffered as a result of the collision or through the loss of the violin.

The £900 claim for hiring is less certain to be recovered. *The Liesbosch Dredger v Edison* (1933) lays down the premise that where a plaintiff suffers a greater loss through some extraneous cause, eg his own impecuniosity, he cannot recover that loss; a plaintiff must always mitigate his own loss. Here Green has to wait for three months until he can afford another violin, although one is available.

Although a short period of hiring may be reasonably foreseeable as a temporary measure, it may be argued that, applying *The Liesbosch Dredger*, Green could not recover the whole claim for £900. However, as in *Perry v Sidney Phillips* (1982) it was said that *Liesbosch* was 'consistently being attenuated in more recent decisions', and in *Mattocks v Mann* (1992) the Court of Appeal stated the case would only be applied in exceptional circumstances, it seems most likely that Brown would be liable for the full amount.

As far as White's claim is concerned, he has suffered economic loss alone; physical damage to the taxi is reasonably foreseeable but will be recoverable not by White but by Taxicab Ltd, the owners. White could rely on *Junior Books v Veitchi* on which to base his claim for loss of earnings, but unfortunately *Junior Books* has been the subject of much judicial criticism (see, for example, *D & F Estates v Church Commissioners* (1989), and *Simaan General Contracting v Pilkington (No 2)* (1988)), and it would not be safe for a plaintiff to rely on *Junior Books* in the future. A similar case to White's is *The Mineral Transporter* (1986) in which a party who hired a ship could not claim for economic loss consequent upon physical damage to the ship.

Violet, as a rescuer, is under no duty to act positively for the benefit of others as a mere passer-by, but since she has attempted to come to the aid of the other parties, she will be owed a duty of care by Brown, whose negligence created the situation which invites rescue: *Haynes v Harwood* (1935); *Baker v Hopkins* (1959). A defence of volenti will be unlikely to succeed against her (*Haynes v Harwood*) since the necessary elements of free-will and consent are missing in the urgency of a rescue. The decision in *Harrison v British Railways Board* (1981) allows the possibility of a defence of contributory negligence against a rescuer who has acted without regard for his own safety, although Boreham J stated his 'distaste' in so reducing the plaintiff's damages by 20 per cent, although in that case the contributory negligence referred to the plaintiff's carelessness not during the act of rescue, but in bringing about the dangerous situation. This defence is unlikely to be successful in rescue cases, although Violet has immediately rushed across the road, so has in that sense acted carelessly. Brown may argue that her action constituted a novus actus interveniens and her injuries are therefore too remote. This argument is unlikely to succeed since a reasonably foreseeable result of his actions is that someone will attempt to aid the parties. Violet, in any event, would also be able to bring an action against the second driver in negligence, as well as (or instead of) against Brown, subject to a possible reduction for contributory negligence.

14

Remedies

Introduction

The law of tort is concerned with redress for the injured party rather than with the punishment of the person liable. The principal remedy in tort is damages which are awarded to reinstate the injured party back to his original person (prior to the tort in question) as far as money is able to this. As a general rule, damages may only be recovered once in respect of one cause of action, with certain exceptions. Damages may take the following forms:

Nominal	where the plaintiff suffers no loss, therefore very little.
Real	reflects the degree of injury of loss suffered.
Compensatory	actual reflection of loss in pecuniary terms.
Aggravated	an additional sum is added over and above the actual sum awarded.
Contemptuous	where the infringement of the plaintiff's right was a mere technicality or was morally justified, and the action should never have been brought.
Exemplary	where the act is oppressive, arbitrary or unconstitutional.
General or unliquidated	need not be specifically proven.
Special or liquidated	specific items of loss or damage which must be proven.

The measure of damages for personal injury includes: pain and suffering, loss of amenity, loss of expectation of life, loss of earnings, medical, other incidental losses, loss of earning capacity, future loss of earnings and future expenses (all as and when appropriate, of course). For loss or damage to property, damages are either the market value at the time of destruction or the cost of repair. Interest and costs are also recoverable. The following cases are relevant in this context: *Hardwick* v *Hudson* (1999) (on pecuniary loss); *Wadey* v *Surrey County Council* (1999) and *Neal* v *Bingle* (1998) (on deductions); *Cox* v *Hockenbull* (1999) and *Jameson* v *Central Electricity Generating Board* (1999) (on damages for fatal accident); *Wells* v *Wells; Thomas* v *Brighton Health Authority; Page* v *Sheerness Steel Co plc* (1998) (on actual and prospective loss of earnings); and *Nykredit Mortgage Bank plc* v *Edward Erdman Group Ltd (No 2)* (1998) (on calculating interest). See also, recently, *Wisely* v *John Fulton (Plumbers) Ltd; Wadey* v *Surrey County Council* (2000) (on special damages); *Heil* v *Rankin* (2000) (on damages generally); *Kuddus* v *Chief Constable of Leicestershire Constabulary* (2001) (on exemplary damages), *Kiam* v *MGN Ltd* (2002) (on the power of the court to substitute damages) and *Warriner* v *Warriner* (2003).

Note also the relevance of the Damages (Personal Injury) Order 2001 when calculating damges for future pecuniary loss. *Geest plc* v *Lansiquot* (2003) dismisses mitigation of loss in calculating damages.

Injunctions are another form of remedy – they are known as equitable remedies which are only available at the discretion of the court. Section 37 of the Supreme Court Act 1981 states the granting of an injunction must be 'just and reasonable'. See, recently, the Court of Appeal case of *British Telecom plc and Another* v *One In A Million Ltd and Another* (1998) where the availability of injunctive relief was discussed. The court may at times award damages in lieu of an injunction. Self help is another form of remedy, for example in abating a nuisance, ejecting a trespasser, self defence to battery, etc.

Questions

INTERROGRAMS

1. What is the distinction between a remedy in tort and a remedy in contract?
2. What criteria do the courts apply in considering whether to grant an injunction?
3. Do the courts take account of the impact of inflation in the future when awarding damages? Should they?
4. How does the law of tort deal with death resulting from negligence?

QUESTION ONE

'English law does not acknowledge a single tort of intention in the same sense that it acknowledges the existence of the tort of negligence.' (Markesinis and Deakin.)

Explain and discuss.

University of London LLB Examination
(for external students) Law of Tort June 2000 Q2

QUESTION TWO

Milly required major heart surgery. The operation was performed by Nora, a leading heart surgeon. She decided to use a new technique which avoided some of the risks of conventional surgery. It had never been performed in the United Kingdom, but Nora had observed it carried out in the United States. Nora told Milly how the operation would be performed, but not that it was a new technique. Although the operation was performed with reasonable care, Milly suffered brain damage. She is now severely disabled, unable to work and requires a great deal of care.

Milly was 22, had just obtained a degree in computer engineering and was about to undertake a graduate degree. Her mother Olivia, who is aged 45, and was a partner in a firm of city solicitors, has given up work to help care for her.

Advise (a) as to any claims in tort, (b) as to the assessment of damages and (c) as to the advantages and disadvantages of a structured settlement.

University of London LLB Examination
(for external students) Law of Tort June 1999 Q2

Answers

ANSWERS TO INTERROGRAMS

1. In contract, the purpose of the award is to put the party in a position that he would have been in had the contract been fully performed, whereas, in tort, the purpose of the award is to put the person who has suffered the loss in the position that he would have been in had the tort not occurred.

2. The courts are normally guided on the principles enunciated by the House of Lords in *American Cyanamid* v *Ethicon* (1975). The following considerations apply:

   a) Is the injury to the plaintiff's legal right a small one?
   b) Is it capable of being quantified in terms of money?
   c) Can it be compensated by a small money payment, ie are damages an adequate remedy?
   d) Would it be oppressive to the defendant to grant the injunction?

3. Yes, the courts do take account of inflation. Hence, in times of inflation, it is obvious that interest must be claimed on damages because there will usually be a considerable lapse of time between the date of the 'tort' and the date of the trial. The court should take into consideration all factors which may reasonably have an impact on the plaintiff's recovery of damages.

4. Where the negligence of the defendant results in the death of another then special rules have been evolved to deal with this issue. At common law, the rule was that death extinguished a cause of action which the deceased may have had against the defendant. At the same time no cause of action accrued for the benefit of the dependants of the deceased. Both these rules have now been abolished by the Law Reform (Miscellaneous Provisions) Act 1934 and the Fatal Accidents Act 1976, so that actions arising out of the death of the deceased are now available.

SUGGESTED ANSWER TO QUESTION ONE

General Comment

This is quite a wide question that requires the student to compare and contrast tortious liability with other forms of tortious liability that are based on intention. There must be a comparative element in the answer, and the discussion should not deal with only negligence.

Key Points

- Introduction
- The basis of tortious liability
- Remedy in tort
- The nature of other liability based on intention
- Remedies in such cases
- A comparative analysis

Suggested Answer

As far as the law of tort is concerned, Salmond and Heuston (*Law of Tort* 5th edn, 1999) contend that 'the law in general asks merely what the defendant has done, not why he did it'. Therefore, it follows that the defendant's motive or intention is irrelevant (usually) to his liability in tort. For example, in the tort of defamation, it is said that the defamatory words must be 'maliciously' published, but this is regarded as mere verbiage. It has been established that even an innocent publication will suffice to give rise to a tortious action for defamation.

Jones (*Tort* 7th edn, 2000) states that malice can have two meanings in tort: first, intentional wrongdoing, and second, improper motive. Intention refers to the defendant's knowledge that the consequences of his conduct are bound to occur, where the consequences are desired or, if not desired, are foreseen as a result. Recklessness for instance is always categorised with intention, where it is used to signify the defendant's advertence to a risk that the consequences will result from his act, although the House of Lords in cases such as *R* v *Lawrence* (1982) and *R* v *Reid* (1992) has stated that recklessness can include some forms of inadvertence.

As Jones rightly observes, as far as tort is concerned the concept of intention has not created the problems that have bedevilled the criminal law. The much wider range of liability for careless conduct or negligence has, to a large extent, removed the need for fine distinctions. In the tort of negligence, if a defendant is responsible when he ought to have foreseen that harm would result from his actions, it becomes irrelevant whether in fact he did foresee the possibility of harm, or even whether he desired it, unlike criminal law, where the culpability or intention must be proved by the prosecution to secure a conviction.

The tort of negligence has, ever since the case of *Donoghue* v *Stevenson* (1932), itself developed into a general principle of liability which is distinct and exclusive from other torts which have some connotation or link or relationship with the concept of intention. In negligence, a duty of care must be owed. That duty must have been breached and must result in consequential damage, either in the form of a physical injury or property damage. If this is the case, then the defendant will be liable to the plaintiff. The usual remedy is that of damages. Negligence can relate to misfeasance or non-feasance, and has nothing or little to do with intention.

But, be that as it may, there are, however, other torts which involve the intentional infliction of harm. These torts will now be analysed briefly. Some of these torts do inevitably overlap with criminal law, for example the torts of trespass to the person and to land.

Battery, for example, is a tort which clearly cannot be committed in the absence of intent. Battery is the direct act of the defendant which causes contact with the plaintiff's body without the plaintiff's consent. The court in *Letang* v *Cooper* (1965) said that intent to harm is an essential element for this tort, and, in *Miller* v *Jackson* (1977), the court held that this particular tort cannot be committed negligently. The House of Lords in *Stubbings* v *Webb* (1993) subsequently emphasised the distinct and separate nature of the tort of trespass.

Trespass to land is defined as a direct interference with the possession of another's land, without lawful justification. One of the essential elements of this tort is intention. The defendant must have intended to enter the land, but need not have intended to trespass. Hence, it is no defence to show that the defendant was unaware that the land belonged to somebody else: *Conway* v *George Wimpey & Co Ltd* (1951). It is, however, a defence to show that he had no intention of entering the land, as in *Smith* v *Stone* (1647).

It was held in *Wilkinson* v *Downton* (1897) that where the defendant intentionally inflicts, or wilfully does, an act calculated to cause physical damage to the plaintiff, and has in fact caused such harm, a cause of action arises in tort.

There are other torts which cover the infliction of economic harm, such as deceit and malicious falsehood, which are also intention based. In the tort of deceit, for instance, the court in *Pasley* v *Freeman* (1789) stated that where a person makes a wilful and reckless statement to another with the intention that the other shall act in reliance upon that statement, and the other does in fact rely on the statement to his or her detriment, liability arises in tort. It must be mentioned that the tort of deceit has similarities with the tort of negligent misstatement and the contractual concept of fraudulent misrepresentation. Deceit, of course, is more appropriate where the parties are in a non-contractual relationship. Malicious falsehood involves the making of a false statement, with malice, to a person other than the plaintiff, which causes damage to the plaintiff; the court in *Ratcliffe* v *Evans* (1892) emphasised the requirement of malice or intention. An honest belief would therefore negate the presumption of an intention: *Balden* v *Shorter* (1933).

The economic tort of conspiracy is yet another tort which requires an intention on the part of the conspirators to pursue a common aim or objective. This was illustrated in *Lonrho plc* v *Fayed* (1991).

Inducing a breach of contract is also an economic tort which requires knowledge and intention on the part of the defendant. The court in *Merkur Island Shipping Corp* v *Laughton* (1983) stated that this tort cannot be committed negligently. Intimidation is another tort which has intention as one of its core elements: *Rookes* v *Barnard* (1964). Another good example would be the tortious act of interference with trade by unlawful means. In *Associated British Ports* v *Transport and General Workers Union* (1989), the court held that it was the presence of an intent to injure which turned a non-actionable inducement of breach into unlawful means.

Whilst the remedy is purely damages in the tort of negligence, for all the other torts requiring intention, the remedy could also include injunctions as well as mere damages. Hence, it is submitted that whilst negligence may be viewed as singular, there is not, on a comparative basis, a simple tort of intention in the same sense.

SUGGESTED ANSWER TO QUESTION TWO

General Comment

This question is relatively straightforward, provided students have revised remedies as well as substantive liability. Students should avoid any detailed examination of elements of negligence which are not in issue, such as whether a duty of care exists in this case.

When discussing the advantages and disadvantages of structured settlements, ensure that the points you raise are fully explained.

Key Points

a) • Discuss Nora's liability in the tort of negligence, in particular the scope of the duty to disclose the risks involved in surgery under *Sidaway*, *Bolam* and *Bolitho*
   • Discuss whether a breach of any duty by Nora caused Milly's loss
b) • Identify the aim of damages in tort and explain the heads of loss relevant to Milly's circumstances, under which damages will be assessed
   • Make particular reference to future loss of earnings, and the provision of care by a relative.
c) Explain the nature of structured settlements, their advantages and disadvantages.

Suggested Answer

a) *Nora's liability in tort*
   If Milly is to claim against Nora in tort, such a claim will be based in negligence upon Nora's duty to give her patient proper and skilled advice, rather than in trespass as a battery which lacks the patient's valid consent. Only if Nora had actively misled Milly concerning the fact that she was unpractised in the new technique for performing heart surgery would an action in battery be likely to arise: *Sidaway* v *Board of Governors of the Bethlem Royal Hospital* (1985).

   It is well established that doctors owe duties of care to their patients, not only in the context of diagnosis and treatment, but also (in limited circumstances) to disclose the risks involved in a course of treatment. This was confirmed by the House of Lords in Sidaway and subsequently by the Court of Appeal in *Gold* v *Haringey Health Authority* (1988).

   In order to determine whether Nora is in breach of her duty to Milly, it is necessary to examine the scope of the duty she owes. The majority of their Lordships in Sidaway held that the proper test to apply in these circumstances is that established in *Bolam* v *Friern Hospital Management Committee* (1957); in other words, the test is whether a reasonable doctor would have acted as the defendant had done. A doctor will be held to have acted reasonably if he acted in accordance with a practice accepted as proper by a responsible body of medical men skilled in that particular art. Not only would Nora's failure to inform Milly that she intended to use a new technique (with which she had no previous 'hands on' experience) have to accord with a practice accepted as proper by a responsible body of doctors, the court would also have to be satisfied that this practice of non-disclosure has a logical basis: *Bolitho* v *City and Hackney Health Authority* (1997).

   It would obviously be rare to find that a body of professional opinion lacked logical analysis. Lord Browne-Wilkinson in *Bolitho* said that a judge would not normally be able to draw such a conclusion without expert evidence, and if the body of opinion reflected an accepted practice in the profession, a judge would not be able to discard that practice unless it could not be logically supported at all.

It is difficult to speculate whether Nora's non-disclosure was in accordance with the commonly accepted practice of a body of responsible doctors. Nora did, after all, explain how the operation would be performed. One body of professional opinion might logically consider that such a disclosure would inhibit the introduction of new and unpractised procedures, as few patients might consent if they were aware that they were the first to be subjected to a new procedure. On the other hand, the court might conclude that it is illogical to assume that patients would not consent to a new procedure which offers a clear reduction in risks compared to conventional surgery.

It should be noted that the minority of their Lordships in *Sidaway* held that the disclosure of some risks are so obviously necessary to an informed choice on the part of a patient that no reasonable prudent medical man would fail to make them. The information not disclosed in this case might well be regarded as essential to allow a patient to make an informed choice; however, it is the view of the majority which has been followed in later cases. As such, there is no duty on the part of doctors to enable patients to make an informed choice in English law.

Assuming Nora were to have broken a duty of disclosure to Milly, it would also have to be proved that 'but for' the non-disclosure, Milly would not have consented to the new technique, and would not thereby have suffered brain damage: *Barnett* v *Chelsea and Kensington Hospital Management Committee* (1969).

b) *The assessment of damages*

Assuming Nora is in breach of a duty of care owed to Milly, Nora's employer will be vicariously liable to pay a lump sum of damages (unless the parties were to agree to a structured settlement: see (c) below). The aim of such an award will be to restore Milly, in so far as money will allow, to the position she was in before the negligence occurred. An award of damages is usually considered in two parts: 'special damages' covering precisely calculable losses, normally arising pre-trial, and 'general damages' which are not capable of precise mathematical calculation and normally arise post-trial. It is also customary to classify losses sustained as being either pecuniary or non-pecuniary.

Pecuniary losses: loss of earnings

These mostly arise post-trial in Milly's case, and will include prospective earnings during any 'lost years' due to a reduced life expectancy and loss of pension rights associated with a future loss of salary.

Milly's future loss of salary is clearly difficult to assess as she has not yet entered the job market. It is likely that, had Milly become fully qualified, she would have been extremely employable and would have attracted a high salary. The court will award Milly a lump sum which, when invested, will be sufficient to produce an income equal to the loss of her future salary. The calculation is approached in two stages. The court will first assess Milly's net annual loss. The difficulty here is knowing how much Milly would have earned upon her entry to the job market (as a computer engineer?). Nonetheless, the court will have to make some assumptions, most probably based upon evidence from someone with expert knowledge of Milly's future intended profession.

The court will then select a multiplier based upon the likely duration of the disability. However, this will not be the same as the number of years Milly will work before retirement following completion of her post-graduate course, because the courts apply a reduction to take account of the possibility that future events might have cut her working life short, eg early death or unemployment. The possibility that Milly might have taken a career break for several years in order to raise children will also be a limiting factor. A reduction is also applied to take account of the fact that a lump sum payment will produce an investment income of its own. Other factors, such as Milly's future promotion prospects, may well increase the multiplier. This factor, together with Milly's young age, means that she is likely to obtain a near-maximum multiplier, perhaps in the range of 16–18.

Medical expenses reasonably incurred

The cost of nursing care and travel expenses to and from hospital are recoverable. The cost of nursing care provided by Olivia can be recovered by Milly herself: *Hunt* v *Severs* (1994). In *Housecroft* v *Burnett* (1986) it was decided that where a relative gives up work to look after the claimant, the court will award reasonable recompense to the carer, but the ceiling on such an award is the commercial rate for providing such care. Thus Olivia will be unable to recover her full loss of earnings, given her former employment as a partner in a city firm of solicitors. The damages awarded in respect of the carer will be held on trust for Olivia by Milly: *Cunningham* v *Harrison* (1973).

Non-pecuniary losses

Milly's non-pecuniary losses include the pain and suffering she has endured both pre and post-trial, her loss of amenity, ie the loss of capacity to engage in activities which she enjoyed before trial, and compensation for her actual injuries. The amounts awarded under these heads are usually assessed by reference to past cases.

c) ### The structured settlement

This type of settlement was developed following pressure from those involved in clinical negligence claims (eg lawyers and insurers) and from tax concessions made by the Inland Revenue. The Damages Act 1996 provided further statutory support. Structured settlements may be suitable in cases such as Milly's where substantial damages are payable, but they can only be made where both parties agree.

Once a lump sum figure has been agreed, the part of the award representing special damages to the date of settlement would be paid to Milly as a lump sum. The remainder is used by the defendant's insurers to purchase an annuity to provide a fixed income stream for the claimant. Variations in payments from the annuity can be built in to cater for various contingencies likely to arise during the life of the claimant.

Advantages of structured settlements

1. Income from the annuity is tax free (benefiting higher rate taxpayers in particular) whereas income from the investment of a lump sum will be subject to income tax. Thus income payments from a structured settlement are likely to be larger.

2. A structured settlement would provide certainty for Milly in respect of her future income, and would avoid the danger that a lump sum might be spent too quickly, leaving insufficient funds for later years.
3. Milly is quite possibly unable to manage the investment of a lump sum herself given the extent of her disabilities, and would be reliant on the goodwill, good faith, and investment expertise of those who care for her to manage her affairs. The use of a structured settlement removes this responsibility from the claimant.
4. Annuities can be set up to protect future income from the effects of inflation.
5. The income from an annuity will be guaranteed to last for Milly's lifetime, even if she survived longer than her predicted life expectancy.

Disadvantages of structured settlements
1. Even though there is flexibility within a structured settlement to vary payments to cater for various contingencies likely to arise during the life of the claimant, once agreed, a structured settlement cannot be modified. This means that there is extreme pressure to structure the settlement correctly at the outset. Predictions concerning Milly's future need for income and capital will have to be made straight away.
2. The amounts payable under a structured settlement may still be inadequate if Milly's prognosis is incorrect.

Suggested Solutions to Past Examination Questions 2001–2002

The Suggested Solutions series provides examples of full answers to the questions regularly set by examiners. Each suggested solution has been broken down into three stages: general comment, skeleton solution and suggested solution. The examination questions included within the text are taken from past examination papers set by the London University. The full opinion answers will undoubtedly assist you with your research and further your understanding and appreciation of the subject in question.

Only £6.95 due November 2003

Company Law
ISBN: 1 85836 519 8

Evidence
ISBN: 1 85836 521 X

Employment Law
ISBN: 1 85836 520 1

Family Law
ISBN: 1 85836 525 2

European Union Law
ISBN: 1 85836 524 4

For further information on contents or to place an order, please contact:

Mail Order
Old Bailey Press
at Holborn College
Woolwich Road
Charlton
London
SE7 8LN

Telephone No: 020 8317 6039
Fax No: 020 8317 6004
Website: www.oldbaileypress.co.uk

Old Bailey Press

The Old Bailey Press integrated student law library is tailor-made to help you at every stage of your studies from the preliminaries of each subject through to the final examination. The series of Textbooks, Revision WorkBooks, 150 Leading Cases and Cracknell's Statutes are interrelated to provide you with a comprehensive set of study materials.

You can buy Old Bailey Press books from your University Bookshop, your local Bookshop, direct using this form, or you can order a free catalogue of our titles from the address shown overleaf.

The following subjects each have a Textbook, 150 Leading Cases/Casebook, Revision WorkBook and Cracknell's Statutes unless otherwise stated.

Administrative Law
Commercial Law
Company Law
Conflict of Laws
Constitutional Law
Conveyancing (Textbook and 150 Leading Cases)
Criminal Law
Criminology (Textbook and Sourcebook)
Employment Law (Textbook and Cracknell's Statutes)
English and European Legal Systems
Equity and Trusts
Evidence
Family Law
Jurisprudence: The Philosophy of Law (Textbook, Sourcebook and Revision WorkBook)
Land: The Law of Real Property
Law of International Trade
Law of the European Union
Legal Skills and System (Textbook)
Obligations: Contract Law
Obligations: The Law of Tort
Public International Law
Revenue Law (Textbook, Revision WorkBook and Cracknell's Statutes)
Succession

Mail order prices:	
Textbook	£15.95
150 Leading Cases	£11.95
Revision WorkBook	£9.95
Cracknell's Statutes	£11.95
Suggested Solutions 1999–2000	£6.95
Suggested Solutions 2000–2001	£6.95
Suggested Solutions 2001–2002	£6.95
Law Update 2003	£10.95
Law Update 2004	£10.95

Please note details and prices are subject to alteration.

To complete your order, please fill in the form below:

Module	Books required	Quantity	Price	Cost
		Postage		
		TOTAL		

For Europe, add 15% postage and packing (£20 maximum).
For the rest of the world, add 40% for airmail.

ORDERING

By telephone to Mail Order at 020 8317 6039, with your credit card to hand.

By fax to 020 8317 6004 (giving your credit card details).

Website: www.oldbaileypress.co.uk

By post to: Mail Order, Old Bailey Press at Holborn College, Woolwich Road, Charlton, London, SE7 8LN.

When ordering by post, please enclose full payment by cheque or banker's draft, or complete the credit card details below. You may also order a free catalogue of our complete range of titles from this address.

We aim to despatch your books within 3 working days of receiving your order.

Name

Address

Postcode   Telephone

Total value of order, including postage: £

I enclose a cheque/banker's draft for the above sum, or

charge my   ☐ Access/Mastercard   ☐ Visa   ☐ American Express
Card number

☐☐☐☐ ☐☐☐☐ ☐☐☐☐ ☐☐☐☐

Expiry date   ☐☐☐☐

Signature: ....Date: ....